Intersexions

Intersexions

Gender/class/culture/ethnicity

Edited by
Gill Bottomley, Marie de Lepervanche
and Jeannie Martin

ALLEN & UNWIN

First published 1991
Allen & Unwin Pty Ltd
8 Napier Street, North Sydney NSW 2059 Australia

National Library of Australia
Cataloguing-in-Publication entry:
Intersexions: gender, class, culture, ethnicity.

   Bibliography
   Includes index.
   ISBN 0 04 442325 X.

   1. Minority women-Social conditions.   2. Social classes.   3. Sex role.
   I. Bottomley, Gillian, 1939–   .   II. De Lepervanche, Marie M.
   III. Martin, Jeannie A.

305.4

Set in 10.5/11.5pt Sabon by Graphicraft Typesetters Ltd., Hong Kong
Printed by Dah Hua Printing Co., Hong Kong

Contents

Contributors

Gill Bottomley, Associate Professor in Anthropology and Comparative Sociology, Macquarie University
Marie de Lepervanche, Associate Professor in Anthropology, University of Sydney
Vanda Moraes Gorecki, Lecturer in Anthropology, James Cook University, Queensland
Margaret Jolly, Senior Lecturer in Anthropology and Comparative Sociology, Macquarie University
Jan Larbalestier, Lecturer, School of Social Work and Social Administration, University of Sydney
Jeannie Martin, Senior Lecturer, Faculty of Humanities and Social Sciences, University of Technology, Sydney
Jan Pettman, Senior research fellow, Peace Research Centre, Research School of Pacific Studies, Australian National University, Canberra
Kalpana Ram, Tutor in Anthropology and Comparative Sociology, Macquarie University
Kathy Robinson, Senior lecturer in Anthropology and Comparative Sociology, Macquarie University
Santi Rozario, Lecturer in Sociology, Hunter Institute, University of Newcastle
Ellie Vasta, Lecturer, School of Sociology, University of Wollongong

Preface

In 1984, in *Ethnicity Class and Gender in Australia*, we attempted to move beyond unitary explanations of Australian immigration and its consequences. As that book's name suggests, we included discussions of class, gender *and* ethnicity, rather than emphasising one perspective at the expense of the others. Although we failed to achieve this aim in all chapters, the book's contributors have provided scholarly and thoughtful alternatives to the unidimensional analyses so dear to social scientists. The impact of *Ethnicity Class and Gender* has been difficult to assess, despite its relative success as a publication. Some writers have dismissed its triple perspective as a 'holy trinity' or a 'litany', implying a form of religious incantation at some distance from our own critical and scholarly intentions. Others have continued to ignore one perspective or another as irrelevant, ideological or just too hard. But several major streams of scholarship have provided much stronger justification for approaches that challenge boundaries and stress interrelationships rather than divisions between ways of knowing.

The additional impetus that stimulated this second book came from those streams of thought. One of these developed in feminist debates concerned with the fragmentation of and perceived biases within the women's movement (see Carby 1982; Parmar 1982, 1989) and in debates about the decline of the 'grand narratives' of social theory (see Pateman and Gross 1986; Fraser and Nicholson 1988). Just as we completed the manuscript of *Ethnicity Class and Gender*, two London-based sociologists published an important paper in *Feminist Review* contextualising feminism within and against the discourses of class and ethnicity (Anthias and Yuval-Davis 1983). This and similar papers have had a mixed reception from feminists, but they have also provoked substantial rethinking, a questioning of the notion of hierarchies of oppression, and a recognition that, in the words of the black American poet June Jordan, 'each one of us is more than what cannot be changed about us' (quoted in Parmar 1989, p. 62). Moreover, accounts that fail to recognise this fact can themselves become forms of subjection, even if they are intended to be liberating.

Another, related, body of thought of importance to the themes of this book is that contained in recent anthropological and sociological post-colonial writing, which, like feminism, has profoundly challenged a number of dominant discourses. Issues of representation have become increasingly important—the political representation of women and members of minority groups, and also their symbolic representation within particular discourses.

This latter concern has led to a healthy scepticism about the very bases of knowledge, and about the frames of reference that inform particular explanations. Broadly defined, this issue of representation is one of the main themes of our book. All of these chapters cover perceived racist, sexist, ethnocentric and class biases in sociological and anthropological writing and in other accounts of immigrant and colonised people, especially women. Although our approaches are critical, we are also concerned to offer alternatives, by combining comparative and specific analyses, by attention to material written or spoken by the people 'being represented', and by examining our own positions as commentators. Most importantly, we are all aware that categories and intellectual frameworks are constructed within relations of domination and subordination. Our aim in this book is not merely to offer a pluralist presentation of 'life's rich tapestry', but to understand the processes by which such relations of power are maintained, reproduced and resisted.

Intersexions, therefore, moves a good deal further than *Ethnicity Class and Gender* in several ways. First, we have included material from beyond Australia that explores the central themes of the book. Four of the chapters draw on fieldwork undertaken by their authors in Vanuatu, Indonesia, India and Bangladesh.

Part of our intention in widening our geographical scope was to introduce a more comparative perspective into feminist (and other) discussions about gender, class, ethnicity and culture. Most of the authors in this book have been trained as anthropologists and are well aware of the limitations and intractability of ethnocentrism. These chapters question accepted categories and offer insights into the processes of defining and contesting hegemonic relations of power based on caste, religion and colonialism, as well as class and gender. Thus, Kalpana Ram's chapter dismantles the apparent unity and homogeneity in the term 'Hindu woman' in her detailed study of the 'untouchable' Mukkuvars of Kerala, whose assertive counter-caste identity emphasises masculine prerogatives and a specific cultural construction of gender. Santi Rozario's chapter raises questions about the notions of purity, honour and community in a Bangladeshi region where Christian women, while enjoying greater mobility than their Muslim counterparts, are still limited by the politics of both Christian and Muslim men, and by class relations. Kathy Robinson discusses the internal and international migration of Indonesian women, showing how cultural expectations and class relations are affected by regional origin, but also how quasi-familial ideas shape relations between employer and employee within, but not beyond, Indonesia. Margaret Jolly's chapter examines the politics of colonialism and decolonisation in Vanuatu, including a historical view of colonialism and the intersection of racism and gender relations, whereby black women were subordinate to white women as well as to men, despite the fact that colonialism was a masculinist project. Some of the consequences of this history are revealed in the poetry and criticisms of a Vanuatuan woman poet and politician, Grace Mera Molisa, some of whose work is included in this chapter.

A second, and related, aim in this book is to examine modes of representation—within social theory, feminism, development theory and discussions of capitalism and postcolonialism, as well as in dominant ideological notions such as caste, domesticity and 'success'. Jan Larbalestier discusses the perspective on Aboriginal identity presented by three Aboriginal women writers, within the context of dominant white Australian definitions. Gill Bottomley also includes literary material in her analysis of studies of 'second generation' Greek Australians, questioning their recurrent definition as 'problems' and drawing attention to a creative energy

that offers an alternative view to that of most social scientists
and policy makers.

Other writers offer assessments of the relations between feminism, multiculturalism, racism and social theory. Jeannie Martin
dissects multiculturalism from a feminist perspective, but also
develops a multiculturalist reading of feminism. Marie de
Lepervanche's chapter focuses on the ideology of the family in
Australia, especially in relation to immigrant women. This chapter and others challenge the private/public dichotomy that sus-
tains the artificial separation of domesticity from other social,
economic and political arenas. Ellie Vasta, discussing her own
research among Italo–Australian women, shows how class, gender and ethnic subjectivities are defined *within* each other and are
sometimes constructed separately from and in resistance to each
other. Vanda Gorecki, similarly, explores the practices of the
Latin American women with whom she worked in terms of the
interrelations of, and contradictions between, aspects of their
employment, 'traditional' beliefs and familial obligations. In the
final chapter, Jan Pettman takes a critical view of racism and
sexism in sociology.

Clearly, a number of themes recur throughout these chapters
and are discussed from several perspectives. There is, therefore, a
degree of overlap in discussion that brings the reader back to
central debates, despite our wide-ranging subject matter. All the
authors are feminist anthropologists and sociologists with a comparative approach to their work. Despite differences in style and
content, the book is an extended discussion around its major
themes, rather than a collection of conference-style papers. Most
of the chapters were written especially for *Intersexions*, and all
their authors share the same determination to question unitary
categories and to demonstrate the processes by which relations
described as 'class', 'ethnic', 'cultural' and 'gender' *intersect* and
interact with each other in complex and specific ways.

Acknowledgements

All the authors wish to thank the institutions and individuals who
helped them with the research on which these chapters have been
based. We are also grateful to Grace Mera Molisa for her kind

permission to republish the poems in Chapter 4 and to the editors of *Migration* for permission to re-publish Ellie Vasta's paper as Chapter 9. Specific acknowledgements are made to Raul Pertierra (Chapter 2), Helen Easson (Chapter 6), Ann Aungles, Stephen Castles, Annie Phizacklea and Sandra Taylor (Chapter 9). We are especially indebted to Helen Easson for her assistance in preparing the bibliography and the final manuscript.

Gill Bottomley
Marie de Lepervanche
Jeannie Martin

1 Moving in from the margins: Gender as the centre of cultural contestation of power relations in south India

One of the central dilemmas of feminist scholarship has become increasingly more pronounced: feminist writings now run the risk of functioning as a mere adjunct to other, more established, discourses such as those of class, and (in the case of India) of caste. The danger is exemplified in the characteristic title 'Women and . . .' (one can fill in the blank in any number of ways), given to so many books and articles published since the 1970s. The notion of 'intersections' attempts to avoid such pre-emptory alliance, as well as the old theoretico-political tyranny of attributing primacy to one structure (usually that of class) over all others. However, the notion implicitly supposes the existence of a number of independent variables (caste, class, ethnicity, gender), all of which are already constituted and may or may not come together ('intersect').

In this paper I propose instead that we attribute a centrality to gender, both as discourse and as social practice—not in the old sense of a causal primacy, but rather in the sense of a field in which a process of 'transcoding' occurs. Jameson defines the preconditions for transcoding as 'the invention of a set of terms, the strategic choice of a particular culture or language, such that the same terminology can be used to analyse and articulate two quite distinct types of objects or "texts", or two very different structural levels of reality' (1981:40). The female body may be

1

viewed as the site at which a 'transcoding operation'—the construction of femininity—may be said to take place as a process
involving castes, classes and ethnic groups in the definition
and contestation of relations of power.

Even the term 'transcoding', with its origins in structuralist
linguistics, is inadequate to quite capture the nature of the relationship I have in mind: femininity is rather a terrain in and over
which a battle rages. Marxism, particularly where influenced by
Gramsci, is wont to point out that classes are not pre-formed
structural entities; rather, they are formed in the process of contestation. Marxism, however, overlooks the sense in which this
contestation is bound up in practice with constructs of femininity
and, more broadly, of gender. By the same token, femininity itself
bears the stamp of this battle: it can be used as a singular abstract
noun (as in 'the Hindu woman' or 'the Hindu construction of
femininity') only as long as we accept the appearance of unity and
homogeneity which is the hallmark of successful hegemonisation
by a class, caste or ethnic group.

I approach the task of taking apart this facade of cultural unity
and highlighting the different, often conflicting, ideological
strands which contribute to making gender such a volatile construct through a consideration of a marginalised south Indian
community, ritually low in caste ranking and also poverty
stricken.[1] In this community, constructions of gender are crucial
to the expression of group identity and, even more significantly,
to the proclamation of a kind of affirmative redefinition of the
dominant caste Hindu view of their community.

The Mukkuvars are fisherpeople. They inhabit a continuous
strip of coastline from the Kerala border down to the tip of Cape
Comorin in south India. As an occupational group associated
with the killing and sale of flesh, they are unambiguously classified as a polluted caste according to the criteria of ritual
hierarchy. In accounts of Malabar society at the turn of the
century, Mukkuvars are placed at a distance from the Brahmans,
Kshatriyas and high-caste Sudras. They may 'adore the deities in
the Brahmanic temples by standing at a distance from the outer
wall' (Iyer 1981:274). Tied to an occupation which places them
on the perimeter of the land mass, the people of the coast find
themselves segregated; they are virtual prisoners within their own
area. 'They were in former times considered an inferior race, and,

as such, precluded from travelling along public roads, and consequently obliged to keep to the sea-coast.' (Iyer 1981:275)

But if the Mukkuvars are polluted untouchables to caste Hindus, that is not how they necessarily see themselves. Instead they present themselves to the outside world as brave, innovative, adaptable to change and capable of cunning in response to challenge on sea or land. Individualism and freedom from unnecessary supervision are so highly prized that any work which entails loss of autonomy is rejected out of hand, despite the long months of seasonal unemployment built into a fishing economy. Such a confident self-presentation, and the individualist values that accompany it, contrasts markedly with the attitudes of other untouchable groups such as landless agricultural labourers. Moffat (1979), writing about a rural caste of untouchables in the same south Indian state of Tamil Nadu, characterises their system of values in terms of the replication of upper caste hierarchical attitudes within the framework of religious culture.

The contrast is undoubtedly anchored in the opposing frameworks of production. Landless labourers are enmeshed in a complex web of interdependencies with land-owning castes and with the priestly Brahmans, which the British colonialists referred to as 'the jajmani system' (Dumont 1980:97–9). The Mukkuvars, on the other hand, depend for their livelihood on the sea—a terrain which offers them both ready, if provisional, escape from caste society and an alternative source of autonomy and identity. It is in the craft of fishing, using only non-mechanised technology, that Mukkuvar values find their fullest expression, with pride of place given to individual skills and knowledge, and to the capacity to learn and adapt to new technological influences.

Although these values are definitive of *caste* identity, such identity is in fact just as gender-specific as the work of fishing on which it depends. Both fishing and the values of individualism are specifically masculine prerogatives. Individualism merges with a marked masculine ideology of strength, virility and valour. Men pride themselves on being the best fishermen on the west coast, and boast of their bravery and skill. The martial and the combative elements of life are highly prized, and oral history is replete with tales of physical bravery, as well as of trickery and cunning. The caste name and the very physical territory the community occupies are legitimated by a story of the services rendered by the Mukkuvars to the king of Travancore in 1741 in his battle against the Dutch. In gratitude, the king offered the Mukkuvars a reward, and they asked for the 'Mukku', or tip of the land.

Masculinity and male work are an integral part of the way in which the community as a whole has tried to maintain its sense of self-respect and dignity in the face of the degrading status offered by caste society. Femininity and female work, on the other hand, present themselves as far more problematic—both to the community itself and to the scholar trying to analyse them. The most striking feature of the sexual division of labour in the fishing community is the complete exclusion of women from the work of fishing and from access to the economic and cultural capital required to perform this task. The most lucrative occupation open to the seafaring community, which is also (as we have seen) the activity central to the community's self-definition, is barred to women.

This exclusion, which is so deeply entrenched that it is taken for granted by the community and by outside observers, depends for its legitimation on a construction of women as 'dangerous'. Fishing, which is in any case hedged about with ritualistic taboos, is seen as particularly vulnerable to women's behaviour and indeed, to their very presence. A woman crossing a man's path as he is setting out to sea is said to make the sea rough. Women must therefore stay out of sight when men are setting out with boats. Young girls will never take the shortest route between coastal villages—a route which lies along the beach-front itself—if they know the men are likely to be launching their craft. Wrongful conduct on the part of women may be held responsible not only for the success of economic ventures at sea, but for the safety and welfare of the men themselves: such a belief has a peculiar and terrible force in an occupation marked by daily risk and uncertainty.

The view of women as dangerous is partly grounded in the rather uncertain basis of male dominance in a fishing community. The very monopoly exercised by men over the economic resources of the sea requires that they absent themselves for long periods from the land-based society of the village. In contrast with agricultural society, where patriarchal cultural rules are buttressed by the actual physical presence of the menfolk, the sexual division of labour in a fishing society leaves women in charge of all activities based in the household.

The close association—even identification—between women and the domestic economy of the household only superficially resembles the association between femininity and the responsibility for familial welfare found in the dominant version of Tamil culture. In the dominant version, women are *of* the domestic sphere, are contained by the interior space of the house, without being able to lay claim to the ultimate decision-making responsibility pertaining to their sphere (Baker-Reynolds 1978). Without necessarily setting out to transgress the dominant codes of Tamil culture, Mukkuvar women find themselves in a very different position. Indeed, their very efforts to fulfil the cultural requirements of ensuring familial stability, survival and welfare force them to assume roles that take them well outside the traditionally female spheres of influence.

Men are unable and unwilling, by virtue of exhausting preoccupations out at sea, to follow through the financial transactions which flow on from the initial auction of the fish catch and which are realised only after their sale at the markets. It is women who keep track of what is owed to their husbands and receive the money, as well as make the decisions regarding the allocation of this scarce cash resource to various urgent familial needs.

Further, women find themselves in the position of having to mediate between the temporal rhythms of production and reproduction in fishing society. The periodicity of fishing is governed by the seasons, tides and winds, as well as by sheer chance. The economic contribution of men is therefore necessarily sporadic and uneven. When there is a spectacular catch, there is a flood of money, while lean fishing seasons mean dearth and hunger in the home. Social reproduction, however, is a continuous, daily process and has a distinctive rhythm of its own which is in direct tension with the vagaries of the fishing economy. This process, which is directly women's responsibility, concerns not only the family's biological survival—and this means finding money for food, clothing, housing repairs and medical expenses—but also the broader strategies of social reproduction involved in marriage, kinship and religious practices. These strategies may involve raising sums of money for dowry, marriage expenses and pilgrimages, payment for the education or training of children, or finding the money to send a son overseas in search of work. The male economy of fishing is of necessity complemented by a women's credit economy. The latter is conducted in relative privacy and obscurity, based on networks of neighbourhood, residence and kinship. The credit economy consists of a multitude of small-scale transactions, with women acting as borrowers and lenders, involving a range of households known to them through association of marriage, kinship, common work experiences and friendships, or through the services of female intermediaries who utilise similar social networks.

The theme of women as dangerous, but powerful, finds ample confirmation in the specific sexual division of labour in the fishing community. The ideology is one which both legitimates women's exclusion from key areas of production, and simultaneously registers the constitution of the feminine as powerful by virtue of the considerable responsibilities exercised by women in the land-based economy. Although the ideological formulation of femininity as dangerous seems tailor-made to the peculiar dilemmas confronting male dominance in the fishing villages, such an apprehension of femininity is in fact far more widespread in the Tamil country. According to recent ethnographic writing, the Tamils traditionally viewed divine power not as transcendental, but as imminent within actual objects and thus as potentially harmful (Hart 1975:42–3; Baker-Raynolds 1978:68–70). These divine forces, called *ananku* by the early Tamils, are malevolent and dangerous, but also capricious and erratic. Ananku refers both to the power and, by metonymy, to those who possess it. There appears to have been an ancient association between women and *ananku*, an association which particularly crystallised around the periods when women's bodies were perceived as 'out of control', due either to biological phenomena such as menstruation and childbirth, or to a weakening of male authority, such as occurs, for example, after the death of a woman's husband. The breasts, loins and outflows of women are particularly credited with possessing *ananku*. This early, rather baleful, view of divinity/femininity seems to have merged with the southern variants of a pan-Indian *sakti* cult, celebrating female energy. In these cults, centring on the female goddesses Kali and the Devi, the feminine roles of wife and mother are regarded as inessential

6

to the conceptualisation of female power. It is quite common in the south to come across accounts of creation where female is taken as first principle and where women's *sakti* is said to lie behind everything (Beck 1974:7). The worship of the village goddess in Tamil country continues to capture the simultaneously destructive and redemptive capacities of the divine. Her worship has been associated particularly with certain forms of epidemic disease (especially smallpox), which she both causes and cures and which may also be seen simply as manifestations of the goddess.

I elaborate this view of the feminine as dangerous and awesomely powerful in some detail because it presents a bold contrast to the more commonly discussed Hindu constructs of femininity as polluted and impure (see articles in Allen and Mukherjee 1982). The inordinate attention paid to this view is a by-product of the scholarly preoccupation with upper caste, Brahmanic codes of purity and pollution. The dominance of these priestly codes is unquestionable. The goddess worshipped in the great Hindu temples is not the maverick and dangerous goddess of the Tamil villages, but a 'consort'—a wifely submissive partner to the male gods Visnu and Siva. The Tamil conception of the feminine is therefore an aspect of a subordinated tradition, but it continues to provide a critical element of tension in the southern construction of gender.

The tensions are particularly acute in the case of a community such as the Mukkuvars, for whom Hindu ideologies of purity and pollution, if adhered to, would entail quite damning implications for any attempt at sustaining a sense of self-respect and dignity. In keeping with the community's general resistance to accepting a lowly status, one finds that pollution ideology is markedly muted. Birth, death and menstruation are attended by rituals which emphasise danger, but not pollution. Menstruation rites show up this selectivity in the absorption of Hindu values very clearly. The first menstruation, which is marked in Tamil society as an auspicious and celebratory occasion, is an important part of the Mukkuvar female life cycle. However, in Tamil society, it is not simply menarche but every menstruation which is marked by ritual—and unlike the menarche ceremony, subsequent menstruations are accompanied not by celebration but by seclusion and a ban on public worship and domestic cooking. Such a practice of monthly

7

menstrual seclusion is conspicuously absent among Mukkuvars. Women cook, go out to work, and attend religious services during menstruation, although women who become possessed by divine grace, as mediums, do draw the line at healing in the name of divinity while menstruating.

In resisting the devaluation of their entire caste, Mukkuvars have had to resist the devaluation of the female body as unclean or impure, for both untouchability and femininity are regarded as analogously impure in the hegemonic paradigm of priestly Hinduism. Indeed, in some texts, fisherpeople are explicitly likened to a menstruating woman in her most polluted phase (Baker-Reynolds, 1978:101–2).

Mukkuvars converted to Christianity as early as 1535. Whatever their reasons for conversion, this has enabled them to consolidate their cultural distance from certain dominant interpretations of Hinduism. In the course of 400 years, the church has constituted itself as a quasi-state, operating within the boundaries of the official state of the day. It has levied its own taxes, adjudicated disputes between one village and another, or between individuals, and generally mediated the relations of people within its own territory with the outside world. Villagers ironically refer to their parish priests as *kutti raja*, or 'petty prince'.

One of the key initiatives taken by the church has been the encouragement of an indigenous and popular Catholicism with a base in voluntary religious organisations and in mass cults surrounding the Virgin Mary and the saints. In 1582, the Jesuits imported from Manila a statue of Our Lady of the Snows, and established in Tuticorin a cult of the Virgin which became a focal point of caste identity (see Roche 1984 and Bayly 1981 for details). The Virgin and the saints have become guardians of village welfare among the Mukkuvars as well. Priests have encouraged villagers to adopt a saint as a village patron, and to celebrate that saint's festival with special community pride. Erected outside each church is a special shrine dedicated to the village's patron saint. The official Sunday sermons are held in the church but, in addition, priests deliver informal sermons at the shrines of the saints.

Men and women alike have elevated the Virgin or Maataa (mother) to the primary position of worship, but whereas for men the relationship to the Maataa is intense and private, relatively unmediated by the church and parish priest, for women the relationship entails social duties and responsibilities. Women are the mainstay of the church, taking it on as part of their numerous obligations. They demonstrate faith through regular attendance, and by organising the social details of church festivals—arranging, decorating, cooking special foods, conducting catechism classes, organising children for their First Communion and so on. With women forming the bulk of their supporters and, at many times of the year, their entire parish, the priests, in emphasising the message of godly love in their sermons, inevitably play on women's responsiveness to the cult of the Maataa. The Virgin's love for her earthly children is the image favoured to help concretise the idea of divine mercy. There are many explicit appeals to the mothers in the audience as intuitively equipped to understand the nature of godly love.

The cult of the Virgin has taken on many of the characteristics of the worship of the Tamil goddess, including the primacy of the feminine and the capacity to cure disease through possession. However, the Virgin shares none of the disorderly and dangerous qualities of her Tamil counterpart; popular iconography in major shrines of the Virgin depicts her as serene, smiling, eternally placid and the embodiment of a purely benevolent idea of the maternal feminine. At the same time, the idea of the feminine as dangerous and powerful is kept alive in Mukkuvar rituals, and is also the refuge of Mukkuvar women in states of illness and possession. Such possession, diagnosed as the entry of the Hindu goddess into the women, is treated as evil and demonic in nature, to be cured by the church or by other women healing in the name of the Christian Virgin.

As far as women themselves are concerned, one could argue that the different ideological strands which are available in this part of south India—woman as polluted, woman as danger, and woman as maternal virgin—may be at odds with one another, but none are particularly liberating in potential. Further, the very nature of their activities, far exceeding the narrow bounds of domesticity and seclusion characteristic of upper caste women, renders Mukkuvar women particularly vulnerable to the hostile evaluations of caste Hindu scrutiny. If men's work allows them a provisional escape from the dominant culture, women's work continually takes them into enemy territory, removed from the social density and cultural singularity of coastal villages. In the course of their trips to healers and Christian shrines, women travel all over the district and even into adjacent districts and states. Domestic space is therefore imperceptibly extended into sacred spaces, a terrain without any strict physical boundaries. Women who work as fish traders enjoy a unique access to other castes and communities in the agrarian hinterland. In their daily movement to and from the marketplace, the women develop social relations with other caste groups and many develop relations of direct barter with agricultural households, exchanging fish for rice and firewood.

However, women's work, particularly the work of fish trading, requires systematic transgression of virtually all locally available cultural encodings of the feminine, whether Hindu or Christian. These women must be continually present in spaces which are defined as 'male': on the sea-front, alongside men from their own community, as well as those from other inland trading communities and castes. During auctions, women must bid in the midst of physical jostling, excitement and aggression. Purchase is followed by a walk through the country roads, and the short-cuts to the markets take women through the paddy fields, along which they return late in the evening. The marketplace is, again, a territory not only of males, but of males from non-Mukkuvar communities. The atmosphere at these markets is not as aggressively and exclusively male as the bazaars of north India, but women who are selling fish must adopt tough and vocal strategies in order to compete effectively.

The threat represented by such transgressions is a double one. Not only are women present on spaces which have been defined as 'male', but they are not there 'under cover' of some feminine role or domestic obligation. Thus the cultural purdah which metaphorically shields women and renders them culturally invisible or protected when they travel to religious shrines, healers or on social errands, or even to the marketplace itself (as consumers and purchasers of items for domestic consumption) is conspicuously unavailable for women who work as fish traders. Traders do not have available any cultural ambiguities about their role which they can exploit to legitimise their activities: when they appear on the beaches and marketplaces, they are there, at least in theory, to perform a role identical to other traders who are male.

10

In the course of their excursions into 'male' and, worse, 'outside-male' space, the fish traders are left in no doubt of the view held of them in the wider society. Distaste for aggressive and haggling 'fish wives' is there reinforced by caste values. Coming back from the markets after a day in the hot sun, fisherwomen who stop at a tea-house are served at the door, and must drink their tea separately, either standing outside or seated in the corner. If they use public transport to carry their baskets of fish to the market, they may be ordered off the bus at the whim of the conductor.

It is therefore women who bear the brunt of the polluted status of Mukkuvars in caste society. Their activities threaten to undermine the very project of carving out some measure of dignity and autonomy for the community as a whole. The various devices of seclusion with which Mukkuvars attempt to restrict their women must therefore be seen as a response to the threat of hostile outsider evaluation, as well as an outcome of their own ideologies of the dangers inherent in women's bodies. The result of these multiple pressures is most clearly evident in the restrictions which govern the most 'public' and potentially damning of women's activities, namely fish-trading. Most of the women who work in this capacity are in their 50s, and more are below 30. All are either married or widowed. In other words, transgressions on to the public male space are simply not permitted where the sexual presence of the woman is regarded as her defining characteristic.

Similar considerations of sexual respectability, ultimately tied to the preservation of the community's respectability, govern the newly emergent division of labour. With the impact of capitalism and wage work, men are travelling further away from the villages than ever before and for longer periods of time, working almost exclusively as a semi-skilled labour force on mechanised fishing vessels in major sea-ports located in other parts of the state, or in other southern states. Women's attempts to earn cash, however, tie them even more firmly to the four walls of the home, in some ways restricting them more than their former roles as household managers. Those women who are both young and unmarried may earn money only within the home. In coastal areas, the activity that most commonly fulfils this requirement is that of weaving fishing nets. Once married, women shift to forms of petty trade which can still be carried out from the front porch of the home or in small shops which are physical extensions of the home. Significantly, the only young women who 'escape' from the coastal villages are those who are educated enough to merit jobs considered 'respectable women's jobs' by the outside world (a miserably limited range: teachers, social workers, typists and clerical assistants). In addition, the girls must have chaperonage—usually provided by the church, which endows them with the training and the job. The social mediation with the outside world which the church offers provides a respectable way out, but carries with it its own set of restrictions. Often 'escape' may mean no more than employment in a strange district in the closed atmosphere of a convent. However, Mukkuvars have no problems accepting educated and trained young women. The prestige of their education, their close connections with the church, and above all the fact that these girls do not compromise the community's dignity, give them an enviable legitimacy and even authority. Cultural constructions of gender and female sexuality in particular are therefore crucial not only in mediating relations of power and legitimacy in the more archaic framework of caste hierarchy, but in shaping the nature of capitalism itself, rendering it a gender-specific historical process. 'Indology', as the scholarly study of India has come to be known, has long been in the grip of an assumption of an overall homogeneity and unity binding the most diverse south Asian communities together. Dumont (1980) argues that alternative identities do not last long in caste society without some compromise being struck with the dominant principle of hierarchy. Such an argument totally dissolves the possibility of long-term conflict, instead presenting us with an overwhelmingly static picture of a stratified society in which hegemony is an achieved fact, rather than a process of continued renegotiation. Recent scholarship, particularly on south India, has been successful in demonstrating that the priestly cultural codes of purity and pollution are not the only ones with widespread currency. There have been vivid and interesting demonstrations of the hardy persistence of cultural difference among the warrior–merchant castes (Mines 1984), the powerful non-Brahman land-owning castes (Beck 1974) and the aristocratic castes (Dirks 1987). However, to seek to simply demonstrate a multiplicity of cultural codes is to contribute to a merely static analysis.

I have argued that the study of gender can provide us with

a means of investigating the dynamic interaction between the elements of different cultural codes and between the social groups through which they function. This can, in principle, be undertaken in a way that is simultaneously an investigation of the constitution of power relations, and an appraisal of the tensions and challenges to which they are subjected.

In turn, such an investigation implies the need to rescrutinise the basis on which we introduce the term 'gender' into our analysis. It is all too easy, particularly in anthropological ethnographic writing, to incorporate gender as yet another static cultural attribute of the tribe, caste or social group under discussion.

In the case of the Mukkuvars, I have undertaken to show how ideologies of sexual differentiation, masculinity and femininity are themselves inherently volatile, since they do not merely reflect other relations of power, but are one of the fundamental ways in which hierarchies of caste and class are constituted, and simultaneously contested and transformed.

2 Ethno-religious communities and gender divisions in Bangladesh: Women as boundary markers

This paper is part of my PhD thesis, based upon anthropological fieldwork carried out in 1983–84 in the mixed village of Doria, located in Dhaka, Bangladesh. The village's religious communities consist of Muslims (50 per cent), Hindus (30 per cent) and Christians (20 per cent). However, data used for this paper involves several other villages in the Palashi Union (local council) as well as Doria. It should be noted at the outset that Christians make up less than half a per cent of the total population in Bangladesh. The fact that 20 per cent of Doria's population is made up of Christians simply means that Christians congregate in this region very heavily, Palashi having one of the oldest Catholic churches in Bangladesh.

My study examined the dynamics of religiously defined communal and gender domination under conditions of rapid socioeconomic change. Analysis of the relationship and conflict among the three religious communities, between different classes, and between men and women in the village of Doria[1] reveals the significance of 'purity' for the maintenance of the hierarchical relationships between and within these social groups.

As the socioeconomic situation changes, more women are participating in outside paid employment. Bengalis[2] can no longer afford to confine all their women to their households. Yet women who join the 'men's world' are disapproved of: their status is still defined in terms of the traditional ideologies of purity/pollution and honour/shame. The ideology of 'purity' is not new in Bengali society. However, owing to the new economic role of women, female sexual purity has become not only one of the main ways of controlling women, but also of justifying and maintaining other relations of domination and subordination—among Muslims, Christians and Hindus; between rich and poor; and among lineages. These inequalities reinforce each other; in particular, communal domination reinforces gender domination.

By detailing and analysing the origin and meaning of *nari andolon*, a Christian women's movement, in a Bangladeshi region, this paper shows how Christian women, while enjoying greater physical mobility than their Muslim counterparts, are constrained by Christian and Muslim men's politics. Elite Muslims keep their women in strict *parda* (seclusion)[3] and use poor Muslims in their power struggle against rich Christians. All these structural conflicts and relations of domination and subordination are manifested through the shared ideologies of 'purity', 'honour', *parda* and 'community'.[4]

Honour/shame, purity/pollution and parda

In Doria the ideologies of honour/shame, purity/pollution and *parda* most directly affect the cultural notions of gender and sexuality (Ortner and Whitehead 1981). Social control of the sexual behaviour of both men and women, but especially of women, has been shown to be related to group solidarity, identity and social hierarchy (Goddard 1987; Davis 1973; Peristiany 1965; Schneider 1971; Pitt-Rivers 1965; Douglas 1966; Turner 1984). This paper argues that the control of female sexuality is also of the utmost importance in maintaining group boundaries and social hierarchy in Doria.

It is beyond the scope of this paper to enter into a detailed discussion of these ideologies, which are not unique to Doria or Bangladesh: they are present in many cultures, although their specific meanings vary. The notions of 'honour' and 'shame' are common throughout Middle Eastern and Mediterranean societies of Christian and Muslim background (Peristiany 1965; Schneider 1971; Pitt-Rivers 1977; El Saadawi 1980), while 'purity' is found almost everywhere, especially in cultures with Christian and Hindu traditions (Allen 1982; Dumont 1972; Yalman 1963; Fruzzetti 1982; Krygier 1982; Harris 1984; Warner 1976). On the other hand, the ideology of *parda* is commonly associated with Islamic societies, although its meaning varies from one Muslim society to another. However, in Middle Eastern and Bangladeshi societies observance of *parda* by women is often a concomitant of the honour of their families or lineages, and is also practised by non-Muslims (El Saadawi 1980; Rozario 1988a).

'Honour' and 'shame' are terms used to evaluate the behaviour of both males and females, but their specific meaning varies with context. Pitt-Rivers (1977) sees honour as having a general structure and as including qualities such as reputation, honesty and loyalty, while 'shame' involves sensitivity to public opinion. These terms apply to general conduct as well as to sexual conduct. In Doria the term 'honour' is clearly a positive quality and is seen primarily as a male virtue in villagers' relations with one another. The term 'shame' has connotations beyond its English equivalent, taking on positive virtues as well as negative qualities. To have 'shame' (i.e. to be sensitive to public opinion) is a good quality which serves to prevent a person from going against the social norm. From this point of view, to have 'shame' is desirable, because not to have 'shame' (i.e. shamelessness) is dishonourable for the person and his/her family or lineage. In Doria, in the course of a day, one comes across the phrases 'she has no *lazza-sharam* (shame)' or 'if she/he had any *lazza-sharam* she/he would not do this' several times. Although these phrases do not always have sexual connotations, in the case of women they are most likely to have them. A woman's 'misbehaviour' does not have to involve sex directly, as an impression of her sexual status is often formed from her day-to-day behaviour, for instance, how she walks, dresses or handles her hair, as well as how she behaves with her family, neighbours, etc.

However, a person may also cause or bring 'shame' and make himself/herself as well as his/her lineage shameful (i.e. result in loss of status). In this sense, shame is negative. In Doria I often came across remarks like 'she is the cause of *lazza* for her family' or 'she has "drowned" her family', meaning 'she is the cause of total loss of honour for her family'. On the whole, the idea of 'shame' acts as a restraint on female much more than on male behaviour. A shameless woman is liable to lose her sexual purity, bringing serious damage to her family's honour, whereas absence of shame in a man is not of such critical importance.

While, in theory, codes of honour and shame refer to the behaviour of both men and women, honour is seen more as men's and shame as women's responsibility. It is the responsibility of women to have 'shame' (e.g. preserve their sexual purity), while men's duty is to protect it. It is through their role as protectors that men's honour is determined. On the other hand, women's status or honour is related to their having 'shame' or preserving their 'purity' voluntarily. It is by voluntarily preserving their 'shame' that women can retain what Abu-Lughod (1986) refers to as the 'honour of the weak' (*hasham*). In explaining why those at the bottom of the social hierarchy (men and women) of Beduin culture accept the ideologies which in fact legitimise their subordination, Abu-Lughod (1986:104) argues that voluntary deference to those in authority is the 'honourable mode of dependency'.

The purity and pollution beliefs which are practised among the three religious groups in Doria have much in common. In all religious groups, women are associated with nature. Beliefs about female pollution (e.g. menstruation, childbirth) are the best example of this. According to Blanchet (1984:30), 'in Bangladesh and possibly elsewhere in Muslim India, the notion of purity and pollution appears in another guise, mainly that of a pervasive philosophical outlook which links purity with auspiciousness and impurity with misfortune, illness and catastrophe'. This philosophical outlook is shared by Muslims and Hindus as well as Christians in Doria. For instance, all three communities believe that various complications of children's and women's disease, illness or death are caused by certain evil spirits (bad air, or *bhut*). They also believe that a woman may come into contact with *bhut* only when outside the confines of the household, (i.e. by not observing *parda*). Hence, in all three communities, the idiom of *parda* is of utmost importance not only to safeguard the sexual purity of women but to avoid other forms of pollution.

Thus the norm of *parda* followed by women in Doria cannot be explained in relation to Islam alone, although Muslim women follow it much more strictly than Hindus and Christians. The

17

ideologies of honour/shame and purity/pollution are integrally related to the practice of *parda* and the latter is often a by-product of these ideologies. *Parda* (i.e. seclusion) means that women do not come into contact with non-related men or with the outside world. This in turn guarantees their purity beyond any doubt and hence the honour of their men, families and other groups including religious communities. Pastner (1974:409) defines *parda* as a 'highly ritualised expression of explicit values, usually referred to as "honour" and "shame", which are directly concerned with the status of women'. Although both men and women are seen as repositories of honour and shame, women are seen as being most susceptible to breaches of these important qualities. El Saadawi (1980) and Mernissi (1975; 1982) convincingly argue that underlying the practice of female seclusion in Muslim Middle Eastern and African societies is a concern about the preservation of the virginity of young girls and their chastity after marriage, on which the honour of a family depends.

In Doria, too, there is a clear relationship between *parda*, the 'purity' of women and the status or honour of their families, lineages and religious communities. This also means that the degree of *parda* observed by a woman is determined by her age, class and religious background.

Nari andolon *(women's movement)*

This nominal 'women's movement', which could have been more aptly called a 'men's movement', was initiated by Christian men to ensure the 'purity' and chastity of their women. It is argued that *nari andolon's* concern about Christian women's 'purity' reflected a deeper anxiety about the Christian communal boundary which was being threatened by its women's increased physical mobility and their interaction with non-Christian men.

The Christian *nari andolon* (women's movement) emerged at a time when the Christian community of Doria and the Palashi region was experiencing various economic, social and political changes. During the last decade a significant number of Christian men had taken up employment in the Middle East and left their wives and children behind for two to three years at a time. A large number of men were also employed in the metropolitan centres and they returned home about once a month. The Jute Works co-operatives and the BRDB (Bangladesh Rural Development Board) co-operatives increased the physical mobility of Christian women considerably. Wives of the men employed in the Middle East and the metropolitan centres, as well as members of the co-operatives, needed to become more mobile, not only in the nearby bazaar but also in the cities. In addition, women whose menfolk were unable to meet family responsibilities (e.g. because of alcoholism or unemployment) sought outside opportunities. In the bazaar and the cities, Christian women were coming into close contact with non-Christians. This increased physical mobility of Christian women endangered traditional notions of women's 'purity' and family honour, as well as blurring Christian communal boundaries. On the other hand, while Muslim and Hindu women were affected by the recent developmental changes, their physical mobility was still very limited, and was usually confined to within the village. Thus, as discussed below, the problems of a minority community of Christians were compounded even further.

The principle of male domination is well established and accepted in Bengali society among all religious groups. However, for Palashi Christians, male domination was being contested by an increasing economically based female independence. As Douglas argues, 'when the principle of male dominance is applied to the ordering of social life but is contradicted by other principles such as that of female independence, ... then sex pollution is likely to flourish' (Douglas 1966:142). This is confirmed by the case of the Christian *nari andolon*. In the past, female sexual purity was important but could be easily guaranteed to maintain family honour. However, as women's physical mobility increased, female sexual purity could not be as easily guaranteed; consequently, it acquired a new and striking significance in maintaining the family's and community's honour.

Thus increased mobility of Christian women, owing to recent socioeconomic changes, has created certain difficulties within the Christian community. Christians, who are marginal both structurally and culturally in the region, welcome many of these changes which enhance their economic position, but the increased mobility of Christian women is considered a problem. The presence of Christian women in the local bazaar was perceived as a

19

threat to men in general, but especially to Christian men, since the complementarity between status and gender categories might have broken down. Moreover, such a situation ultimately threatened to weaken the position of Christian men even further in the Muslim/ Christian power structure. However, the Christian community makes inconsistent demands of its women. Men and women attend the same church together, although they sit separately. Christian men, however, are not happy when their women go to the bazaar, which is recognised as male space. The source of this inconsistency for Christians is a consequence of living in a Muslim dominated society; the Muslim definition of the bazaar as male public space also applies to Christians. Christians normally do not make such a strict ideological division between the sexes, although they are influenced by the Islamic institution of *parda*. Because Muslim women refrained from going to the bazaar, Christian men saw their women as being accessible to and hence compromised by Muslim and Hindu men in the bazaar. Indeed, claims that several Christian women had run away or had 'affairs' with Muslim men were taken to confirm fears concerning the vulnerability of Christian women in the bazaar.

Palashi church records show that since 1971 some 35 Christian women married Muslim men and became Muslims. There were also four Christian men who married Muslim women and converted to Islam. In intermarriages, the trend seemed to be for Christians to convert to Islam. Thus the Christian authorities became particularly concerned about sexually fertile unmarried women and married women whose husbands were away as wage-earners in the Middle East or in the city. Women in these categories were without a male guardian, particularly one responsible for controlling their sexuality.

The *nari andolon* was initiated by some Christian men to address this problem. Some important points about its origin should be noted. In one of its meetings, the mission *samity*[5] discussed the problems of the increased mobility of Christian women. The members of the mission *samity* expressed concern about the increasing number of women marrying non-Christians as well as about the interaction of married and unmarried women with non-Christian men in the bazaar. In increasing numbers, women were freely going to the bazaar in order to use the services of the bank, doctors or tailors, or to purchase groceries. This interaction, however, was also bringing non-Christian men into their households, often in the absence of the menfolk: for their purchases women were using credit, and the non-Christian shop-keepers were calling into the Christian women's houses to collect debts. It was alleged that such visits were leading to unnecessary familiarisation between the Christian women and the non-Christian men. The mission *samity* decided that elderly women (i.e. the mothers) should be given the responsibility to control the movement of their younger women: daughters and daughters-in-law.

When, however, men first raised the matter concerning the presence of women in the bazaar, women pointed out that their men did not carry out their responsibilities regarding the bazaar (i.e. buying the household necessities) and therefore women were obliged to frequent the bazaar. Women argued that alcohol consumption was responsible for men's irresponsible attitudes towards the family and that they had to go to the bazaar to buy jute strings (to make jutecrafts) or other necessities because their menfolk spent their time drinking when they were home at weekends or on holidays.

Subsequently, some leading Christian men talked the women of their village into organising a protest movement against alcohol. Their argument was that since each 'alcoholic' man had either a wife, mother or sister, women were in the best position to tackle the problem. This movement later became known as the *nari andolon*. Its earliest members came from the only three villages without any non-Christian inhabitants, and gradually Christian women from other villages also joined the *nari andolon*. Non-Christian women were not invited to join.

The explicit goals of the *nari andolon* (as recorded in their minute book) were:

1 to stop oppression of women;
2 to guide young men and women towards the right direction in life; and
3 to solve all social ills by such measures as:
  a stopping families who made business out of making alcohol;
  b preventing free mixing of Christian women with unwanted, unknown and non-Christian men; and
  c preventing women from going to the bazaar.

21

However, the issues discussed in the *nari andolon*'s meeting mainly involved male alcohol consumption and the allegedly disreputable way of life of some women. These issues referred to goals number 2 and 3. Goal number 1 (i.e. 'stop oppression of women') was never a real issue to the male organisers of the *nari andolon*. It was used to justify the use of the words *nari andolon* (women's movement). Excessive consumption of alcohol—which gave rise to various family problems (e.g. financial difficulties, physical violence and mobility of women in the bazaar)—*was* recognised to be a problem. However, women were blamed for their husbands' habit of excessive drinking and the onus was placed on them to solve the problem. Women were told to act in such a way (e.g. by prayers, sacrifice and obedience to men), to enable the problem of alcohol to be solved. In one of the meetings, *nari andolon*'s members (guided by male organisers) discussed the reasons behind men drinking alcohol excessively, and they concluded that Christian men drank because their women (both married and single) were mixing or eloping with Muslim men.

Mothers were blamed for much of the young women's 'disreputable behaviour'. It was claimed that because mothers could not control their young daughters or daughters-in-law, the latter could go to the bazaar and indulge in activities which ruined the name not only of the individual or the family but of the Christian community as a whole.

Reference was also made to unmarried women wearing unsuitable clothes (e.g. tight-fitting *salwar kameez*), which interfered with their 'modesty' and 'purity'. Moreover, the *salwar kameez*, traditionally worn loose, was used only by Muslim women and its adoption by Christian women was very recent. Thus, underlying the criticism of wearing *salwar kameez* by women of adult age was not only the concern about lack of the 'modesty' and 'purity' of women, but also a concern about the Christian identity and the community boundary.

As will be seen, *nari andolon* was not so much concerned about the oppression of women; on the contrary, it was involved in the maintenance of female subordination. Moreover, alcoholism was only one of many factors that led to women's increased mobility. Very few men were alcoholics and only a few women's increased mobility was a consequence of their husbands' alcoholism or excessive drinking. Most women's mobility has to be understood by referring to the recent socioeconomic changes in the region. However, women used alcoholism as an excuse to justify their entry into the bazaar, the male space. Thus women remained trapped within a false framework: they could only cite alcoholism as a pretext, despite the fact that they really wanted mobility for other reasons. As a result, the focus remained on alcoholism, not on women's need for or entitlement to mobility. On the other hand, the male organisers of the *nari andolon* took up the issue of alcoholism not only because it led to women's increased mobility, but also because alcohol consumption was negatively perceived by the Muslims. Christians had been drinking alcohol for a long time but they began to perceive it as a real problem only recently when the relationship between the Christians and the Muslims became sensitive. Together with Christian women's increased mobility, which endangered their 'purity', alcohol consumption was also threatening the honour of the Christian community in relation to the Muslims. Hence it is no surprise that these two concerns were simultaneously expressed through the *nari andolon*. When mission *samity* expressed concern about women's increased mobility, women defined the problem as alcoholism and men defined it as lack of 'purity'.

Apart from a handful of wealthy women, a large number of poor women (who were contravening the norms of 'female dependence' and 'purity', and were the real target of the *nari andolon*) became involved in the movement. This has to be explained by the fact that *nari andolon* had started as a protest against men's excessive consumption of alcohol and was popularly known as 'movement against alcohol' (*moder birudhey andolon*). However, in reality it turned out to be a protest against the alleged 'misbehaviour' of women (i.e. their nonconformity to certain traditional values of female dependence).

The first general meeting of *nari andolon* that I attended was held in early January 1983. There were 44 women representatives from several villages in the Palashi mission. Two men, one young (Shujit) and another middle-aged (Parimal), were centrally connected with the *nari andolon*. It was they who initiated the *andolon* and nominated the representatives from individual villages, as well as choosing the members of the central committee. The president of the central committee was under their control and never acted without consulting them. Parimal and Shujit decided what should be discussed during meetings, at which, far from remaining neutral or in the background, they were the main speakers. Parimal criticised women's behaviour in the bazaar where they had to interact with Muslim men. In an effort to curtail women's entry into the bazaar, Parimal made a few suggestions as to how women could obtain jute strings without going to the bazaar. It should be emphasised that in organising the elderly women into *nari andolon* in order to restrict the physical mobility of younger women in the bazaar, Parimal was expressing the concerns of the whole Christian community.

The only woman who spoke in that meeting was the president, Shefali. Her concerns were along the same lines as Parimal's. She criticised women who, she claimed, went to see the local priest frequently, sometimes in the late evenings, between 8 and 9 o'clock. Shefali was using the ideology of 'purity' to control the mobility of poor women who often did go to see the priest to ask for financial help.

It is important to note that Shefali herself came from an affluent background and lived in one of the very few brick houses in the mission. Thus she would not have needed to see the priest for financial help. Shefali's criticism of women going to see the priest was an instance of the affluent using the ideology of 'purity' to heap abuse on the poor and thereby to control their behaviour. The women who went to see the priest were either widows with several dependant children or the wives of alcoholic husbands who suffered great financial strain. Such women found it impossible to manage without assistance from the priest or the Vincent de Paul Society. Except for emergencies, women usually went to see the priest in the mornings, the time set aside by him specifically for the purpose. In addition, some women, aged in their 30s and 40s, had to frequent the bazaar to buy jute strings or other groceries. Owing to financial problems, it was also they who used credit and as a consequence, non-Christian shopkeepers sometimes called into these women's households. Thus *nari andolon*, in its attempt to control the physical mobility of women, was adversely affecting the situation of the poorer women and their families.

At another meeting of the *nari andolon* held in a different village, similar points about women's 'misbehaviour', such as inappropriate clothing worn by young women and the mixing of women with non-Christian men, were discussed. It was stressed that Muslims were 'outsiders' (*bijati*—i.e. outside the community) and 'troublemakers'. A well-known Bengali saying, 'making the way for a crocodile by excavating a canal', was often used in relation to Christians inviting Muslims to their houses. In this context, the saying implied that it was the Christians' own fault that they were in trouble as they invited the Muslims to come into their households. Repeated use of this Bengali saying at the *nari andolon* meetings was a reflection of their anxiety about the Muslims, who were not only politically dominant but who were now 'taking advantage' of the Christian women. This posed a great challenge to the honour of the Christian men who became concerned about the 'purity' of their women and the communal boundary.

It should be noted here that when mission *samity* members initially raised the problem of increased mobility of Christian women in the Palashi bazaar, they did not necessarily link women's mobility to men's alcoholism. Hence, when a *nari andolon* was initiated, apparently to address the problem of alcoholism, mission *samity* members found it difficult to come to terms with it. On the one hand, by emphasising the need for obedience, modesty, immobility and the 'purity' of women for the benefit of their families (men) and the good of the Christian community, *nari andolon* was advocating the significance of male domination to maintain the identity and boundaries of the Christian community. Yet ironically, in order to work towards that goal, a certain amount of physical mobility of women was inevitable (e.g. the weekly or fortnightly meetings, attended by women of several villages). Hence, to some members of the mission *samity*, *nari andolon* was interfering with certain traditional values of the family, such as women's roles as housekeepers, childbearers and rearers, lovers and carers of husbands. These men were of the opinion that the only solution to alcoholism was love and modesty of women in relation to their men. The logic is that if women love their men they will obey them and curtail their mobility outside the house. That is, immobility of women would guarantee their 'purity'; the honour of the men would thus be guaranteed and they would not be tempted to indulge in alcohol consumption. In this way, the physical mobility of women created by their participation in the *nari andolon* brought to the fore the very concerns (i.e. women's 'purity') that *nari andolon* was founded to protect.

In late 1983, *nari andolon* invited a number of prominent figures from the Christian community (the archbishop, the local priest, the ex-president of the regional Christian youth association as well as its current president and some educated men from neighbouring missions) to their general meeting. While the archbishop and the local priest encouraged women's efforts to stop 'alcoholism' in the mission, other invited guests tried to discourage any kind of *andolon* amongst women.

The ex-president of the Christian youth association, an educated man, justified the excessive drinking habit of men. He argued 'the mental state of a man without a job is the same as the mental state of a woman without a husband', indicating the two most important things in a man's and a woman's life respectively. Arguing that drinking was not necessarily bad, he said that Jesus Christ himself encouraged drinking. The major point made by this speaker was that the cause of unhappiness in a family was 'loss of character' (*charitrahinata*). (Discussing one's character usually refers to one's sexual purity, and it is the purity of women that is of utmost concern, whereas a man, having had a number of 'affairs', may still remain a desirable groom.) He further added that a 'liberated' attitude in relation to women of the Christian community posed the main problem, leading to a 'loss of character' of women. Hence, according to him, a man drank when he was depressed either because he did not have a job or because his wife, sister or daughter had impaired her 'purity', thereby ruining his honour. Such an analysis of excessive consumption of alcohol was in line with the explanation of the *nari andolon* and represented the prevailing ideology of 'purity'.

Different meanings and functions of nari andolon

The socioeconomic changes which led to the dispersion of the Christian community in Doria caused it to feel threatened and insecure. The anxiety of the community was reflected in the emphasis its members began to place on various symbols in order to distinguish themselves from 'others' as well as to create a sense of belonging, of identity.

Some of these symbols (examples of which are given below) originated in Dhaka city, the seat of the archdiocese. They revealed that the concerns of the mission *samity* in Palashi reflected the anxiety and insecurity felt by the wider Bangladeshi Christian community. During the last decade a number of new associations, which may be viewed as symbols, were generated within the Christian community. 'Symbols refer to things which stand for or represent something else and allow those who employ them to supply part of their meaning' (Cohen 1985:14). In this sense, the following associations and rituals, including the *nari andolon*, had varying meanings to different members of the Christian community:

• In Dhaka city, an 'unmarried Christian women's association' was formed and its members attempted to perform functions similar to those of nuns. Most members were aged 25 and over and had to live in the city because of their employment. They met regularly to pray, and to discuss different problems of the Christian community. They often visited the households of Christian women who had married Muslim men in order to influence them to return to the church. They also visited sick people and prayed for their recovery. This association was formed by churchmen. The church was concerned about the increasing number of Christian women marrying Muslim men and the structure and function of the 'unmarried Christian women's association' was meant to 'create a consciousness of community' (Cohen 1985:53) and thereby to prevent women eloping with non-Christian men.

• Similarly, in 1979, a 'Bangladeshi Christian nurses' guild' was formed. Most of the Christian nurses were employed in the metropolitan centres, especially in the city of Dhaka. They came into direct and frequent contact with non-Christians through their daily activities and most of the Christian women who married Muslim men were nurses. The 'Christian nurses' guild' was formed in response to this state of affairs. Their meetings and conferences were marked by religious authorities (e.g. the bishop, priests and nuns) giving speeches about how to be a 'good Christian nurse'. Problems of Christian nurses deserting the church (*bipathey jaoa*—i.e. to leave the church by marrying non-Christians) were always discussed. Clearly the function of the nurses' guild was similar to that of the 'unmarried women's association': to reinforce the Christian communal boundary.

• In 1976 a 'Christian *jubo sebadol*' (Christian youth service team) was also founded. Two of its aims were 'to promote the Christian faith among the youth' and 'to create a brotherly relationship among them' (D'Costa 1981:34). Here again the aim was to create a consciousness within the community so that the young people would not easily stray from the community's standards. Lacking common spatial and social boundaries, Christians were symbolically represented as a unit.

• During this period there was also a considerable increase in the frequency of Christian rituals. One of the most important of these was known as the 'charismatic prayer session'. In these sessions a group of people got together in a private house or a church and said their prayers, asking for strength from the Holy Ghost so as to be able to lead a 'good' life, as well as engaging in Bible reading and discussing the problems of the Christian community. These 'charismatic prayer sessions' spread to the Christians in the villages, including Palashi mission. In addition, Christians in Doria and Palashi began to organise informal prayer sessions and the saying of mass in private households. These increased religious activities reflected the insecurity and anxiety the Christian community was experiencing and were a means for strengthening and confirming the Christians' identity.

It is within this context that the meaning and aims of *nari andolon* need to be understood. As in the abovementioned examples—the 'unmarried Christian women's association', the 'Bangladesh Christian nurses' guild', the 'Christian youth service team' and the 'charismatic prayer sessions'—the aims of the *nari andolon* were also to create a consciousness of the Christian community as distinct from non-Christians. By expressing concerns about Christian women's mobility in the bazaar and the metropolitan centres, their contacts with non-Christian shopkeepers and the elopements with Muslim men, the *nari andolon* was drawing attention to the problems of communal boundary. *Nari andolon*'s aims were to control the mobility and thereby protect the 'purity' of Christian women, and thus to maintain the communal boundary.

However, *nari andolon* involved the playing out of a range of different interests and different issues were involved for its members and others associated with it: men versus women, rich versus poor, old versus young. As Cohen (1985:71) argues, 'the same symbol can "mean" different things to different people, even though they may be closely associated with each other as members of the same community or bearers of the same culture'. The same was also true of *nari andolon* in its role as symbol. As a boundary-expressing symbol, it was shared by all, but it served different functions and meant different things to men and women, elderly and young women, wealthy and poor women; to members of the mission *samity* (elderly men); to the priest; and to the organisers of *nari andolon*.

As mentioned, as large number of women initially came forward to join the *nari andolon* in order to address the problem of men's excessive drinking, which was seen to be responsible for certain financial difficulties and physical violence within their families. Although most members of the *nari andolon* were elderly women, their different interests became apparent once *nari andolon*'s aims were set out more clearly. The interests of the wealthy women were the same as those of the male organisers. *Nari andolon*'s immediate goal was to prevent women entering the nearby bazaar. Understandably, this clashed with the interests of the poorer women, who depended on the Jute Works as a major source of income, or women who were compelled to frequent the bazaar for various other reasons (banks, doctors, groceries). But these women could not openly voice their opinion because *nari andolon* was dominated by the male organisers (Parimal and Shujit) and some wealthy women who gained status through their leadership roles.

Young unmarried women, who were not members but a target group of the *nari andolon*, saw it as directly interfering with the physical mobility they were enjoying through their membership of the Jute Works and BRDB women's co-operatives. For *nari andolon* it was of utmost importance to control the physical mobility of these women, to prevent them from eloping with Muslim men and to protect their 'purity'.

The above divisions and conflicts between women reveal the

different orientations of *nari andolon*'s members. Men were sometimes able to exploit these divisions between different categories of women. Wealthy but elderly women saw *nari andolon* as a means to enhance their own status through leadership roles. Their desire to control the physical mobility of poorer and young women was parallel to this leadership role and their identification with the aims of the male organisers. However, ironically, their leadership roles entailed greater freedom of physical mobility which was inconsistent with an important aim of *nari andolon*. Some of these women often travelled to the metropolitan centres to attend meetings associated with various religious functions. Their mobility was sometimes criticised by other potential leaders. Thus the ideology of 'purity' was not only used by men to control women; it was equally used by women themselves to control one another. It was through the ideology of 'purity' that different tensions and conflicts amongst the women manifested themselves.

Nari andolon did not mean the same thing to all men, either. Mission *samity* members were in a dilemma about *nari andolon*. On the one hand they were prepared to allow it to continue its activities, which were in line with male interests. Yet some men were against *nari andolon*'s existence. In order to attend the meetings of the central committee, representatives from different villages had to walk several miles. Hence, although the aims of *nari andolon* coincided with the interests of the mission *samity*, some men were not happy that it also increased the physical mobility of their women. However, because members of *nari andolon* were mainly elderly women, it did not create the same problem as it would if the members were young. Christian women who were beyond their childbearing age enjoyed a certain degree of physical mobility in Doria and its surrounding villages.

The local priest, on the other hand, viewed *nari andolon* as similar to the other existing organisations, (e.g. St. Vincent de Paul, Daughters of Virgin Mary), and thus as a ready source of various kinds of social work for the benefit of the mission.

Despite the differing interests and meanings attached to *nari andolon* by the abovementioned groups, they all acknowledged *nari andolon*'s role in symbolising the Christian communal boundary. It was ultimately as a communal boundary-expressing symbol that *nari andolon* was able to continue its existence, despite initial opposition from one of the most powerful organisations of the church, the mission *samity*.

Conclusion

Through the *nari andolon*, men were trying to ensure the 'purity' of their women as well as to maintain the boundary of the Christian social structure. Use of women for this purpose is understandable in that the view of women as moral police is a basic tenet of Christianity (Summers 1975) and other religions. One of the major functions served by *nari andolon* was the boundary drawn between 'good' women and 'bad' women. Wealthy members of the *nari andolon* who could afford not to frequent the bazaar were chosen as moral guardians, to control the physical mobility of poor and young women. Summers' (1975) analysis of the two stereotypes of Australian women, as 'damned whores' and 'god's police', makes very good sense in this respect. The poor and young women, who most commonly frequented the bazaar, were placed under tremendous pressure to avoid being categorised negatively.

By using the ideology of community, reinforced through the ideologies of 'purity' and 'honour', the Christians as a minority group gave expression to a concern about the stability of a boundary that was increasingly being threatened by the marriage of a growing number of Christian women outside their community.

When Christian women appeared 'available' to Muslim men (i.e. through non-participation in *parda*), Christian men felt compelled to 'protect' their womenfolk (and their own claims to those women) by imposing institutions similar to those of Islam in order to control the movement of 'their' women. The result was that the Christian community, through its desire to retain a religious identity, adopted similar institutions to those of the dominant community. Yet, for men, the problem was that they did not have the power within their own community to impose these restraints on their women. The *nari andolon* can be seen as an attempt by the men in the community to apply these restraints.

Finally, this paper has been an attempt to show the integral relationships between gender domination and the wider social structure, (e.g. class divisions, religious divisions, lineages and families) in a Bangladeshi region. Analysis of the *nari andolon* has made it clear that women's subordination cannot be understood in isolation from other social divisions. Thus within Western feminism there is a growing recognition that the theory of the common oppression of women is problematic. The fact is that women are divided by their class, race, ethnic and religious identity and also 'exploit, oppress and discriminate against each other' (Ramazanoglu 1989:95; Anthias and Yuval-Davis 1983; Newton and Rosenfelt 1985).

The use of women as status indicators by families and other larger groups, hindering those women's personal and economic independence, is also not unique to Bangladesh. Although the ideological mechanisms vary from culture to culture, women are used as carriers of group identity and boundary in most societies. Using women as boundary markers serves to maintain the hierarchical structure of a society, by means of gender, class, religious, ethnic or racial divisions. Similarly, it can be generalised and argued that in all societies with social hierarchies (including those based on class), notions parallel to that of purity/impurity—ability/inability and success/failure—are part of the legitimating discourse of the dominant group.

3 Housemaids: The effects of gender and culture on the internal and international labour migration of Indonesian women

Migration has been a feature of many of the diverse societies of the Indonesian archipelago, but was severely limited before the high age of European colonial penetration, in particular the era of direct colonial control which began in the nineteenth century. In this island world, population movement had been limited by a lack of transport, so the beginnings of European trade provided much of the incentive for increasing volumes of population movement. People moved first to the new port cities, with their mixed populations serving inter-island and international trade, and at a later stage of colonial exploitation, moved into mining and plantation areas.

The 1930 census, the earliest source of information about Indonesia's population, shows the greatest volume of movement was from (already overcrowded) Central Java, to the mines and plantations of Sumatra (Hugo et al. 1987:172). This early wave of migration exemplified the process, described by Miles (1987), of the critical link between migration and forms of unfree labour in the early phase of primitive accumulation in the development of capitalism. The lack of economic compulsion for the people of Sumatra to seek work in the new sectors of the foreign-dominated economy necessitated a search for labour elsewhere in the archipelago, in this case leading to the recruitment of indentured labour from Java (see Stoler 1985).

However, not all aspects of Indonesian migration can be understood in terms of the need for labour. The propensity for high levels of migration is one of the characteristics used to differentiate ethnic groups in Indonesia: hence images have emerged of the migratory Minangkabau (from Sumatra) and the seafaring Bugis (from South Sulawesi), for whom long-term absences from their native villages in far-flung regions of the archipelago are commonly regarded as fundamental cultural traits. In a well known typology, Hildred Geertz (1963) divided Indonesian cultures into two types, the centrifugal and the centripetal, the former essentially throwing off its members, the latter drawing them in. The classic centripetal society is Bali. In this typology, the inland people of the island of Sulawesi are also regarded as archetypically centripetal, whereas their neighbours, the coastal Bugis, are seen as essentially centrifugal. The 1930 census showed that while 10.5 per cent of the Bugis were outside their homeland, only 0.2 per cent of the inland-dwelling Torajans were outside their native territory (Hugo et al. 1987:224). These differences seem to have a cultural basis, and cannot be accounted for simply by economic or sociological causes. Also, they are not just scholarly typologies; ethnic stereotypes in the Indonesian popular consciousness enshrine these differences between ethnic groups.

The societies for which outmigration is a culturally determined proclivity are characterised by a particular form of male migration: long-term male absences, with the women staying at home and perpetuating the village economy and society (most notably the Bugis and the Minangkabau). In the case of Bugis migration, it has been argued that the impulse comes from the constraints this highly status-conscious and competitive society places on the upward mobility of lowly born males. They seek fame and fortune on distant shores (Lineton 1975).

The growing incidence of internal and international labour migration in Indonesia, associated with the development policies of the New Order government, which has encouraged both foreign investment and labour movement overseas as ways of absorbing Indonesia's growing labour force, has been characterised by a growing number of women migrants. While most of this movement can be seen as 'spatial movements of people to different sites of class relations' (Miles 1987:6), gender differences significantly affect the motivation and choices of migrants. There are different pressures on men and women, related to social, cultural and economic aspects of gender difference. These gender differences vary between ethnic groups; indeed, culturally specific variations in gender-defined behaviour are significant in defining ethnic differences in Indonesia. (The Bugis, for example, link an exaggerated concern with female modesty to notions of family honour and shame, regarded as fundamental to their cultural being.) In addition, these population movements take place in a sex-segregrated labour market, so the opportunities and experiences of male and female migrants differ.

This paper takes up two case studies of female labour migration in contemporary Indonesia: Torajan women from the interior of Sulawesi to the coastal cities and Indonesian (mostly Javanese) women to the Middle East (principally Saudi Arabia). In both these cases, the occupation most available to these women is working as housemaids, reflecting sex segmentation in the organisation of labour on a national and international level. There are important differences in the experience of women in the two situations which exemplify the significant ways in which culturally specific assumptions about appropriate gender relations affect the migration process.

Domestic service

Domestic service has been dealt with to a limited extent in the development studies literature, usually in discussions of urbanisation. It is not only that the growth of employment through industrialisation attracts migrants to the cities, but also that the rural crisis, with increasing population and land shortages, propels people to leave rural areas in search of work. The varied economic life of the city can provide niches, often in the so-called informal sector, when work opportunities have dried up in the countryside. Governments in poor countries tend to spend a disproportionate amount of money in funding services in the urban areas, and this further attracts migrants from rural areas (Lipton 1977). The limited and often capital-intensive industrialisation which has occurred cannot absorb all of this relatively surplus population, and so a characteristic of Third World economies is the growth of a large service sector (many governments are pinning their hopes on tourism as an important growth area). It is this area which tends to provide employment for women.

Latin American cities were identified by Ester Boserup (1970) as having a higher proportion of women migrants, many of them in domestic service, than other Third World countries. A number of women scholars have studied domestic service in Latin American cities, and the main issues in this discussion (most of it in Spanish) have been summarised by Jelin (1977).

Domestic service has been an important occupational alternative for young women (Jelin 1977:131), especially for rural women arriving in cities on their own, looking for work. (Women who come with their families, she comments, are more likely to carry out unpaid domestic work for their own households (Jelin 1977:131).) In urban areas in the Third World, domestic activities are not heavily socialised and are still carried out in a subsistence fashion in the home: tasks include washing by hand, ironing with primitive tools, sewing and shopping daily for unprocessed food. This creates an occupational niche for young women who can take on the servant role as an extension of their previous socialisation to domestic subsistence activities (although, for rural migrants, domestic service in urban areas tends to expose them to new household gadgets and routines). Unlike industrial work, this work is always available.

Domestic service provides an opportunity for young women to leave their families and natal villages and gain some autonomy, some control over their own lives (Jelin 1977:136). Indeed, it has been suggested that the higher rates of female urban migration in Latin America can be explained by women's lack of autonomy, and by the male control represented in 'machismo' (Jelin 1977:134; see also Gorecki's chapter in this book). In the Indonesian case, migration to the cities provides a way of young women avoiding family control, especially over matters such as choice of spouse. This is not to deny the significance of poverty, lack of services and limited opportunities for education and employment in the villages of origin as motivating factors affecting both men and women.

Women migrants move into the service sector because of a lack of alternative female waged work, especially the more highly paid industrial work. In a variation on the pattern found amongst most of its Asian neighbours, the Indonesian government, instead of setting up special industrial zones to attract foreign investment in manufacturing, has encouraged the establishment of factories in rural areas with high rates of landlessness. The workers are still predominantly young women, but they live under the 'protection' of their families and traditional village leaders (see Wolf 1984).

For young women with little education, domestic work is something for which they are fitted by their female socialisation. A Philippines study found that female domestic servants tended to be young, unmarried, poorly educated and from low status and rural backgrounds. They had few marketable skills, and so had to settle for jobs with low prestige and low pay (Palabrica-Costello 1984:240).

The origins of domestic service in Indonesia

Domestic service has always been a feature of the modern urban centres which have grown up as a consequence of European trade in the Indonesian archipelago. In its earliest form, both native and *mestizo* households were characterised by large numbers of retainers of slave status. However, the social position of the slaves cannot be understood as analogous to New World slavery (Reid 1983). Domestic slaves lived in the household and were involved in an intimate way with the daily life of the householder and family. Jean Taylor (1983) describes the social world which grew up in Batavia (now Jakarta). Until the nineteenth century, when the Dutch East Indies were under the control of the Dutch East India Company, Batavia was characterised by a *mestizo* culture, which was heavily adapted to the characteristics of native culture, including an emulation of the hierarchical practices of the native courts. This included the use of household slaves (1983:70). However, the end of company rule and the beginnings of a more bureaucratic colonial culture in the nineteenth century changed the character of this *mestizo* society. In 1818, the new regime banned international commerce in slaves to the colony, and by 1855 slavery was banned within Indonesia (1983:125). Subsequently, slaves were 'thinly disguised' as free servants (1983:132). Taylor describes the gradual disappearance of advertisements for slaves in the 1850s as 'one more indication of an increasingly authentic Dutch style of living in Indonesia' (1983:129). However, she does not tell us if this was accompanied by payment of wages to household servants, the beginning of a modern form of service based on wage labour.

The origins of this peculiar form of work, which shares some of the traits of production for self consumption and some of the traits of waged work through the money payment, historically relate to the introduction of new forms of production and new social relations of exploitation in the period of colonial expansion, although domestic service is not unrelated to forms of work existing in pre-capitalist society.

In contemporary Indonesian village society, young women are recruited into households to do unpaid domestic work. This might take the form of fictive adoption, or occur through drawing on kin ties (perhaps a younger sister or a niece.) This entails an obligation on the part of the household to provide for their sustenance, and (usually) to provide for at least limited education. Young men might experience similar forms of incorporation as household workers, for example through fictive adoption or through institutions such as bride service. Such relations of servitude are, at least in Sulawesi, often inherited from generation to generation. Like slavery in the precolonial context, they are an aspect of hierarchical social relations in the local community.

In the pre-colonial courts, servitude was extremely common, in such forms as slavery and concubinage. These were not merely impersonal economic relations; the slave often lived on intimate terms with the owner's household, and could claim a position of trust. The significant fact which delineated their unfree status was that they were not free to move to another place of work or to follow another master, as was the free man who was a client of the master (see Warren 1981).

Domestic service in contemporary Indonesian cities is an excellent representation of the contradictory nature of social relations in a society developing along capitalist lines in the periphery of the world system. It is a contractual relation, like the wage labour relation, with personal services being performed in return for a wage. However, other aspects of the relation reflect familial assumptions not usually associated with waged work. These assumptions of relations on a familial model are held by both householder and servant, and seem to replicate some of the assumptions underlying these relations in village society, where real kin ties were often involved in master–servant relations.

Internal migration: Torajan women in the cities of South Sulawesi

There is a growing form of out-migration in rural South Sulawesi, which owes more to the changes associated with the economic policies of the current regime than to long-cherished social and cultural patterns: that of the mountain dwelling Toraja of the interior, traditionally 'centripetal' non-migrants. Indeed, Volkman comments:

> For the Toraja ... there are no historical precedents for extensive migration, nor are there traditions which view the prospect of distant travel with relish. On the contrary, highlanders traditionally shunned unnecessary movement, preferring to stay close to their significant centres: the *tongkonan* [clan houses] ... Rituals reinforced the centripetal tendencies of Toraja life by periodically reconcentrating dispersed family members at the centre, and kinship ideally did the same, as preferred marriage 'returned to the house'. (1985:132)

There are some historical precedents for the outward movement of Torajans in the late nineteenth century slave trade, when many were captured by Bugis and sold to the lowlands. In the 1930s, more Torajans were forced to leave for the city or for areas to the north in quest of jungle products in order to pay taxes to the colonial government. However, the major outmigrations have occurred since the late 1960s, when the foreign investment policy of the New Order government led to the opening up of job opportunities in mining and extractive industries in Sulawesi, Kalimantan and West Irian. In the mining town of Soroako, to the northeast of Toraja, for example, Torajans were disproportionately represented amongst the unskilled labourers in the company labour force. Household servants (maids, cooks, nannies and gardeners) were almost exclusively Torajan (see Robinson 1986). (I was told that Torajans also dominated the domestic service category in a large foreign-owned copper mine in the distant province of West Irian.) The quest for employment extends also to the timber industries of Kalimantan, and there is illegal migration to the neighboring Malaysian state of Sabah. Political stability, as a consequence of the quashing of an Islamic rebellion (also in the late 1960s), facilitated this outmigration (Volkman 1985:134).

The migrants' purpose, according to Volkman, was often

expressed as 'looking for money' (1985:135). Apart from providing a livelihood for impoverished rural dwellers, money has the
added potential of being translated into symbolic capital through
the purchase of goods which confer status, but especially through
the 'ultimate demonstration of value and honour': sacrificing
buffalo at funerals (Volkman 1985:135).

Torajan migration differs from Bugis migration in that both
men and women leave. In Volkman's survey of outmigration from
a Torajan village, women were as numerous as men (1985:137).
In the environs of the Soroako nickel project, the proportions of
men and women from Toraja were very similar. An examination
of Torajan migration is a unique opportunity to investigate
female migration for, as Fahey (1988) has commented, studies of
migration have principally been on male subjects.

There are now considerable numbers of Torajans living outside
of their mountain region. Toraja has also become a popular
tourist destination, and visitors to the picturesque region may find
it difficult to accept that poverty is a principal motivation for
migration. The best-known area of Toraja is near Rantepao, in
the valley of the Sa'dang River. These villages have rich irrigated
rice fields on the river plain, many of which can be double
cropped with the new 'miracle' rice. Nonetheless, in this densely
populated Shangri-La, there is not enough land to go around, and
many leave for the city. However, the tourists rarely visit the
remote mountain villages where there are even more pressing
reasons for outmigration. Here there is little rice grown and the
villagers subsist on a variety of carbohydrate staples grown in dry
fields. Their income is supplemented with a small amount of cash
cropping. I visited an impoverished area in the western part of
Tana Toraja. We reached our destination after walking for more
than two hours from the end of a vehicular road, where there is a
weekly market. Public vehicles venture there one day a week, on
market day. The rugged foot track passed no other villages. The
village residents lived in a number of scattered hamlets, each of
only a few households. The most remote were not nucleated
settlements, but single houses amongst their scattered gardens
over the mountainous terrain. On market day, people make the
long walk to the market site, with their few goods for sale (a few
handfuls of coffee or passionfruit) and return with tea, sugar,

soap and other small items. These people have become dependent on the remittances of those living in the cities for the commodities of the modern marketplace, such as clothes, towels, torches, lamps and even foodstuffs like oil and sugar. Many of the village girls work as domestic servants in the city and acquire these goods as gifts from their employers, as well as buying them with their wages. These items are as important as cash remittances in the Torajan economy. Hence the outmigrating young women make important economic contributions to the village, and enhance the living conditions of their families.

Work is a strong motivation for most migrants, but for many the driving force is education. (Torajans are also proportionately over-represented amongst the students in the provincial university, where places are obtained by a highly competitive public examination.) But motivations of men and women differ in Torajan migration. For Torajan women, migration can be a way of avoiding obligations and expectations of family, especially concerning marriage, but also over schooling. A number of young women I knew in the city had run away from their families after a conflict of expectations, and had done so with the confidence that they could obtain domestic work in the city.

One case involved a young woman from the impoverished area described above. There was no elementary school in her remote village until 1978: she began school at that time, when she was about 12. Her family were extremely poor, and she had been 'fostered' by another family when she was small, whom she served as a kind of servant. When she wanted to continue schooling after Grade 3, her foster parents refused permission. There was a young man living in their house, also in a servile relationship. She hadn't realised it, but he was performing bride service in order to secure her as a wife. When she became aware of this, she ran away. A classificatory aunt, who worked as a domestic servant, was visiting the village. The young woman accompanied her to the city and found work. At the time she was about 15. She said that she was a very hard worker so her foster parents were angry when she ran away.

She has continued to behave as a 'dutiful daughter', but towards her real parents, not her foster parents, against whom she still bears a grudge. She has regularly sent her parents money, which they have set aside to build a house (referred to by them as 'her' house). She and her friends, mostly from the same area in Tana Toraja, participate in an *arisan*, a revolving credit association. They arrange the payouts to members to coincide with visits home, so they have money to take with them.

The usual pattern is one of chain migration, with young people leaving to join relatives or people from the same village in the cities. Once they reach their destination, the jobs available to men and women differ. Occupational specialisation by ethnic group is common in the cities and towns of South Sulawesi. In the case of the Soroako nickel project, Torajan men tend to come to work as wage labourers, while Bugis men are less likely to come as labourers, especially those who have originated from the areas best known for outmigration (see Lineton 1975). These people dominate the local market. Almost all of the domestic servants in the mining town are from Tana Toraja, whereas indigenous Soroakan, Bugis and Makassarese women are rarely found working as domestics. This is explained by strong notions about the protection of female honour, and an abhorrence of relations of servitude, seen as antithetical to the highly developed notions of honour and dignity characteristic of these ethnic groups. Particular kinds of gender differences are an aspect of the preoccupation with differential identity in South Sulawesi. Torajan women are heavily represented in other service areas, such as nursing: they are more pragmatic than Bugis or Makassarese in their choice of occupation.

In the provincial capital, Ujung Pandang, similar occupational segmentation occurs along ethnic and gender lines. Torajan men are well known as artisans—for example, roadside shoe repairers are all Torajan (Abustam 1975), as are many silversmiths and rattan furniture makers. They rarely own the enterprises, but provide the skills for small manufacturing enterprises, often owned by Chinese entepreneurs. In a similar vein, Torajan men rarely work as *becak* (pedicab) drivers, an occupation which is the province of rural Makassarese. Ideas about appropriate female behaviour and appropriate work conditions which are specific to certain ethnic groups in Sulawesi affect the segmentation of the workforce, so the majority of household servants in Ujung Pandang originate from Tana Toraja or the neighbouring region of Duri.

Domestic service in contemporary Indonesia

This section examines conditions of domestic service using data collected from interviews with, and observations of, a number of young women working as domestic servants in Ujung Pandang, the provincial capital of South Sulawesi. This account looks at their view of the job, their expectations about their conditions of work, including relations to their employer, the organisation of the working day and forms of remuneration. In examining the life histories of these women, it is clear that both the forces which cause them to leave the rural areas and their experience of the urban labour market are influenced by class and gender.

As in the Philippines study cited above, the majority of household servants in Ujung Pandang are young unmarried women. (In the mining town of Soroako, every household also has a garden boy (usually Torajan) but this is not so common in the city.) The servants live in the house under conditions similar to those experienced by children. Their food and clothing are provided and their movements outside the home restricted, taking place only with the permission of the householder. Given the anomalous situation of having in the home unrelated young unmarried women whose honour must be safeguarded, it would seem that these assumptions are important to safeguard the reputation of both servant and householder, for honour is a serious matter in South Sulawesi. The relationship is usually a highly personalised and even intimate one, although status differences are never disregarded.

Employers can also take responsibility for the education of the servant. For young women of rural origin with poor formal education, this would be most likely to take the form of sewing lessons. However, another common pattern involves an employer taking in a young person and putting them through school, even university, while they live in the house and perform some domestic tasks.

The familial assumptions are important for daily harmony, due to the intimate nature of the relationship, with servants living in the same domestic space. Newspaper reports from Jakarta indicate that these assumptions are breaking down in that urban jungle. There are numerous reports of servants stealing goods of great value, and even kidnapping children. There are also accounts of servants being treated badly, including reports of physical abuse. Whereas in the smaller city of Ujung Pandang household servants are recruited by word of mouth, with women already in employment calling (*panggil*) others to work with them or for their boss's friends, in Jakarta recruitment through agencies is common. Hence the initial encounter does not follow the personalised familial pattern.

The assumptions about the protective nature of the relationship mean that the women are, to an extent, exchanging one set of oppressive family relations for another. However, they still maintain basic control of their lives. It is, after all, a contractual relationship and they can leave at will (and frequently do).

Conditions of work

The common pattern (reflected in the organisation of work in Ujung Pandang) is that servants live in, and have duties which may extend around the clock. They are on call all the time, although their actual duties may take only a few hours per day. Although they are formally free, assumptions about the familial nature of the relationship, combined with their low status, mean that they do not leave the house without permission. This is an aspect of the control of their labour power, but also reflects an assumption that they are part of the household, and as unmarried women are not free to go out and about in the world. In my experience, servants expected such concern and protection from their employees. For example, one of my servants brought her nervous prospective husband to meet me, casting me in the role of her parents and older kinspeople.

Within the household, servants have well developed ideas about the division of labour (the apportioning of household tasks). Cooks are generally more highly paid and of higher status than maids, and within the daily functioning there is a strong notion of division of tasks. Conflicts arise if, for example, a slow worker expects a quicker worker to finish her work, hence intruding on what she sees as her rightfully earned leisure time.

Servants also have well developed ideas about fair reciprocity for their services, something which is not totally encompassed by monetary remuneration. The employer has to provide for their subsistence, and this has to be at an adequate level. There is also an obligation to provide clothes, including a formal expectation of one set of new clothes per year (at Christmas or the Muslim feast of Idul Fitri, depending on the religion). There is a notion that an employer and employee should '*cog-cog* (be harmonious)' and women will leave, rather than suffer an unhappy relationship. This seems to be so important in domestic service because of the familial assumptions about the nature of the relationship, and the enforced intimacy which results from the sharing of domestic space.

In the case of the foreign employers in the Soroako nickel project, many saw the relationship as a straight contractual one: service in return for the wage. They expressed a disinclination to pay the extra month salary at Christmas, and often did not see the necessity of feeding their employees (see Robinson 1986:250). Such behaviour was seen as mean (*kikir*) and as a denial of taken-for-granted contractual obligations in the employer–servant relationship.

A Torajan servant who is unhappy with her employer will 'vote with her feet'. A common ploy involves the fictive funeral. Torajans are often called back to their villages for funerals which are the most important ritual events in their culture, and demand participation by close kin. A woman who wishes to leave her place of employment will '*minta izin* (ask permission)' to return home, for a funeral or some other family crisis, and then simply fail to come back. (A refusal of such a request, even if it were false, would be a breach of the assumptions surrounding the 'understanding' between domestic workers and employers.) After a few weeks, the employer realises that the servant has effectively resigned.

Although good servants are in high demand, this does not seem to translate into a collective ability to demand higher wages. Perhaps, in a good relationship, the non-monetary component of remuneration is more subject to covert bargaining about such things as the quality and quantity of food and clothes provided, generosity with leisure time and leave, access to television and so on. It has been argued that the lower wages for domestic service relative to other forms of urban employment are offset by the fact that servants' subsistence needs are usually met, and that they benefit from gifts and access to aspects of the middle-class lifestyle, such as television (Palabrica-Costello 1984).

According to Smith (1973 cited in Jelin 1977:136—7): 'It has been asserted that domestic service provides one of the few opportunities for upward social mobility within the broad spectrum of the lower class.' This assertion has never been clearly demonstrated, but it has generated discussion about whether domestic service provides a stepping stone to waged work in the formal sector, or whether it is an occupational dead-end. (The kinds of industrial work available to young women in the newly industrialising countries lead us to question whether such employment is in fact superior.) Palabrica-Costello concludes that, in the Philippines, domestic service is clearly not a career occupation. Fewer than one in twenty of the women servants were over 30 years of age (1984:241). She attributes this to an almost universal rejection of married servants, due to the requirement of living in, and the almost round-the-clock demands. However, we also have to ask about the aspirations of the women themselves. Of those I knew in Ujung Pandang, most did not see service as a long-term 'career', and aspired to marriage and parenthood. One young woman who had worked for about ten years in the city was actively pursuing possibilities of marriage. She commented: 'You *'rugi'* (lose out) if you don't marry and have children. Who will care for you when you are old?' Another commented: 'Why should I keep working until I'm old and don't have any strength, so no-one will want to employ you? Who will feed you, especially if your parents are dead?'

An older unmarried woman, who had experienced a number of mental breakdowns which she attributed to love magic employed by a spurned suitor, worried about her future as she had no children, and hence no one to care for her in her old age. She was keen to build a house so a niece or nephew would be willing to live with her.

Although these women do not see domestic service as lifelong employment, the way out through marriage is difficult because they are no longer willing to settle back into a rural village, having enjoyed city life. They stand out in the villages with their stylish clothes and confidence. In the city, they live their lives in a web of Torajan social relations, revolving around the church and their city-based kin. This network is the source of potential spouses.

They maintain close ties to their natal villages, revitalised at

46

regular intervals by visits home, especially at the time of significant life crisis events like funerals. The money and gifts they take home on these visits, and the agricultural produce they bring back to the city, serve to maintain these relations. However, filial piety does not seem to stretch to marrying a village boy selected by their parents. Their independence having been established, they are reluctant to give it away , even for the sake of marriage.

For these young women, the changes in their lives through pursuing work in the city are contradictory. On the one hand, the familial assumptions surrounding their employment offer the paternalistic protection of the family, but on the other hand, they are in the position of being free workers, and have achieved some independence from the strictures of family relations. As Hantrakul has argued for Thai prostitutes, their independent actions and economic autonomy challenge many of the customary definitions of female behaviour (see Hantrakul 1989). The international migrants discussed below find themselves in a situation where those familial kinds of protection are absent, where they find themselves exploited both as workers and as women.

International labour migration: Indonesian women to the Middle East

In recent years in Indonesia, some public concern has developed about the working conditions of the growing number of Indonesian women being recruited as domestic servants to the Middle East. The nature of the public outcry reflects the assumptions surrounding the institution of domestic service in Indonesia, as well as underscoring the significance of the gender bases of the migrant experience.

From 1983 Indonesia joined several other Asian countries in allowing recruitment of its nationals to work in the Middle East. By September of that year, it was estimated that there were 47 000 Indonesian nationals working in Saudi Arabia, and there were hopes that the number would double in the following year (*Berita Buana* 22 September 1983). The scheme was viewed with enthusiasm: the Indonesian ambassador to Saudi Arabia, for example, commented that it would both lead to increased work opportunities for Indonesians, and earn valuable foreign exchange. (He claimed that workers were able to send up to 60 per cent of their salary as remittances to the home country: *Berita Buana* 19 August 1983.) However, the high hopes of the Middle East as a source of jobs for skilled workers were not realised. Indonesia was a latecomer into the market, which had absorbed thousands of construction workers from countries such as the Philippines, Thailand and Pakistan. For the poorly skilled Indonesian male workers who were initially recruited, there were few job opportunities. One area of expansion in the Saudi economy was for domestic workers, and by 1984 the majority of Indonesian migrants were women, mostly working as housemaids. A survey of a sample of 400 Indonesian migrants revealed that 78 per cent were women. Their reported ages were between 25 and 34. Of these women, 26 per cent had never attended school, while 63 per cent had some primary school education, and almost all came from the rural areas of Java. Most had no previous employment experience as housemaids, or any relevant training (Cremer 1988:76). Indonesian women were able to slot into this niche in the Saudi Arabian economy because the countries which had supplied the male construction workers—Bangladesh, the Philippines and Pakistan—had not undertaken to allow the recruitment of women as housemaids due to perceived problems in 'worker protection' (Cremer 1988:77).

Indonesia attempted to offer some protection by limiting recruitment to a number of companies licensed by the Ministry of Manpower. They were not allowed to operate directly in the villages, but had to recruit through newspaper advertisements, and from amongst job seekers registered with the Department of Manpower. The workers had to be offered contracts specifying minimum wages and be provided with insurance, as well as pre-departure training and orientation (Cremer 1988:78). The agency was responsible for their travel, with costs met by a recruitment fee paid by the Saudi employer. The fact that Indonesians are Muslim made them acceptable for deployment in Arab households (Cremer 1988:81). However, none of the women was able to speak Arabic. The women were attracted by advertisements promising high wages and light work, as well as the prospect of a possible pilgrimage to Mecca (*Kompas* 12 May 1984; Cremer 1988).

In a very short space of time, there was as outcry in the

Indonesian press about the conditions under which these women were working, including complaints of beatings and sexual exploitation and accusations that the women were not being paid the promised wages. The Indonesian Embassy was accused of not carrying out its duty to protect its citizens. Indeed, the embassy could not even advise how many Indonesian citizens were working in Saudi Arabia. The public outcry reflected the assumptions underlying domestic service in Indonesia, in particular the invocation of familial relations as the appropriate model. Their exploitation and abuse were seen as more heinous than the exploitation of workers in an industrial workplace. The workers' isolation in the homes of their employers and their silence due to their inability to speak Arabic facilitated the exploitation but also made it more shocking, as such vulnerability would demand the protection of the paterfamilias in Indonesia. Local laws offered no protection to domestic servants (Cremer 1988:81).

The Indonesian ambassador published an article which reported that between January 1984 and February 1986 there had been 3600 complaints to the embassy from Indonesian housemaids: complaints of long hours, payments below the contractual wage, beatings and sexual abuse. He likened their condition to slavery (Cremer 1988). Some reports claimed that their travel documents were held by the bosses.

In May 1984, the Islamic organisation Muhamadiyah publicly demanded that the government stop the recruitment of women to the Middle East because of these undesirable practices, and the fact the government, through the embassy, seemed incapable of providing any protection. It was thought that many of the women were illegal migrants, not even having the formal protection of a system of recruitment through the licensed operators (hence the difficulty in keeping track of them) (*Kompas* 12 May 1984).

Public opinion, as represented in the newspapers, demanded that the government intervene, acting in an appropriately paternalistic manner to safeguard the wellbeing of its citizens abroad. The government did not share this view, resisting the demand to intercede with the powerful Saudi Arabian government. The Minister for Labour tried to impose a ban on workers speaking to the press about mistreatment abroad (*Tempo* 20 July 1985) and ultimately declared that workers who went abroad would do so at their own risk (*Kompas* 17 January 1986). Although the Indonesian government usually defines its role in relation to society in a paternalistic manner (see Robinson 1989), in this case it rejected the demand from its citizens to act to protect some of their number in an area of life where paternalism is seen as appropriate: the protection of young women working as servants.

As in the case of the Torajan women in Ujung Pandang, the motivation for international migration was poverty, but the occupational niches available were defined by gender. Also, the exploitation to which migrant women were subjected, especially sexual abuse, was gender specific.

Domestic service is regarded as 'unskilled' labour because it requires no formal education. However, women are regarded as more suitable than men for this work precisely because they have had skills training as part of their female socialisation. Domestic service operates as part of the informal, or unregulated, sector of the economy. The conditions of work—often in isolation in the employer's home—have great potential for exploitation. Cultural constraints are significant in mitigating this potential, in particular assumptions about the familial nature of the relationship and the need for protectiveness on the part of the employer. The outcry in Indonesia over the treatment of the women in Saudi Arabia points to the viable nature of these assumptions. Within Indonesia the women have access to some resources, in particular their families and their social networks, giving them a limited degree of power in negotiating work relations and work conditions—something which is lacking in the case of international migration. Torajan women in Ujung Pandang are protected by cultural assumptions which are reproduced in the context of the reality of the woman's capacity to escape an invidious situation. In the Middle East they are regarded as 'other' and outside the protection afforded women of Saudi households. Cultural credos about male responsibility to protect female honour are not adhered to in the case of the Indonesian domestic workers abroad, whereas they do appear to influence the way female servants are treated at home. There have been no revelations in the press about ill treatment of male workers in the Middle East. The domestic servants were ill treated because of their vulnerable status as unregulated workers in the home, and because they were women.

With worsening economic conditions in many parts of the world, increasing numbers of people, and particularly women, are going to be drawn into highly exploitative service sectors of the world economy (most notably domestic service and prostitution). Their experience must be understood in both class and gender terms, in order that appropriate political strategies can be found in addressing these problems. For example, banning sex tourism is no solution to the problems of poor women in Thailand. They themselves call for decriminalisation of prostitution (see Hantrakul, 1989).

The issues of poverty and exploitation need to be addressed more thoroughly in terms of culturally determined gender relations as well as economic inequalities. In internal migration, Indonesian women obviously benefit from regional and familial networks as well as the 'familial' mode of domestic work. Both of these, however, are absent from the international experience, which is clearly exploitative in formulation and practice. The 'push' factors of migration need to be addressed. But the specifically female dimension to the migrant experience also requires far more attention and understanding.

MARGARET JOLLY

4 The politics of difference: Feminism, colonialism and decolonisation in Vanuatu

Women's Liberation or Women's Lib is a European disease to be cured by Europeans. What we are aiming for is not just women's liberation but a total liberation. A social, political and economic liberation. Our situation is very different to that of the European women. Look around you and see, especially in town. Hundreds of our women slave everyday for white women. They cook, clean, sweep, and wash shit for crumbs from European women. European women thought up Women's Liberation because they didn't have enough to do, and they were bored out of their minds. They wanted to be liberated so they could go out and work like men. They were sick of being ornaments in the house. They hate their men for it. That's not our position at all. Our women always have too much to do. Our women never have the leisure to be ornaments. Our societies are people oriented so we care for one another. Our situation also affects men. (Molisa 1978:6)

These are the words of Grace Mera Molisa, in a speech delivered to the First National Conference of Vanuaaku Women on Efate, 1978. In 1990, Molisi was Private Secretary to Father Walter Lini, Prime Minister of Vanuatu from independence in 1980 to the present. In this chapter I examine her views on feminism and colonialism as expressed in her essays and volumes of poetry. I will situate these in the broader context of the views of black feminists in America and Britain, and of other Pacific and Aboriginal spokeswomen. Her views cannot be dissociated from the experience of colonial history in the Pacific and the problematic

52

ways in which European and indigenous women were brought into association in the course of that history. A greater understanding of that history is needed in the theoretical and political attempts by Australian feminists to appreciate the politics of difference *between* women.

Plurality and power

The politics of difference mean recognising ethnic and class differences between women as a starting point for feminism, rather than as an embarrassing afterthought. Moore has recently shown the problems of assuming identity between the interests of all women in a way that denies ethnic and class differences (1988: 7–11). Universal models of woman are often grounded in the experience of white, bourgeois women. This is why many 'women of colour' experience the women's movement as imperialist—since the political issues and the theoretical concerns which are central to white feminists may be marginal to them. Rather than admitting the plurality of women's different situations and thus the need for different feminisms, white feminists have tended to presume that their politics are more sophisticated and developed, thus condescendingly treating other women as constrained by 'tradition', feudalism or underdevelopment (Bhavnani and Coulson 1986; Bourne 1983; Carby 1982; Thornton Dill 1983).

As Moore (1988:7–8) and Bhavnani and Coulson (1986:81) insist, dealing with ethnic difference does not just involve dealing with ethnocentrism, but also with racism, since relations of race and ethnicity are implicated in relations of power. Thus the problem is not just that political and theoretical differences exist between white women and women of colour, but that these differences can reflect real conflicts of interest. In the American context, conflicts have surfaced over the white bourgeois character of demands for paid work and equal employment opportunities for women, and controversies about 'abortion on demand'. For example:

> The bourgeois individualistic theme present in the contemporary women's movement led many Black women to express the belief that the movement existed merely to satisfy needs for personal

self-fulfillment on the part of white middle-class women. The emphasis on participation in the labour force and escape from the confines of a home, seemed foreign to many Black women. After all, as a group they had had higher rates of paid labour force participation than their white counterparts for centuries, and many would have readily accepted what they saw as the 'luxury' of being a housewife. At the same time they expressed concern that white women's gains would be made at the expense of Blacks and/or that having achieved their personal goals, these so-called sisters would ignore or abandon the cause of racial discrimination. (Thornton Dill 1983:133)

The very freedom white women had to get good jobs often depended on black women doing their housework. Similarly, abortion on demand was not so compelling for black women in a country where doctors and the state had been only too willing to abort or sterilise them. Amos and Parmar (1984) point out that the present controversies about forced sterilisation and the use of Depoprovera for black women in the United States are simply the culmination of decades of eugenically informed birth control—promoting white women's fertility while constricting that of black women (1984:13).

For Britain, Amos and Parmar (1984) and Bourne (1983) argue that black feminists have different approaches to the family, sexuality and the state, and that white feminists have often displayed extreme insensitivity to this in political campaigns. The family, analysed as a major site of white women's oppression, has for many black people been a crucial site of struggle and survival. Black families have been ripped apart by slavery and labour migration, and those different family forms which evolved in response to these pressures (e.g. female-headed households, extended families) have been pathologised and seen as inhibiting of women. Similarly, sexual liberation has not been so central to black women, because there have been more pressing issues of economic or political survival, and because black women were already cast as oversexed and licentious, in opposition to white women (see also Nkweto Simmonds 1988). Bhavnani and Coulson (1986) allege that feminists have colluded with the state's criticism of 'arranged marriage' as a way of denying entry to migrants and in moves against male violence in 'reclaiming the night' (1986:84–5), precipitating public hysteria about black male sexuality, which was thus linked to rape and street crime (see also Bourne 1983:13–14).

In Australia, in the early phase of second-wave feminism, there was a similar suppression of class, ethnic or party-political divisions which were seen as divisive of sisterhood. I have a strong memory of such debates being quashed at a plenary session of the first Women and Labour conference at Macquarie University in the mid-1970s. It was Mothers' Day, and there was much waving of white chrysanthenums—a beautiful celebration of our shared sisterhood or weapons brandished to police difference? Partly as a result of challenges from migrant and Aboriginal women, our movement has matured and proliferated since, but there is still a fundamental problem of recognising difference. The newly formed National Foundation of Women is presently struggling to make itself more accessible to all women—regardless of class, colour, age or sexuality (Denoon 1989).

Such political questions cannot be dissociated from theoretical attempts to deal with the complicities of gender, race and class (Bottomley and De Lepervanche 1984; Anthias and Yuval-Davis 1983); (Jenette et al. 1987, Pettman 1988). The former writers suggest that, rather than dealing with these as three autonomous systems which relate only through mechanical accumulation, we should treat them as intersecting and complicit. Thus, rather than a description of the triple oppression of being a woman, black and working class, we would presume that class and ethnic categories are gendered, that gender and race have a class character, and that gender and class have a racial dimension. The intersection of these systems in practice has been explored in Anthias and Yuval-Davis's work on women migrants to Britain and by black American writers such as Angela Davis (1971, 1982). Importantly, this is not just intersection in terms of personal experience, but in terms of structural complicity, for example in relation to the state.

The politics of listening to indigenous voices

It is in this political–theoretical context that I want to approach the words of Grace Mera Molisa's quoted at the beginning of this paper, and examine the usual responses of white Australian feminists to such assertions. A first defensive response is to question the veracity of these images of white women and European feminism. We might argue that this view of white women in the colonies is at variance with historical evidence, which shows white women in the colonies of the Pacific and Australia to have been hardworking and socially active, hardly bored creatures devoted to leisure and self-adornment (Knapman 1986; Dixson 1976; Daniels and Murnane 1980). Moreover, we might add that this stereotype hardly fits many white women from working- and lower middle-class origins in the countries of Europe from which women came to the region. We might also argue that feminism in our experience is a much more expansive and differentiated movement than the portrait of women's liberation proffered by Molisa. Women's lib evokes a liberal individualist feminism, associated with an early phase of American feminism. But at the time of Molisa's speech, and much more so since, this has been only one kind of feminism. Feminism has always been politically plural. Debates between radical and socialist feminist positions, between those espousing a politics of difference and those espousing a politics of equality, between those embracing lesbian separatism and those maintaining that heterosexuality and feminism were compatible—these controversies have been vital to our movement (Eisenstein 1984). In many countries, a collectivist orientation in feminism has been as strong as an individualist one, and in European countries such as Italy and Greece feminism has been closely allied with socialist or social–democratic movements for economic and political liberation (Bottomley 1986; 98ff.).

Despite the force of such arguments, it is important to get past this first defensive response and understand *how* and *why* the contrast between white women and black women is being drawn so strongly. As Australian feminists, we face a particular political problem in our relations with Aboriginal women in Australia and with Pacific women within and outside Australia. There is the general problem of white feminists dealing with Australian women of colour, the rainbow spectrum of ethnic identities resulting from a long process of migration. But the problem is more acute with indigenous women because they identify us not so much as the Anglo inhabitants of Australia, but as the white invaders of their lands. There is a strong and persistent sense of racial difference and conflict born out of the history of colonialism in our region. The politics of colonialism and decolonisation impede easy alliances with Aboriginal and Pacific island women. This is, as we shall see, not just the archaic heritage of a bygone age, but a politics which persists to the present.

This is obvious in these words of Grace Mera Molisa proclaiming the irrelevance of European feminism. But on what grounds is European feminism dismissed? 'Women's liberation' Western style is seen as inappropriate because it deals with personal liberation, with individual autonomy rather than questions of collective liberation or communal autonomy. It is seen as partial because it deals with women's liberation apart from broader issues of social, economic and political liberation. It is seen as irrelevant, since it addresses the situation of white women, not the very different situation of black women. White women are portrayed as leisured and bored, 'ornaments in the house', who desire to get out of the house to go to work. Ni-Vanuatu women by contrast, do not have the time to get bored nor the leisure to cultivate themselves as ornaments. They work hard, not just for their own families, but in the households of European women, doing domestic work for a pittance.

Similar sentiments have been expressed by many Aboriginal spokeswomen in this country and by some women holding high political or bureaucratic positions within other Pacific states such as Papua New Guinea (Burgmann 1984; Sykes 1975; O'Shane 1976a; Johnson 1984a; Rooney 1989; Grimshaw 1981; Larbalestier 1977, 1980 and this volume). The grounds on which European feminism is dismissed are also rather similar (and parallel opinions have been expressed by women of colour in America, Britain, and in international forums). Firstly, European feminism is said to be too preoccupied with individual autonomy and personal psychology rather than the values of community and kinship. Secondly, and related to this, black women often defend the family as the site of cultural survival and resistance to white occupation. Thirdly, it is said that European women are too preoccupied with issues of sexual liberation and reproductive freedom, which they view with suspicion, if not hostility. Fourthly, whereas European women proclaim the necessity of getting women out of the house and into the paid workforce, non-European women have always worked both within and outside of the home, and moreover have often performed domestic work for European women (see Alenyse Ward (1987) for a painful evocation in her novel *Wandering Girl*).

Some Aboriginal and Pacific Island spokeswomen go further and assert that the position of women prior to European occupation was, if not equal to that of men, separate and complementary. The indigenous relation of men and women is portrayed as being one of harmony and co-operation, not conflict (e.g. Rooney 1989; Johnson 1984a). Thus the contemporary problems of male domination and violence by Aboriginal/Pacific island men are seen as the result of the ravages of colonialism. Unemployment and poverty, alcoholism and despair are consequences of political emasculation and paternalism (but see Langton 1989). Finally, it is argued that the primary struggle is for the Aboriginal/ Pacific nation and that raising the problem of women will compromise the unity of that struggle or divide the nation. This is sometimes linked with the view that the problem of women can be dealt with afterwards or that the problems of sexism are minimal compared to the dire problems of racism, poverty, underdevelopment and the struggle for survival.

Unlike some Aboriginal and Pacific spokeswomen, Grace Mera Molisa does not claim that women were indigenously the equals of men, or that contemporary male domination is only the product of colonialism, or that naming women's subordination is divisive of national unity. Though suspicious of the relevance of European feminism and strenuously advocating the need for an autonomous movement of Ni-Vanuatu women, she does assert that many of the indigenous cultures of Vanuatu were male dominated, that present problems represent a compounding of Melanesian and European misogyny and that women must struggle to keep the issues of gender on the agenda in the post-colonial state.

Let us look more closely at her speech made to the First National Conference of Vanuaaku Women at Efate in 1978. Here she asserted that women were oppressed both by traditional structures and by introduced structures of church and politics. She pointed to the way in which sons were preferred over daughters, despite the fact that women were valuable because of their economic, sexual and reproductive roles. In summation, 'in traditional society there is nothing a woman can't do, except enjoy equal status with men' (Mera Molisa 1978:2).

Moreover both the Christian church and Western-style politics were, she claimed, 'male-oriented and male-dominated' (1978:4). She suggested that in both Biblical representations and contemporary Christianity women were auxiliaries, 'complete only when paired with a man'. Eve was made from Adam's dispensable rib; God sent his son not his daughter; and the twelve apostles were all men. The Biblical figures of Mary, Mary Magdalene and Martha were all subservient, suffering and passive. Within the comtemporary churches, elevated positions in the hierarchy were exclusively male—'Pope, Archbishop, Bishop, Priest, Deacon, and Elder'—while 'women slavishly keep the church house clean, raise funds for the church, look after the visitors, give gifts for the needy ... Anything in the name of the church, women will do but to share some of the power the men enjoy. No! No! No!' (1978:5).

In the political processes prior to independence, Molisa saw women as being without power. But she argued that this had to be changed in the process of attaining independence; it could not be delayed until afterwards. 'Otherwise our achievement of Independence will only be a half-victory. A victory for the freedom of men but not of women' (1978:6). She here draws a direct analogy between the European colonisation of indigenous people and male power over women. Just as the tentacles of the colonisers are difficult to disentangle and break free from, so are those of men over women. Men, like colonisers, are not likely to relinquish their privileges easily. So women must fight, using their powerful role as mothers and educators, in moulding and re-educating their daughters and their sons and thereby collectively transforming the political culture.

Her more optimistic hopes, and those of several others within the ruling Vanuaku Pati, have not been realised in the independent state of Vanuatu. Her concern about the persistence of male colonisation of women in the post-colonial state is clear from two recent volumes of her poetry, *Black Stone* and *Colonised People* (Mera Molisa 1983 and 1987). There are some interesting differences between the dominant themes and concerns of these two volumes. The first balances the tension between the achievement of nationhood and the perils of neocolonial existence, with only a couple of poems making reference to the situation of women. The second focuses on the problem of women in the post-colonial state: whereas men are free in the independent nation, women are still colonised.

In *Black Stone*, the nation of Vanuatu is evoked in images associating people, place and the geological forces of volcanic eruption and solidified lava. In *Vanuatu* she talks of the land as ageless and primeval, creating place and people in perpetuity (1983:7). In the title poem, instead of a temporal image of eternity, she evokes the spatial equivalent of immobility.

> Black Stone
> Molten lava
> solidified
>
> solid
> jagged forms
> starkly
> awe inspiring.
>
> Black Stone
> immovable
> immobile
> Black Stone.
> (1983:8)

Political forces of nationalism are seen to emanate from the true people of the place. The Vanuaku Pati is defended not as a 'self-interested petty bourgeois dissident urban fringe' but as a 'rural mass movement' ('Victim of Foreign Abuse', 1983:13). Foreign observers and overseas media are castigated for their ignorance and their negative reportage of Vanuatu:

> Why ram
> Freedom of the Press
> down our throats
> when our networks
> and media
> of drummed
> tam tam speech
> are as free
> as the air
> transporting

and broadcasting
information?

What truth
is there
in the definitions
and descriptions
by an Outsider
who has never met
nor seen us
and is totally
ignorant
of our habitat
and environment?

Metropolitan
journalists
flock to Port Vila
crawling the bars
sniffing the farts
of other
transient scavengers
and go away
experts
on Vanuatu politics.
('Newspaper Mania', 1983:15)

The impregnable fortress of Melanesian solidity, manifest in the condensation of people and place, the solidified lava stone of the nation, is opposed to the transient predations of foreign observers. And the foreign values of democracy and press freedom are counterposed to the indigenous values of consensus, the one the tyranny of the majority over the minority, the other the harmonious conciliation of all views. The value of traditional leadership is revered in the person of her grandfather, a combination of philosopher, judge, diviner and doctor—'master of melanesian mysteries' (1983:10).

But in the same volume, the mess of meanings and the multiple uses of 'custom' are evoked, especially as they affect women:

'Custom'
misapplied
bastardised
murdered

61

> a frankenstein
> corpse
> conveniently
> recalled
> to intimidate
> women
> ('Custom' 1983:24)

The image of women in this volume is often of women as victims. 'Marriage' portrays men as parasites sucking women in order to flourish, meanwhile transforming:

> nubile form
> to formless blob
> of vegetating glob.
> (1983:27)

'Pregnant Blues' depicts a state of misery and loneliness. The woman in childbirth writhes in agony alone as the cocktail circuit and the rounds of politics proceed. Only the 'boundless bosom' of God, of Tangaroa, offers her solace.

But though women may have been victims, Molisa looks forward to a time when women have a commanding Presence. Leitak and her Biblical compatriate Mary are envisioned as 'a stately pair', dignified, gracious, 'Ladies of Precedence', models for Ni-Vanuatu women leaders. Still these strong models of women politicians are qualified by a sense of how love and personal life are often sacrificed to political pursuits:

> On the Altar
> of popular
> political
> will
> lie
> the ashes
> of
> Love.
> ('Estrangement' 1983:29)

Molisa portrays politics as a nasty game—not just as played by the self-interested secessionists, land speculators and French collaborators involved in the moves to impede independence (see Beasant 1984), but as played by all politicians. Gluttonous power induces stupor and dissociation from the grass roots; inexperience and indecision yield incapacity.

> Half-Baked
> politicians
> by accident
> of history
> play Big Man
> at State expense.
> ('The Mooted Motion' 1983:58)

Molisa's second volume of poetry, *Colonised People*, published seven years after independence, amplifies this critique of men and the post-colonial state. In the introduction to this volume she highlights this fact: 'Vanuatu is now free of foreign colonial domination but Ni-Vanuatu women are still colonised'. This para-dox informs the title poem:

> Vanuatu
> Supports
> Liberation
> Movements
> for
> the Liberation
> of
> Colonised people
>
> Clear
> articulations
> of support
> for
> freedom fighters
> in East Timor
> West Papua
> French Polynesia
> and Kanaky
> Vanuatu
> Womenfolk
> half
> the population
> remain
> colonised
> by

the Free men
of Vanuatu

Womenfolk
Cook, Sew,
feed, clothe
housekeep
homemake
childbear
healthcare
passively
following
orders
instructions
commands

Women
are treated
as if
having no brain
as if
having no thought
as if
having no feeling
as if
incompetent
and incapable

Man's
colonial
domination
of Woman
is exemplified
in the submissive
subservient
obedience
to Man's rule
and authority
which takes
Woman Vanuatu
for granted
as
a beast of burden.
(1987:9)

Later in this poem she focuses on the horrendous statistics of male violence towards women in Port Vila, in particular the abuse of pregnant women. The gruesome details of such cases—bashed skulls, haematomae, ruptured spleens and haemorrhages—are all recounted, reinforcing an image of women as the victims of violent men. But in this volume she also stresses the responsibility women have not to become victims, to throw off their 'slave mentality' and to support other women in their fight for freedom and dignity. Those women who make it to high positions deserve support and not criticism from other women. She suggests that Hilda Lini, and by implication herself and others in high positions, has been subject to envy, innuendo and resentment.

Women, she asserts, are central, not marginal, to society. Talk of integration of women in national development presumes that women are 'new-comers to the planet', 'new-arrivals hanging in the wings'. Women's marginality in relation to the state and paid employment is clear from the statistics she presents—tables which show the virtual absence of women in Parliamentary, bureaucratic and professional positions. Women are for the most part typists, cleaners, dressmakers, teachers, service workers and shop assistants (1987:19–22). But in reality, women's contribution as mothers, teachers and workers is central to public as much as to domestic life. The central value of such work must be recognised. Men and women must learn to tolerate and to respect each other's contributions. Here, in contrast to *Black Stone*, she espouses the value of democracy, but a democracy founded on considered discussion, conciliation and consensus in both familial and Parliamentary arenas.

In order to appreciate these views enunciated by Grace Mera Molisa in her essays and poems, it helps to know a little more about the history of European colonialism in the Pacific, and the depth of Australia's own colonial and neo-colonial involvement in Vanuatu (see Thompson 1980; Bishop and Wigglesworth 1982). We should not be too surprised that European feminism is dismissed, even if the judgment seems unduly harsh in assimilating all European feminisms to a bourgeois concern for personal freedom. Nor should we be surprised, given the preponderance of Ni-Vanuatu women as domestic servants, that white women are portrayed as lazy and exploitative mistresses.

Such arguments have to be dealt with by Anglo-Australian feminists and not avoided out of a sense of ethnic shame or the frustration of sisterly sympathies. We need to go a lot further in appreciating the long history of colonisation and of decolonisation which underlies such positions. In this history I suggest there is an extraordinary complicity between the constructs of race and nation and the construct of women. I want to explore this through four themes.

The complicities of gender and race in colonisation and decolonisation

Firstly, European imperial expansion and the conquest of other countries was a masculinist project. The ways in which other races/nations were identified and dealt with were intrinsically related to perceptions and adjudications about the position of women. Secondly, effecting transformations in the position of women and introducing self-conscious programs of 'improving' the position of women was basic to the colonial project. Thirdly, colonial history brought colonising and colonised women into association in very problematic ways—in situations where their capacities for identification as women were often overridden by race and class differences. Where similar interests as women were perceived, this was often on the part of white women rather than black women, and the model was often one of maternalism. Fourthly, decolonisation and nationalist struggles, although they might have used women as personnel or as symbols of solidarity, were often masculinist projects. The decolonising relation was often construed as black men taking off the manacles or the mask of the white man (Fanon 1965, 1967; Manonni 1956). Post-colonial states, like European states, are not just statistically dominated by men but also basically represent male interests and projects (Pateman 1988).

I will now consider these themes in terms of the particular colonial history of Vanuatu. Most Australians know little about Vanuatu except as a tourist destination. For thousands of years before Europeans 'discovered' it, this archipelago of Pacific islands was inhabited by people Europeans have labelled 'Melanesian'. Its people made a living through growing taro and yams, herding pigs, fishing and foraging for forest products. They traded goods and cultural items through the use of ocean-going canoes. They lived in houses made of bamboo and thatch and had clothes fashioned from pandanus and bark. Their settlements were small, their neighbours being typically close kin. In some areas, descent was traced matrilineally, in other areas patrilineally, but everywhere kinship was tied to ideas of occupation and residence. Thus people and land were merged in indigenous conceptions of the place (Sope 1975; Beasant 1984:2; Bonnemaison 1984:1). Polities were small and unstable, but often deployed hierarchical principles. In the northern islands, rank was achieved primarily through the exchange and sacrifice of pigs, while in many southern islands there were hereditary chiefs. Religion everywhere focused on the ancestors—who were identified as sacred beings and as primordial deities who had created the natural and the social world. In this island world, women were centrally significant as food producers and as mothers. In some of the northern islands they took rank like men, but women were in varying degrees marginalised from politico-religious activity, from exclusivist men's houses, from the rituals of fertility and warfare and from the drinking of kava. In some of the southern islands, despite women's central significance as workers in irrigated taro cultivation and as bearers of children, many female infants were killed and widows were strangled on the death of their husbands.

Into this world came the European explorers De Quiros (1606), De Bougainville (1768) and Cook (1774). It was Cook who conferred the name the New Hebrides on these islands. Throughout the colonial period they were known as the New Hebrides or Nouvelles Hébrides, a duality which signals the singular misfortune of being a condominium, a joint colony of Britain and France. British involvement was in large measure determined by imperial interests emanating from Australia. This involved the mercantile interests of Burns, Philp and Company alongside other smaller planters, traders and labour recruiters operating for the sugar plantations in Queensland (Thompson 1980:5). It also involved the prosyletising interests of some Protestant missions, especially the Presbyterians of the colony of Victoria. New Hebrideans achieved national independence under extraordinarily difficult circumstances—in the face of French colonists, American speculators and conservative groups such as the Phoenix Foundation, who promoted secessionist movements on the islands of

Santo and Tanna (Beasant 1984; McClancy 1981). At independence, the country was renamed Vanuatu, literally 'our land'. It is still governed by the party and the leader who led the country at independence—the Vanuaku Pati under the prime minister, Father Walter Lini, but there has been much recent turbulence because of the struggle between Lini and his erstwhile comrade in the party and in government, Barak Sope.

Engendering Colonialism in Vanuatu

In Vanuatu, as elsewhere, colonialism was predominantly a male affair (see Callaway 1987; Knapman 1986). The project of European exploration, of discovering other races in the Pacific, was manifestly masculinist, not just in the sense of male adventure, conquest and enlightenment knowledge, but also in the way in which others were perceived. The construction of the race, and the adjudication of its state of relative savagery or civilisation by explorers such as Cook (1774) and De Bougainville (1768) was intimately related to how these men saw indigenous women. So in the diaries and logs of these voyages we see the development of a racist iconography, which continues to afflict not just academic anthropology but also the self-consciousness of Pacific peoples. I refer to the dichotomy of Polynesia versus Melanesia: light-skinned, civilised, chiefly noble peoples as against dark-skinned, anarchic and ignoble savages (Smith 1960, 1985; Thomas 1989; Keesing 1988; Jolly n.d.d.). Essential to this dichotomy was the contrast between Polynesian women—elevated, beautiful, lazy and licentious—and Melanesian women—degraded, ugly, beasts of burden and sexually sequestered by their men. In terms of this racist iconography of Pacific women, Ni-Vanuatu women were regularly classified as Melanesian, with the exception of the lighter skinned women of Ambae, who were sometimes assimilated in the category of Polynesian (Jolly n.d.b.).

From the early nineteenth century onwards, European colonisation began in earnest, with the extractive industries of whaling, *beche de mer* and sandalwood trading, and later the establishment of European missions, plantations and the recruiting of labour for the overseas plantations of Queensland and Fiji (often referred to in the literature as blackbirding). These processes wrought dramatic but contradictory effects in the lives of women.

On the one hand, missionaries were dedicated to the 'improvement' of women's lives, not only by ending practices which they saw as barbarous but by promoting models of womanhood based on domesticity. Starting first in the southern islands of Aneityum, but then progressively moving north, L.M.S., Presbyterian, Anglican and Marist missions tried to end practices such as widow strangulation, polygyny and bride wealth, and tried to divert women's energies from hard work in the gardens to maintaining households and children. They endeavoured to reform both conjugal and parental relations, in an effort to encourage good Christian families (Jolly and Macintyre 1989; Jolly n.d.a., n.d.b.).

On the other hand, traders and labour recruiters had an interest in women as labourers and sexual partners. Although the early sandalwood traders, whalers, planters and labour recruiters mainly dealt with men, there was a significant minority of women who became labourers on plantations in Queensland and Fiji, and later on plantations within the archipelago (see Jolly 1987). Although it is important to deconstruct the ideological association of women labourers or domestic servants as perforce prostituting themselves to white masters, from the mid-nineteenth century some Ni-Vanuatu women became the sexual and/or domestic partners of white men, and bore children to them.

These different perceptions of the place of Ni-Vanuatu women, and the different relations to them not only divided missionary and mercantile interests, but also British and French interests in the archipelago. French colonial officials and even French missions were much less devoted to keeping women at home (in both senses), and were more accepting of women both as labourers and as sexual partners on European plantations. British colonial policy forbade the recruiting of women (at least without the consent of both husband and chief) and British colonial culture was less open and accepting of sexual and reproductive relations between European men and Ni-Vanuatu women ('Asterisk' [Fletcher] 1923; Young n.d.).

However, for both the British and the French, the colonial interaction was for the most part a male–male affair. Insofar as European and indigenous women were brought into association, this happened in very problematic ways, with the problems only sometimes deriving from sexual competition for white men. There has been a tendency to focus on woman–woman relations in the

69

colonies in terms of the power white men exert over black men through the patterns of asymmetrical access to women. Issues of sexuality and reproduction were critical here as in all colonial situations, but although both white and black women's sexuality and fecundity was marshalled in the male struggle for power, women came into relation with each other not just as sexual rivals or as sexual and reproductive icons of a male struggle for power.

Women established close relations across the colonial divide—most clearly in the context of Christian missions. For example, in the history of Presbyterian missions in the south, it is clear that white women established intimate friendships with women who came as converts to the mission station. The latter often worked as domestic servants or as assistant teachers in mission schools where women were taught reading, writing and arithmetic alongside the niceties of housewifery. Such relations were typically matronising—the white woman cast herself as the mother to the black woman as child (Jolly n.d.a.). In discussions of colonialism, condescending racism has often been labelled paternalism, and there has been much psychological and psychoanalytic speculation about the familial model of father and son in the colonising and decolinising relation (Manonni 1956). Here I point to the salience of maternalism. This is not, however, directly parallel to paternalism, precisely because race and gender relations intersect in a different way for women.

White women as a race subordinate and even oppress black women but white women, like black women, are subordinated by their menfolk. It is this tension between the distancing character of racial hierarchy and the identifying potential of womanhood which is so clear in the writings of these white women. The maternal idiom is an ideal way to negotiate this tension; by construing the relation as one of mother and daughter the white woman maintains a superordination, coupled with an identification which actually amplifies control by making it familial and intimate. In the missionary households, perhaps, the extra effect of suppressing a sexual relation with the husband was unnecessary, but in other colonial households this familial model might have rendered such liaisons 'incestuous'. Black women, in this situation, did not necessarily collude in such a definition of themselves as daughters, or 'girls' (Cock 1980; Gaitskell 1982).

Finally, the politics of decolonisation and the construction of the nation of Vanuatu in resistance to whites was primarily a male enterprise. The crucible of anti-colonialism was the male experience of labouring on plantations and in particular the male experience of working for the Americans in World War II (White and Lindstrom 1989). It was men rather than women who had direct experience of working for colonial masters on plantations both overseas and within the archipelago. Women constituted a minority—varying between 6 and 10 per cent in the labour trade to Queensland for instance. As well as allegations by some that earlier forms of labour recruiting constituted kidnap and slavery (but see Jolly 1987), conditions on these plantations were often very hard in terms of the hours of work, the poor rates of pay, diet, living conditions and health. Thus it was men who experienced the more rabid forms of economic exploitation and overt violent racism. But such experiences also brought them into closer relations with their white masters—relations which often combined a bitter sense of exploitation with envy, begrudging respect and even personal affection. Men gained a much more intimate knowledge of European culture and of the outside world than was available to women. It was also men who partook both of a pan-Melanesian consciousness and the sense of different and sometimes hostile ethnicities which developed in such contexts. This was much fostered through the development and stabilisation of a Melanesian lingua franca, in the case of Vanuatu, *bislama*. Most women did not participate in circular labour migration up until the 1960s and had little or no fluency in *bislama*. They were thus not directly involved in the development of a broader consciousness of ethnicity and of the anticolonialism generated by such encounters.

The propensity for opposition to the colonial authorities was amplified in the male experience of working for the Americans in World War II. This may not easily appear as a liberating experience, but relations which Ni-Vanuatu men established with Americans were crucial in their eventual challenge to the conjoint colonial authority of the British and the French. As elsewhere in the Pacific, the Americans were perceived as inordinately powerful and wealthy, but also as generous and familiar compared to the British and the French (White and Lindstrom 1989). Ni-Vanuatu were struck by the fact that there were black men in these forces, and that on occasion black men were giving orders to white men. In many places the Americans in general, and the black Americans in particular, were seen in mythical terms as the returning ancestors (Jolly n.d.c.). This particular convergence of colonial history and myth gave a particular force to the post-war resistance to the condominium.

The nationalist movement was, however, relatively slow in emerging—partly because of the impediments posed by the split between Anglophone and Francophone interests and partly because of the poor state of schooling and tertiary education in the archipelago. Those who did achieve tertiary qualifications at institutions in Australia, New Zealand, Britain and France were crucial in the leadership of the emergent nationalist movement, and in the leadership of the anti-independence political parties. These were predictably mainly men, although there were from the start a few articulate and influential women politicians, such as Hilda Lini and Grace Mera Molisa. Within the Vanuaku Pati, there was a strong women's wing and when after a very difficult struggle for independence, the Vanuaku Pati won power to govern, strong policies on women were soon developed and legislated. But as in most post-colonial states of the Pacific, these have slowly been forced into the background as dealings with the seemingly more urgent problems of secessionist movements, national development and political instability usurp attention.

Conclusion

In this paper, the class dimension of feminism has been backgrounded, in foregrounding the intersection of race and gender. But clearly class is crucial even to understand the position from which both Grace Mera Molisa and I are speaking. Grace Mera Molisa has, primarily through educational mobility risen to high office in the bureaucratic and political elite of Vanuatu. Although she did not attend the Anglican school on Ambae until the age of ten, she made rapid progress, being in 1969 the first Ambae woman to attend secondary school (in New Zealand) and then ten years later the first Ni-Vanuatu woman to head a co-educational boarding school. In 1977, she was the first Ni-Vanuatu woman to obtain a University degree, and in 1983, the first to publish a book. Throughout the 1970s she had a high profile in church, party and international politics—speaking at the ordination of the First Bishop of the Independent Anglican Church of Vanuatu, to the Congress of the Vanuaku Pati, and to international Women's Conferences in Suva and Mexico City. She was the only woman on the National Constitution Committee and the first woman to be appointed to a senior government post.

She thus speaks from a distinctive class location—from within the bureaucratic elite of Vanuatu. Her views in part reflect this— although I would not see her class position as the primary determinant of her attitude to feminism as Johnson has argued for the 'government women' of Papua New Guinea (Johnson 1984a, 1984b; cf. Hau'ofa 1987). Clearly her views are not necessarily shared by other Ni-Vanuatu women, who for the most part live in isolated villages, without her educational, economic or political advantages. But though her views cannot be taken as typical, because of her powerful situation she has more hope than most of influencing the future course of women's lives in Vanuatu.

My own class origins and present class situation also no doubt inform my views on feminism. Like Grace Mera Molisa, I have reaped enormous advantages through the mobility afforded by education. The daughter of a working class family, I was the first to do well enough in my secondary schooling to win a scholarship to University and then fortunate enough to have studied anthropology at a time when good jobs could still be had in the academy. My present position as a researcher affords me the time and resources to write a colonial history of the country where I did my doctoral field work in the early seventies. My approach to feminism is shaped as much by the pursuit of my profession as an anthropologist as by my class location in an intellectual elite.

But of course although we are both intellectuals in our respective countries, Australia and Vanuatu are very differently situated in the class relations of the contemporary world system. Despite the recent economic problems of indebtedness and the decline in manufacturing, Australia is still a rich and powerful nation within the Pacific region. Vanuatu by contrast is a poor and relatively powerless one. No wonder then that the image of colonialism, be it the neo-colonialism of developed and underdeveloped nations still informs our relationship.

In juxtaposing the voice of a Ni-Vanuatu woman, Grace Mera

Molisa, with that of my own, a white Australian feminist working on the colonial history of Vanuatu, my aim has been partly to introduce her views and her poetry to an Australian feminist audience. But how does one do this without engaging in what Spivak has criticised as First World feminists purporting to 'give voice' to Third World feminists (1988a, 1988b), but in fact controlling their voices through authorial authority and easier access to international publication: a kind of feminist ventriloquism? In this case I think Grace Mera Molisa's voice is too strong and distinctively different to mine to be so controlled. The spectre which Spivak presents to us is, I suggest, only avoidable by not trying to understand or to represent the lives of women other than ourselves. I think, despite the hazards, that exercises such as this are essential to opening up and confronting the differences between women. I hope both our voices assist attempts to develop a feminism which starts from difference, and which is equally concerned about racial, class and women's oppression.

5 Through their own eyes: An interpretation of Aboriginal women's writing

Recent discussions of minority group oppression have stressed the issue's complex dimensions (e.g. Anthias and Yuval-Davis 1983; Bottomley and de Lepervanche 1984; Curthoys 1988; Larbalestier 1980; Ramazanoglu 1989). Writers have paid less attention, however, to the ways in which minority group knowledges are constituted. As well, little consideration has been given to the process of cultural representation in contexts which are embedded in relations of power. Examining these issues is another way of dealing with questions about the foundation of knowledges and issues of representation raised by both Gillian Bottomley and Margaret Jolly in this volume.

In this chapter I focus on the recent writings of three Aboriginal women: Ruby Langford's (1988) *Don't Take Your Love to Town*, Sally Morgan's (1987) *My Place* and Labumore: Elsie Roughsey's (1984) *An Aboriginal Mother Tells of the Old and the New*. I explore the ways in which inequality is represented in their writings and look at how such representations are constrained by non-Aboriginal discourses. In the words of one black British writer, I am interested in the ways Aboriginal women 'are caught between white prejudice, class prejudice, male power and the burden of history' (Ngcobo 1988:1).

Black writing and European discourses

'Black' writers in Australia have not been preoccupied with considerations of the multi-dimensional bases of inequality. Nor have the differing experiences of women and men generated debate and discussion, as is the case among minority populations in other parts of the world (e.g. Evans 1985; Giddings 1985; Ngcobo 1988). This is partly related to specific Aboriginal understandings of Aboriginal oppression in Australian society. Further, contemporary black literature in this country is a relatively recent phenomenon (Davis 1985:12).

Modern 'black' writers focus on the experience of being 'black' in a racist society. That is, they see racial oppression, rather than class or gender oppressions, as the overriding issue in their struggles for social justice (O'Shane 1976; Sykes 1989; but see Briscoe 1989). Pat O'Shane, for example, regards racism as particularly important in the context of Aboriginal women's relationship to a 'white' women's movement which attempts to convince Aboriginal women that 'sexism' is what the fight is all about (1979:33). O'Shane is not suggesting that inequalities of class and gender are not important (see also Boyle 1983; Langton 1988b). At issue is the failure of many writers to appreciate the overwhelming significance of racism for the oppression of Aboriginal people. It is a subject which has received considerable attention in some recent feminist writings (e.g. Barrett 1988; Hooks 1982; Ramazanoglu 1989; Stasiulis 1990).

Aboriginal writers seek to circumscribe representations of Aboriginality by generating and controlling their own forms of cultural expression. The dominating theme of the first National Aboriginal Writers' Conference in 1983 was the issue of Aboriginal control of the growing body of unique Aboriginal literature seeking 'to come to grips with and define a people' (Davis and Hodge 1985:1; see also Gilbert 1977; Shoemaker 1989). Aboriginal people are concerned to recount their history and life experiences, and to represent their culture in their own way.

For Colin Johnson (Mudrooroo Narogin) 'it is not only what is said that is important, but how it is said, especially in the case of Aborigines, who until recently were denied a voice and a discourse of their own' (1987:32). Johnson cites Elsie Roughsey's work, along with that of Robert Bropho (1980), as an example of an Aboriginal author who has 'to some degree' managed to 'seize the dominant position for Aboriginal discourse' so that the Aboriginality of the text is assured (1987:29,31).

The struggle for Aboriginal people to generate and control all representations of Aboriginality is ongoing. As the subordinated inheritors of the colonial condition, however, they are inevitably locked into the constraining 'voice' and relentless 'gaze' of the European 'other' (cf. Ariss 1988).

European discourses on 'Aboriginality' have had and still have powerful effects. Not least of these is the notion of a 'true/authentic/real' Aboriginal cultural identity (e.g. Beckett 1988; Cowlishaw 1986; Davis and Hodge 1985; Johnson 1985; Langton 1981; Larbalestier 1988; O'Shane 1976). The implication of such ideas is that some Aborigines are seen to be more 'real' than others. Beckett states the consequence of this emphasis on 'authenticity' in the following way (1988:194):

> Compared with, and at times comparing themselves with, the 'real Aborigines', Aboriginal people are caught between the attribution of unchanging essences (with the implication of an inability to change) and the reproach of inauthenticity. (See also Davis and Hodge 1985:3–4.)

Aboriginal interventions into the representation of Aboriginality have much in common with feminist writings in terms of their impact on our understanding of history and society. Attempts by both feminist and Aboriginal writers to create their own discourses, however, are fraught with difficulties and contradictions (cf. Ariss 1988; Johnson 1988; Pateman and Gross 1986; Pateman 1988; Threadgold and Cranny-Francis 1990).

Aboriginal writers, like feminists, seek to construct a new and 'positive conception of non-subordinated difference . . .' (Johnson 1988:95). Aboriginal interventions directly challenge European representations; however, such challenges operate within a dichotomous view of Aboriginality. Threadgold (1990:1), commenting on current feminist theory, states that Western thought 'is a discursive and representational construction of the world in binary forms such that one term is always regarded as the norm and highly valorised, while the other is defined only ever in relation to it and devalorised'. She argues that working within such dichotomies establishes a double bind so that, despite attempts to reverse or neutralise them, we are still left with their implications. I will return to this issue at the end of the paper.

What are the implications of these issues for our understanding of the ways in which patterns of inequalities are represented in Aboriginal women's writings? Issues of cultural identity directly relate to people's experiences of class, race and gender and the ways in which such experiences are articulated. All experience is mediated by and through cultural norms, ideologies and practices.

Ruby Langford, Sally Morgan and Labumore confront what they see as the dominant oppression in their lives. For Labumore it is the destruction of Aboriginal ways and the imposition of 'white' ones; for Morgan it is the suppression of Aboriginal history and the absence of knowledge about her Aboriginal heritage and identity; and for Langford it is being poor, being female and being 'black', although not necessarily in that order of importance.

Labumore's book is not nearly as well known as *Don't Take Your Love To Town* and *My Place*: Langford's and Morgan's books were widely promoted and have sold well. Labumore, Langford and Morgan grew up under very different circumstances. Labumore was born in 1923 on Mornington Island (Goonana) in the Gulf of Carpentaria, which was established as a Presbyterian Mission in 1914. Langford was born in 1934 at Box Hill Aboriginal Reserve, Coraki, in northern New South Wales. Morgan, the youngest, was born in 1951 in Perth, Western Australia and has a BA from the University of Western Australia.

Despite differences in content and context, Langford, Morgan and Labumore all deal explicitly with issues of Aboriginal identity and experiences of being 'black' in Australian society. Each of the women explicitly addresses a 'white' readership. Each is concerned to promote better understanding between Aboriginal and non-Aboriginal people. Each, in one way or another, operates within the shadow of various non-Aboriginal discourses, where the conditions of being Aboriginal were, and still are, constituted.

An Aboriginal mother tells of the old and the new

Labumore is mission educated and after World War II married the well known painter and author Goobalathaldin (Dick Roughsey). They have six surviving children. Her manuscript was edited

78

by Robyn Horsman and Paul Memmott. The editing was undertaken so the work would be 'acceptable for commercial publication, and accessible to the average White Australian reader'
(Roughsey 1984:240). Labumore was consulted throughout the
editing process and 'the unique flavour and flow' of her narrative
was maintained (1984:241). One reader, however, found her
Lardil English difficult (Binnion 1984). While the language is
perhaps initially disconcerting for English-speaking readers, it is
also direct, powerful and imbued with compelling imagery.

Labumore's work is shaped by contrasts. She is constantly
contrasting the past and the present; 'tribal ways' with mission
ways; and life on the mission with life in the bush. Her contrasting of past and present has a distinct Durkheimian flavour. The
time before Europeans is one of moral and spiritual integration,
Labumore explains: 'Those days were so wonderful. Everybody
was happy, full of laughs and fun. Laws were so strictly kept and
obeyed. Everybody lived as one real people. Lardil, my people,
lived a fine life with all they had.' (Roughsey 1984:1) But, finally
'... crept in a white man, with all its different hard life, with laws
of Government, that drove away all our good ways of living'.
(1984:1)

The book opens with a statement of identity: 'I'm a full blood
Aboriginal ...' (1984:1). She goes on to tell of her 'tribal' people
who were never 'selfish or mean, nasty or greedy'; they were not
'myall'; they were not 'wild tribes' and they were not 'savages'.
Some people said they were, however, because the 'White man'
wanted to come to Goonana (1984:1–3). While Labumore is
clearly aware here that European labelling of Aboriginal people is
politically motivated, she does not question the racist connotations of the notion of 'full-blood'.

Labumore becomes an inmate of the dormitory system when
she is about 8 years old. The dormitory system is alienating and
strictly regimented: 'Dormitory life was hardships of all different
way to make you feel sick, tired, friendless ...' (1984:86). She
recounts that the children were unaware of their tribal related-
ness, that they were locked up when sleeping or resting in the
dormitory, that they were worked hard and were never free from
one sickness or another and that the older girls and boys were
flogged until they bled (1984:12–17). Her critique of dormitory
life does not stop at physical hardship. She complains that '[o]ur

time of doing or learning was just enough and no more than to that, just half way' because the Europeans were not prepared to allow Aborigines the chance to become the 'Whiteman's' equal (1984:87).

However, in a Dickensian mode, life is seen as having 'good times as well as bad times' (1984:17) 'rough cruel times' with 'good and bad mixed to-gether' (1984:28), while Christmas was always a time of greatly anticipated and actual happiness for all. Over the years, Labumore comes to enjoy the dormitory life, and even to become best friends with some of the missionaries. In retrospect, the 'tough' mission days are seen to have endowed her with strengths and a positive outlook. She is helped, however, by both missionaries and 'tribal' elders to learn about the 'real true life' (1984:24–5).

The 'good and bad' of the dormitory experience emerges throughout the narrative, as does mention of a 'tough' and wonderful bush life away from the mission. The past life of the 'tribal' people is an idyllic time and place for Labumore, while the bush life she experiences, if not always idyllic, does enable her to learn the ways of her people in a context of freedom from European surveillance.

Binnion maintains that Labumore's narrative, with the merging of past and present, exhibits confusion because of 'her non-linear thinking' (1984:86). There is, however, another way of reading this temporal merging. The realities of 'white' injustice and 'white' intrusion form a constant thread in the narrative (Roughsey, 1984:44, 87, 88, 98, 161, 175, 179). Throughout the book these realities are juxtaposed with an ideal tribal existence, which is sometimes symbolised by reference to a pre-European existence and at other times by reference to her own direct experiences of bush life. There is no confusion here on Labumore's part, but a very clear and at times painful acknowledgment of her experiences of subordination and cultural oppression.

The mixing of past 'tribal ways' and present experiences indicates the constraining effects of non-Aboriginal discourses. Labumore's narrative is shaped by her understanding of the European ordering of Aboriginal/European relationships and the ways in which Europeans 'understand' or (from her viewpoint) fail to understand Aboriginal cultures. This is patently clear with Labumore's explanation of the killing of the Rev. Robert Hall.

Hall was killed by Peter, who was born on Mornington Island, but as a young lad went to the mainland and moved about with mainlanders, who were not like the 'tame' Lardil. Peter also worked on cattle stations, spoke English and understood European ways. He returned to Mornington Island, asked for tobacco, and when told that nobody smoked on the island became upset and killed the missionary.

Peter, having entered 'the life of civilization', knew killing was wrong. Also, if he had stayed and lived with his Lardil people, 'he would not have known to kill a white man' (1984:46). Because of his experience with the mainlanders, he grew up to see killings and death and this gave him the heart to do what he did.

For Labumore, the Lardil people had their own laws and customs and were peaceful, 'tame' people. She read that other Aboriginal people were savages and 'did lots of killing' (1984:45). Such savage people had come at one time to Mornington Island to war against the Lardil. Aboriginal 'savagery' in general is explained in terms of bad leadership and in relation to strangers entering their country, threatening a previously peaceful people and stealing their women and killing. Consequently strangers are not welcome in 'the country of a black fellow' (1984:45).

Labumore explains that Peter is upset because he had smoked on cattle stations. She does not suggest that Peter is in fact challenging the right of the missionary to tell him what to do, that he has a right to smoke when and where he wants to and that the missionaries are in fact strangers in 'black' country. Instead her explanation is shaped by constituting Lardil law and customs as having as great a 'civilising' effect as Christianity ('white' civilisation). It is a challenge to the abstract and generalising premise of 'white' superiority and a clear claim to cultural equality. Nevertheless, her challenge is firmly located in the evaluative parameters of a 'black/white' opposition.

The often-expressed claim by Aboriginal people that Europeans do not understand their culture is another way of demanding European acceptance of its worth and value. Labumore claims that the 'White man' can never understand and learn about their tribal ways because if they did they would realise that the Lardil did not need 'White man laws' (1984:87,95). The stressing of cultural equality is also a criticism of European intrusion in the first place.

In the context of the killing of the missionary, however, Labumore accepts that the generality of Aborigines may be, or may become, 'savage'. Killing is uncivilised behaviour. However, other Aboriginal groups, not the Lardil, are uncivilised. So while the writer recognises the political dimension of European designations of 'savage' and its equivalents in one context, she does not fully explore the implications of such designations in another. Labumore is quite clear, however, about the subordination of the Lardil people.

The lament for the past values and ways of the Lardil is also a reflection on the pain of the present. This is particularly so for the young generation who know little or nothing of Lardil culture. Labumore explains that:

> the young generation came forward and wanted their own way, and spoilt every customs, culture and laws. They thought these were just foolishness, and would not grasp them. They expected only to love and claim their own parents. But what about the real life that the tribes had ... the true decent friendship they had for all people. (1984:182)

Many people assume tribal law is a 'waste of life' because of the missionary presence (1984:185). They are unable to live with both Lardil and European laws and 'feelings of mixed life have changed into a drifting clouds ...' (1984:185). The 'careless neglectfulness' of the young 'is narrowing their life to become useless' (1984:190).

With missionary education and European laws, the Lardil thought they were aiming for a better life. The reality was that they found themselves 'rounded by wire nettings and fences, and we found living in this modern life, we had lost' (1984:234). For Labumore, the Lardil people have not only lost the moral integration that comes with living as 'one real people', they have also lost out in being 'treated fairly and equally' (1984:234).

Labumore's work is seen as a 'lament for the traditional way of life of her people' (Merlan 1988:63) and as providing insight into the shattering consequences of European intrusion (Binnion 1985). Her work is all of these things, but most importantly, Labumore's narrative is also a process in which she seeks to come to terms with, and define, the conditions of Lardil existence: past, present and future.

Labumore seeks to understand the past in relation to the present and future by constituting and circumscribing Lardil culture, both as a standard of value, and a guide for a better tomorrow. She aims to discredit European images of Lardil people and Lardil culture. At the same time, 'white' culture is both a point of comparison and, in the guise of Christianity, a site of convergence and revitalisation of an equal, if not superior, Lardil cultural integrity. The author addresses the reader thus: 'So now you can read with the most interest and learn from it, so we may closely contact with love, ... and all unite as one in God's big vast of land. That's why God has sent His Son ... to teach us all to live the same as my people of Lardil' (Roughsey, 1984:236).

On the other hand, because they left the wonderful and life-enhancing tribal existence and marched forward into a life 'that really is hurting us', they do not 'care to go any further' (1984:235). Nevertheless, despite their history of subordination and loss of tribal existence the Lardil people will eventually understand that:

> the future lies for the good of them to inherit the days and years to come, and make it better for the two kinds of laws that are now right in the door of our life, to live with what we know is safe and good and obey all the laws that have been given to us for a better use. (1984:236)

For Labumore, while the completeness of past tribal life is gone, the memory of it will last forever (1984:239). At the same time, with merging of both Lardil and European laws, the Lardil may be able to live as 'one real people' again in a better tomorrow.

Don't Take Your Love to Town

Ruby Langford's book is written in standard English, the final version of the manuscript being produced over a two-year period with the assistance of European poet and prose writer Susan Hampton. There is nothing in the narrative, however, to suggest that Ruby Langford was not in complete control of the work. It is a lively, reflective and totally engaging book.

Langford's book is dedicated to 'every black women who's battled to keep her sense of humour'. Her life is a struggle: a battleground on which she fights to sustain herself and her children. Her weapons are tremendous energy, courage, determination and humour.

The book has three main points of reference: the author's childhood, her life with the fathers of her children and the experiences of 'middle age'. Langford expresses feelings of alienation from her Aboriginal heritage, but it is her childhood that forms a significant focal point in the narrative. Her childhood experiences provide a point of departure and comparison for her adult existence. This is particularly so in relation to the men in her life.

Ruby Langford, a descendant of the Bundjalung people of northeast New South Wales, grew up in extended family households. Her parents were married when her mother was 16 and Ruby was 6 months old. Her childhood was happy, loving and secure despite the fact that her mother left home when Ruby was 6 and her other sisters were 4 and 2.

Her father, his brother Sam and her uncle Ernie Ord all act as parental figures. They are family men who provide continuing emotional and financial support for Ruby and all their dependants. Such family men are atypical of the younger generation. Ruby and her female friends have to deal with physical abuse, drunkenness and male irresponsibility in caring for their families (e.g. Langford 1988:58,80,62,64,68,96,105,118,143). Most of their children's generation experience a similar pattern of gender relations.

Unlike the men of Ruby's generation, both Sam and her father are in regular employment. Her father's pattern of employment takes him away from his daughters, but he keeps in contact and regularly contributes to their upkeep. Ruby describes her father as a tall, proud, family man, the best friend she ever had who was always there when she needed him (1988:3,71,101).

Langford's most formative years were spent at Bonalba with Sam and his wife Nell, who was the only mother Ruby and her sisters had known (1988:71). Her father and Sam were among the few remaining Bundjalung speakers. Bonalba is in the region of Bundjalung and Githebul country, and both European township and Aboriginal landscape merge for Ruby as her 'belongin place' (1988:61,242–3). The small rural town in New South Wales is a close-knit community, free from prejudice towards its few black inhabitants (1988:12). In retrospect, the town's ambience is seen as providing Ruby and her sisters with the strength 'to deal with all the troubles later on' (1988:230).

Ruby is educated at the local primary school and for two years at Casino High School. A few months after leaving school, Ruby and her sisters move to Sydney. There they live with their father, his second wife 'Mum Joyce' and their children, in a one-bedroom flat in Redfern. The second union lasts eighteen years until the death of Ruby's father following a heart attack. He is 44 at the time of his death (1988:46).

Ruby, like her mother, is pregnant at 16. She has nine children by four different partners and is a grandmother at 37. Her two eldest children, Bill and Pearl, suffer accidental deaths while still teenagers. Another son, David, dies in his early 20s from 'acute narcotism' (1988:227).

Ruby's first sexual and domestic relationship plummets her into adulthood and her battles begin. She battles with the irresponsible men in her life, poverty, hard physical labour and discrimination. It is the beginning of a pattern of existence that sees her travelling around with her current partner and children between country and city, in search of work. She comments that: 'These days we'd be called fringe dwellers but in those times we were just bushies, and plenty of people lived like that, poor whites as well as blacks.' (1988:84) In middle age Ruby wonders what life would have been like if she had been born rich instead of dirt poor and black (1988:221).

Class inequalities are seen by Ruby as providing common ground for 'black' and 'white'. The non-Aboriginal friendships she makes, female and male (including the Bonalbo residents and her second partner and 'bushie' Gordon Campbell), are with 'ordinary' working people like herself (e.g. 1988:97,123, 128,140). The identification of Aborigines as ordinary working people is not to subsume her Aboriginal identity with class. Living at Katoomba and Green Valley, away from her Koori friends, is seen as a lonely and isolating experience (1988:126,176–7).

The importance Ruby places on her Aboriginal heritage, as well as her feelings of alienation, emerge clearly as she reflects on her life with Gordon Campbell and Peter Langford:

I felt like I was living tribal but with no tribe around me, no close-knit family. The food-gathering, the laws and songs were broken up, and my generation at this time wandered around as if we were tribal but in fact living worse than the poorest of poor whites, and in the case of women living hard because it seemed like the men loved you for a while and then more kids came along and the men drank and gambled and disappeared. One day they'd had enough and they just didn't come back. (1988:96)

Despite such treatment, the men are not without redeeming qualities (e.g. 1988:70,100,102,169).

Langford shares with Labumore the pain of coping with a younger generation that is 'hurting' and whose life is seen to lack purpose. The condition of alienation for young men is seen in the life history of her son Nobby. His experiences reflect the relationship between the criminal justice system and 'black' Australians (e.g. Foley 1984; Cunneen and Robb 1987).

Nobby attends the funeral of his 16-year-old sister in handcuffs. He is 14. At 15 he is truanting, thieving and generally running amok (Langford 1988:163). He graduates from boys' homes to gaol and joins the now well known and devastating cycle of incarceration, police bashing, drinking, depression, attempted suicide and unconscionable arrest. Nobby survives, but as Ruby points out, prison breaks people's spirits and it is 'killing our sons like war' (1988:224).

Don't Take Your Love To Town ends with the author suggesting that her book might give the reader an understanding 'of the difficulty we have surviving between two cultures' (1988:269). The idea that Aboriginal people are living 'in-between' is underpinned by a notion of 'authentic' cultural forms and by racist categorising, both of which have been an important part of European representations of the 'white/black' dichotomy.

That Ruby Langford has internalised the parameters of this hegemony is further illustrated when she describes her visit to Uluru (Ayers Rock). Visiting Uluru helps her to expand her experiences of the Aboriginal heritage. It was the first time she had seen her people in 'their tribal state' and on reaching Uluru she expresses her pride and awe in being 'just a portion of this race' (1988:232,233,234). At the same time, she articulates the cultural gap between her city life and the life of the tribal people of the Centre. She and people like her couldn't survive at Uluru and the tribal people 'couldn't survive in our half black half white world' (1988:235).

The visit to the centre is both an affirmation of a common Aboriginality: '[I]t made me think of our tribal beginnings, and this to me was like the beginning of our time and culture' (1988:234), and an acknowledgment of a cultural chasm. Most importantly, the Aboriginal people living in the Centre are seen by the writer as representatives of a tribal past, of an 'authentic' Aboriginal existence. She belongs to a people 'in-between'; they belong to the 'real' Aboriginal world of tribal living.

In August 1987 Ruby Langford finally has a room of her own to write her life story. She moves into Allawah, an Aboriginal hostel for 'people who had raised their families and didn't want to become live-in baby sitters for their kids' (1988:267). Ruby tells her youngest son that, if we 'fill our lives with meaning, then we will be able to find contentment in ourselves' (1988:250). Writing her book has obviously helped her to do this.

My Place

Aboriginal relationships are constituted in a struggle against policies and practices which undermine attempts by Aboriginal people to live with dignity and independence as 'black' Australians. Ruby Langford's Aboriginal identity, while problematic for her in terms of cultural authenticity, is an integral and publicly shared part of her existence. In contrast, Sally Morgan's book deals with people whose existence is imbued with secrets, silences, shame and denial.

Morgan's mother Gladys and grandmother Daisy decide to protect Sally and her siblings from what they see as the fearful consequences for the children if they find out about their Aboriginal heritage. For these women the experience of living and being 'black' is a shameful, unworthy and degrading one. Their feelings of shame and fear are shared by others. As Marnie Kennedy explains (1985:25): 'Aborigines never felt free—freedom of mind, soul or heart. It lurks deep within us and we are forever afraid.' Sally's non-Aboriginal father Bill (a war psychosis victim who commits suicide when Sally is 9) is part of the conspiracy of silence.

Until the advent of 'multi-culturalism' in the 1970s, 'real' Australians were constituted as being pale-skinned inheritors of a

British tradition. When Sally is asked by her school friends where her family comes from, Gladys tells her daughter to tell her playmates that they are Indian. Sally's playmates are satisfied: 'They could quite believe we were Indian, they just didn't want us pretending we were Aussies when we weren't.' (1987:39) Daisy and Gladys do not want the next generation to suffer shame, fear or bitterness. They would rather pretend to be strangers in their own land.

Sally eventually learns why her mother and grandmother wanted to deny their Aboriginal identity. Her search for, and affirmation of, her Aboriginality is a painful process for all the family. Despite the emotional cost, it helps to lessen the burden of the past for the older women. Such positive affirmations of Aboriginality, however, are more liberating for Gladys than for Daisy.

The burden of history, racism, class and gender oppressions is so great for Daisy that she has never told her daughter anything about her past life. At first Daisy refuses to help Sally in her search for knowledge about her Aboriginal family, claiming it makes her sick to talk about the past (Morgan 1987:161). It is only when Daisy is dying from lung cancer, and her brother Arthur and daughter Gladys have told their stories, that she agrees to tell Sally 'some things' about her history (1987:319). The dying Daisy tells her grand-daughter: '. . . all my life, I been treated rotten, real rotten. Nobody's cared if I've looked pretty. I been treated like a beast. Just like a beast of the field. And now, here I am . . . old. Just a dirty old blackfella.' (1987:352)

Daisy's story highlights a common pattern of sexual exploitation of Aboriginal women in the pastoral regions of Northern Australia and as domestic servants everywhere (e.g. Huggins 1987/88; McGrath 1987). Daisy Corunna (1900–1983) is born on Corunna Downs Station in Western Australia. The station owner, Albert Howden Drake-Brockman, has two children with Daisy's mother, Annie Padewani, Arthur and Daisy (Talahue). Daisy is taken to Perth when she is 14. According to Daisy, her mother was told that her daughter was being sent away to school and would eventually return to Corunna Downs. She never sees her mother again. Instead, Daisy is established with the Drake-Brockman family as a maid of all work, cook and nanny. The Drake-Brockmans claim Daisy as one of the family (Morgan

1987:154,169,334). Daisy tells Sally a different story: 'Oh, I knew the children loved me, but they wasn't my family. They were white ... I was black, I was a servant. How can they be your family?' (1987:334)

Daisy's experience of powerlessness and alienation is profound. Like other Aboriginal servants, she is sexually exploited, raped and made to feel ashamed of being 'black' (1987:337). Daisy has two children by European men: the first child is taken away from her and the second child, Gladys, is sent to Parkerville Children's Home in 1931 when she is 3. Gladys leaves the home at 14. Mother and daughter finally live together when Daisy leaves the Drake-Brockman home, obtains a job as a restaurant cook and shares a house with another woman.

Daisy's story has two versions, not an uncommon occurrence in the history of 'black/white' relations. The Aborigines tell one story; the Drake-Brockmans another. The latter version is that Daisy was taken from the station by Howden's second wife, Alice, at Annie's insistence. Alice tells Sally that Annie wanted her daughter away from the station so she would not have to marry 'a native' (1987:168). According to Alice, Daisy was sent back to the station for a holiday with Howden, and saw her mother, and was happy (1987:168). Alice claims that the family does not know the name of Gladys's genitor (1987:169). Both Alice and her daughter, Judy, tell Sally that her grandmother's father was a station worker called Maltese Sam. Judy, unlike her mother, claims knowledge of Gladys's genitor. According to Judy, it was Howden's friend, an engineer called Jack Grimes (1987: 155).

Both women see their relationship with Daisy and Gladys as familial, kindly and beneficent. Daisy was the 'devoted' family servant (1987:169). They are probably no longer in ignorance of Daisy's feelings about the relationship.

Daisy dies with her secrets and never reveals to either daughter or grand-daughter the name of Gladys's genitor. Morgan herself makes no direct comment on the veracity of either version. She recounts that her uncle Arthur insists the 'whites' are lying (1987:157), and there are hints in the narrative that Howden himself may have fathered his own daughter's child (1987: 157,158,340). Readers are left to draw their own conclusions.

Conclusion

Mudrooroo Narogin (Colin Johnson) maintains that Ruby
Langford and Sally Morgan's works are of the 'battler' genre
and reflect community and family (1990:162–3). In contrast,
Labumore's narrative 'is political in the sense that it questions
the very fact of White dominance in Australia' (1990:163). For
Mudrooroo Narogin, both Langford and Morgan avoid any
political confrontation and their life stories cannot be used as a
political weapon to challenge the hegemony of 'white' Australia
(1990:163).

Australians in general are profoundly ignorant of Aboriginal
history and the experiences of Aboriginal people in this country.
The very act of writing their lives is a challenge to the ways
in which Aboriginality has been constituted in dominant 'white'
discourses. In contemporary Australian society, 'living black'
and writing about it can be seen as a process of political confrontation.

One of the inevitable outcomes of the politics of cultural representation for Aboriginal people is that the articulation of Aboriginal identity and Aboriginal culture is constituted in relation to
representations of 'white' identity and 'white' culture. Cultural
boundaries are constituted in essentialist terms. Such race/culture
boundaries are seen as unproblematic. Thus, while Aborigines
have reversed the 'white/black' dichotomy and constituted 'black'
in positive terms, they are still left with an understanding of their
experiences, of being and living 'black', in relativist terms. Labumore and Langton's narratives and Morgan's positive affirmation
of her Aboriginality are informed by the Western parameters of
a 'black/white' dichotomy. Aboriginal experiences of oppression
are, in part, also shaped by this double-bind.

The writings of Labumore, Langford and Morgan highlight the
complex and multi-faceted phenomenon of Aboriginality in Australia. Cultures are created, transformed and represented under
various political, economic and historical conditions (Bottomley
1981; Johnson 1985; Langton 1981). All usages of the term
'culture' 'involve abstracting from a seamless web of social life'
(Worsley 1984:60). Subordinate groups find ways of expressing
and realising, in their articulation of 'culture', their subordinate
position and experiences (1984:55). The calls by Third and

Fourth World people for the creation of specific cultural forms are constitutive of relations of power, of colonial histories and of European hegemonies (cf. Johnson 1985:27–8).

Aboriginal social relations are fragmented and embattled in Australian society: Aboriginal women and men are both collectively and separately affected by its patterns of inequality. Aboriginal social relationships are also sites of convergence for such inequalities, including those of cultural imperialism.

The works discussed in this paper indicate that Aboriginal ways of living are not isolated domains of separate development. Labumore, Langford and Morgan each refer to a common cultural heritage: to a particular Aboriginal tradition as well as a shared heritage of conquest and survival. They also write of different, individual histories of struggle, accommodation, resistance and adaptation. Their writings show ways in which European-derived cultural forms, including European forms of inequality, are embedded in their own social relations.

The writings of these women attest to specific cultural intersections: the experiences of Aboriginal people may be seen to challenge an understanding of culture and identity in dichotomous terms. At the same time, a 'black/white' dichotomy informs the writers' understanding of these experiences. Labumore is the only writer directly reflecting on, and attempting to resolve, the issue of cultural intersections and difference.

Aboriginal people continue to define themselves in terms of a 'black/white' opposition. The 'white' side of the dichotomy represents the oppressive, life-denying 'other'. In this context 'cultures' are seen as standing in relationship of domination and subordination to one another and in struggle with one another. Aboriginal representations of Aboriginality in dichotomous terms reflect both the burden of history and the continuing pattern of disadvantage and discrimination shaping the conditions of living and being 'black' in Australian society.

Processes of reinterpretation and representation are ongoing. They reflect both the place of Aborigines in Australian society and their struggles to change and determine that place. Whatever the outcomes, the representation of Aboriginality is directly related to the collective and concrete struggles of Aboriginal people (cf. Johnson 1988:95). However contradictory, writing 'black' is part of these struggles.

91

GILL BOTTOMLEY

6 Representing the 'second generation': Subjects, objects and ways of knowing

In *The Migrant Presence*, Jean Martin referred to the enduring frames of reference that stand in the shadows behind definitions of public knowledge in Australia (1987:26). More specifically, Martin explored public knowledge about migrants and 'ethnics' as a form of control, including those representations that were sympathetic but potentially stereotyping. Martin's theme revealed her own sensitivity to the political aspects of academic work in this field, but also her sensitivity to the interplay between class, culture and the relative powerlessness of those being represented. More recently, Jeannie Martin has criticised Marxist analysts for considering migrant women in Australia only 'in their role in production, that is as honorary males or a sub-category of male' (1984:121). Writing in Britain, Floya Anthias and Nira Yuval-Davis offered a more comprehensive critique, noting not only the tendency of Marxists to reduce ethnic and gender divisions to some form of class divisions, but also that of feminists to render ethnic and sometimes class divisions invisible in assuming unitary and biological roots of sisterhood:

> All three divisions have an organizational, experiential and represen-
> tational form, are historically produced and therefore changeable, are
> affected by and affect each other and the economic, political and
> ideological relations in which they are inserted. Relations of power
> are usually found within each division and thus often the existence of
> dominant and subordinate partners. They are all therefore framed in

relation to each other within relations of domination ... It is not a question therefore of one being more 'real' than the others or a question of which is the most important ... it is clear that the three divisions prioritise different spheres of social relations and will have different effects which it may be possible to specify in concrete analysis. However, we suggest that each division exists within the context of the others and that any concrete analysis has to take this into account. (1983:65)

As explained in the Introduction, a similar perspective informed our earlier book *Ethnicity, Class and Gender in Australia* (1984), and continues to structure this present volume. In this chapter, I will examine some concrete analyses of 'second generation Greek Australians' with several aims in mind. One is to examine the frames of reference of these analyses; another is to develop a more multi-dimensional framework that can take account of the complexities of migration and settlement, and of social relations and identity formation in a highly diverse society, as well as the inter-relation between class, gender, ethnicity and culture. While agreeing wholeheartedly with the above critiques of uni-dimensional explanations, I also believe that the development of more adequate explanations is hampered by a failure to question the foundations of knowledge as well as the problems of representation. The political question of representing (or misrepresenting) the 'other' has been raised elsewhere in this volume, especially in the chapters by Margaret Jolly and Jan Larbalestier. This has been a major theme of feminist and anti-colonialist discourse, and of other anti-dominant critiques, and was strongly articulated by Edward Said in his influential study *Orientalism* (1987). However, Said was also aware of the possibility that 'a double kind of possessive exclusivism could set in' to such critiques; 'the sense of being an excluding insider by virtue of experience (only women can write for and about women, and only literature that treats women or Orientals well is good literature), and ... by virtue of method (only marxists, anti-orientalists, feminists can write about economics, Orientalism, women's literature)' (Said 1986:15). This is certainly a tendency in analyses of class, gender and ethnicity, which results in competing claims to the 'correct' form of knowledge. One of the techniques used in this competition over ways of knowing is to exclude or elide certain concepts and perspectives—as Martin, Anthias and Yuval

Davis explained. 'Concrete analyses' often proceed as though other perspectives, and even other writers, do not exist. These exclusions may be conscious—for example, the result of a decision to ignore a perspective because the writer is an 'outsider' or a 'Marxist' or a 'culturalist', or in some other category considered to be illegitimate. But many are not so conscious; some are the consequences of shoddy scholarship and some arise from the very methods employed, as in positivist analyses of data that assume a certain truth value in themselves. In all these cases, the bases of knowledge need to be questioned more thoroughly. Frames of reference are revealed as much by their absences as by their particular emphases.

Another important technique is the separation of subjective and objective ways of knowing, where one form is assumed to be superior to, but distinct from, the other. In this chapter, I propose to demonstrate not only the falseness of such a separation, but the constant inter-referencing of subjective and objective accounts. Moreover, an avowed dedication to subjectivity or objectivity obscures the fact that we are all 'spoken' by the words and concepts that we use. Thus, feminists have questioned the androcentric bases of knowledge (cf. Caine, Grosz and de Lepervanche 1988) and of Western rationality (cf. Lloyd 1984). Writing has also been subjected to scrutiny. As Italo Calvino pointed out in an essay on 'The Right and Wrong Political Uses of Literature':

> we can no longer neglect the fact that books are made of words, of signs, of methods of construction. We can never forget that what books communicate often remains unknown even to the author himself, that books often say something different from what they set out to say, that in any book there is a part that is the author's and a part that is a collective and anonymous work.
>
> This kind of awareness does not influence literature alone: it can also be useful to politics, enabling that science to discover how much of it is no more than verbal construction, myth, literary topos. Politics, like literature, must above all know itself and distrust itself. (1989:99–100)

I believe we can broaden Calvino's advice to a much more general scepticism about received categories and ways of knowing, while recognising that we ourselves have been, to some extent, constructed by them. I am arguing here from what I have called an 'anti-categorist' position, embodying a suspicion of oppositions and boundaries based on too-ready categories or claims to a privileged authenticity. This is not at all a neutral relativism, but an attempt to understand the construction of forms of knowledge. It is worth remembering that the word 'category' derives from the Greek verb 'to accuse publicly'. This gloss sometimes remains in categorising, although it may go unrecognised.

Part of my intention, then, is to develop a more distrustful account of knowledges about people who are often described as 'second generation migrants', although they are also first generation Australians. I will concentrate on Greek–Australians because of my own familiarity with the subject of Greek migration, but also because I believe that ethnospecific analyses can offer a deeper understanding than that provided by generalities about migrants or 'ethnics'. I will, therefore, move between discussions of conceptual frameworks and examinations of specific writings. Finally, I intend to blur genres of writing, using literary sources as well as those derived from the social sciences. I have always done this, in teaching as well as research, partly because literature can provide insights and subtleties rarely found in social science material. Despite their different aims and possibilities, I believe that it is also important to recognise the inter-referencing of these two genres, as writers such as John Berger and Raymond Williams have noted. More directly, Anna Couani, an Australian of Greek–Polish extraction, has explicitly referred to the sociological aspects of her own position, and the difficulty of recognising these in writing from a 'self-consciously non-Anglo perspective' (1989:16).

As Anna Couani implied, and I suggested above, writers like myself are indeed constrained by sociological language and preconceptions. Some of these constraints will become apparent in the analyses that follow, where I will also examine those arising from the explicit or implicit perspectives already mentioned.

Subjects and objects

One of the pervasive divisions in the social sciences is that between subjective and objective accounts of social phenomena.

This division is obviously pertinent to questions about representation and claims to legitimate knowledge, but it has more general significance in the very construction of knowledges. Although this significance has been recognised by a number of social theorists, including Berger and Luckmann (1969) and Giddens (1987), and explored by feminist writers, it has been most thoroughly elaborated on by the French sociologist Pierre Bourdieu (1977, 1986, 1987). A recurring theme in Bourdieu's work has been, in his words, the objective limits of an objectivism that grasps practices from outside, as a fait accompli, rather than examining the theoretical and social conditions within which practical knowledge is developed (1977:4). On the other hand, a subjectivism that privileges lived experience obscures the fact that 'the truth of social interaction is never entirely in the interaction as observed' (1987:153). It is therefore necessary to go beyond the artificial opposition between structures and representations and to develop a kind of relational thought. Bourdieu suggests that, where subjectivism reduces structure to interaction, objectivism deduces actions and interactions from structure, assuming the existence of unified groups and a homogeneity of conditions. While the objectivist perspective is necessary, social scientists must recognise that social reality is also an object of perceptions (including their own) developed within specific constraints.

This kind of relational approach is caught, to some extent, by our emphasis in this volume on 'intersections', although we also need to be aware of the complexity of categories such as class, gender and ethnicity. The need for reflexivity, for a sensitivity to the perspective of the viewer as well as the viewed, is one that I raised in the introduction to this chapter. If we also take into account the fact that knowledge is usually contested in the struggle for social power, it becomes even more important to distrust ready categorising. Bourdieu, for example, points out that:

> Class or class fraction is defined not only by its position in the relations of production, as income or even educational level, but also by a certain sex ratio, a certain distribution in geographical space (which is never socially neutral) and by a whole set of subsidiary characteristics which may function, in the form of tacit requirements, as real principles of selection or exclusion without ever being formally stated (this is the case with ethnic origin and sex). (1986:102)

96

More generally, I believe that some of Bourdieu's concepts, especially the notions of habitus and of cultural and symbolic capital, indicate a pathway through the unproductive dichotomies of subjective versus objective, ethnicity versus class and structure vesus culture that appear in much sociological literature. Bourdieu explains that biological individuals carry with them their present and past positions in the social structure in the form of dispositions that are marks of social position: 'The history of the individual is never anything other than a certain specification of the collective history of his group or class' (1977:86). Accordingly, 'habitus'—history become nature—is the process whereby those who occupy similar positions tend to possess a similar sense of place. It acts as an intermediary between social positions and practices that represent the world as structured, producing meaning through categories of perception and appreciation that are themselves socially produced. So objective relations of power are generally reproduced in relations of symbolic power and both are indissolubly linked to the process of producing meanings, values and practices. I will return to these concepts later, when discussing the material about second generation Greek–Australians.

Sociological studies

Over the last twenty years, much of my own work has been motivated by an interest in the ways in which people are socially constructed and construct themselves, especially in resisting pre-definitions and categorisations. In *After the Odyssey* (1979), I was mainly concerned with notions of 'Greekness' and 'Australian-ness' and their negotiation within specific social fields. I used historical, sociological and literary sources in an attempt to outline what Greekness might mean and studied some of the institutions within Sydney's Greek community. I also undertook detailed studies of 23 people who were born in Australia or who migrated to Australia as small children. These studies included long interviews (between eight and ten hours with each person), network analysis, an attempt to graph each interviewee's social field and participant observation wherever possible. Although this study was completed fifteen years ago, I believe that the questions it raised, the framework of inquiry and the research methods are still relevant to more recent concerns with representation and the constitution of subjectivity. Theoretical formulations are now more sophisticated, but methods and techniques have lagged behind the theory.

In *After the Odyssey*, I suggested that we could study some of the processes of identity formation, including cultural resistances and transformations, by looking at:

1 people's location within social and political systems and their patterns of interaction;
2 the cultural content of their activities;
3 the perspective that explains and guides this experience—their definition of the situation.

In particular, it was important to see how these three interrelated.

The study demonstrated that more than half the interviewees were included in community-type social networks that 'sustained a social environment based on kinship, friendship, shared experience and mutual understanding' (1979:129). These networks were important in maintaining and enabling commitment to Greekness, as were participation in ethnic institutions, visits to and contacts with Greece and marriage to Greek spouses. In exploring the interviewees' self-identifications and their perceptions of how they were identified by others, I found a remarkable degree of self-awareness, probably related to a sense of coping with (at least) two cultural milieux. Some of their coping strategies were developed within what I called 'areas of conversation' with others who confirmed a particular definition of reality. I also found that class position, status aspirations and gender were at least as important as ethnicity in the construction of these identities.

Several points emerged from this brief re-excavation:

1 These second generation 'subjects' were both constructed by and actively constructing their social and cultural universes.
2 The constraints, oppressions, limitations and possibilities created by social structures were based on class and gender as well as other variables, such as country versus city living and the size and knit of kin groups.
3 It was clearly essential to try to understand the interplay between such structures and people's perceptions of and relation to those structures.

In later research, I have maintained this 'subjectivist objectivism' (Bourdieu's term) in studies of the relevance of feminism to Greek–Australian women and girls (Bottomley 1983, 1984a), including further investigation of class and cultural limits and possibilities. I also analysed the 'traditional' practice of dowering brides but, instead of assuming some essentialist notion of cultural continuity, placed the practice in the context of class and status mobility, and of the structure of taxation and financial law in Australia, as well as Greece (Bottomley, 1985). More recently, I have written about the intersections of gender, ethnicity and class in Greece as well as Australia (1986, 1990). In all these studies, I have been concerned to avoid assumptions about the priority of any of these categories, and to recognise that cultural practices are always contested, always in process, and never coterminous with 'ethnicity' (itself a contested notion). Almost invariably, culture and ethnicity are conflated in migration studies, the result being a homogenising of diversity and a neglect of the fact that class and gender are themselves culturally constructed.

The implication that culture equals ethnicity also leaves unquestioned the cultural practices of the 'non-ethnics' in Australian society, although these are obviously crucial in the struggle for cultural capital. Some of the more anthropologically informed researchers have offered more sophisticated delineations of culture, but this aspect of their work has received little recognition (cf. de Lepervanche 1984a; Humphrey 1984; Hampel 1987).

Much of the Australian material is directly policy oriented, pragmatic in orientation and hence impatient with complex notions of culture or with the need for multi-dimensional frameworks. But this orientation can, as Jean Martin suggested, become another form of domination, or at least of pre-definition. In a recent survey of ethnic youth, for example, Cahill and Ewen (1987:84) commented on 'the weight of the literature which sees immigrants in general and ethnic youth in particular as problems, problems, problems'. They agreed that major issues such as unemployment, language difficulties and special educational needs should not be under-emphasised. But they also argued that ethnic youth have many assets, such as bilingualism, biculturalism, adaptability, access to firm moral frameworks and a commitment to Australia's future. These conclusions were developed from the authors' research and long experience in ethnic and youth affairs.

They explained the lack of appreciation of these assets in terms of Anglocentric notions of Australian identity, and the inability of agencies and organisations to cope with the complexity of Australia's population. The shadows behind policy and practice become apparent at these levels. The perceived lack of understanding and adaptability is also compounded in the training of those who administer policy and the determined monoculturalism that still prevails in the education system.

The argument advanced by Cahill and Ewen is an important one. They are not suggesting that ethnic youth face no special disadvantages, but that the definition of ethnic youth as inevitably being 'problems' is often ethnocentric and unimaginative. At a personal level, this definition can also be oppressive. A number of Greek–Australians have commented to me that they find accounts of their purported problems more oppressive than their own experience would suggest. This movement from general statements to particular experiences is another of the difficulties of the subjective/objective dichotomy and is often encountered in feminist discussions, where the applicability of universal statements to specific women or men is a thorny issue that requires careful dissection.

Another general survey looks specifically at patterns of disadvantage among the children of overseas-born migrants as well as the migrants themselves (Castles et al. 1986). The authors point to a shortage of historical data and a general lack of information about Australian-born children of immigrants, as well as the need to disaggregate material in terms of birthplace, forms of migration, age and gender, in order to define the concept of disadvantage, especially when comparing different cultural orientations to 'success'. From their report, it appears that the offspring of Greek migrants show both a high rate of occupational mobility (11.6 per cent in the professional/technical category, compared with 1.8 per cent of the first generation) and a relatively high rate of unemployment (8.9 per cent) (Table 32). Similarly, the Greek-born population aged 15–24 had a high participation in 'post-compulsory education', but also a relatively high proportion of early school leavers (1986:43), making the category of 'Greek youth' effectively bimodal in this respect.

Castles et al. reiterate the shortcomings of available data about ethnic youth, women and migrants generally. They do, however, illustrate some of the specific ways in which young women of non-English speaking background are disadvantaged. There is, for example, 'unambiguous evidence that the aspirations of parents and their children ... are higher for boys than for girls' (1986:47). The authors suggest that parents may believe that schooling for girls is a matter of prestige rather than career training and that teachers' lower expectations of girls contribute to the girls' own limiting of aspirations. Thus gender may be more important than ethnicity in this context, but the two are clearly intertwined.

Most of the social science material about the second generation is concerned with education. The debate about ethnic disadvantage in education has become more intense as multiculturalism comes under attack. Summarising arguments against ethnic disadvantage, Kalantzis and Cope argued that these could be used 'to fill the policy vacuum created by fiscal cuts' (1988:40). Although the effectiveness of multicultural programs may be questioned, the issues they attempted to redress 'are still real and pressing' (1988:40). Kalantzis and Cope argue that the authors whom they criticise fail to disaggregate the category of non-English speaking background (NESB), to recognise that school retention rates are not in themselves indicators of high performance, and to take into account the class context as well as the ethnic composition of schools. At the same time, there is evidence of a sizeable gap between aspirations and performance of NESB girls. Kalantzis and Cope urge a new form of multicultural education, aimed at social equity and at directly tackling the pressing problems of racism (1988:55).

Some other scholars of the second generation and education have also been careful to recognise the intersection of ethnicity with class and gender. An early and sensitive example was Isaacs' *Greek Schoolchildren in Sydney* (1976), which combined studies of families and schools. Isaacs' interrelated discussion of inner-city living, playground culture, expectations of parents and teachers, overt discrimination against 'wogs', the relevance of Greekness and of rural origins, and the effects of sexism still stands as a valuable but neglected model for researchers. She raises important questions about the unquestioning Anglocentrism of education authorities and teachers, and the possible consequences of cultural diversity. Her partly ethnographic method also enables her to include the perspectives of the 'subjects' of her study.

Another partly ethnographic study was undertaken by Maria Strintzos (1984), who interviewed eighteen Year 11 girls from three Melbourne schools, including an inner city co-educational school with a high proportion of Greek students (83 per cent), a state co-educational school with 35 per cent and a girls' grammar school (10 per cent Greek). Strintzos was interested in the girls' ideas and practices of both family and Greekness, and found that, despite differences between 'good' and 'bad' girls, and between class backgrounds, these girls maintained the centrality of the notions of honour and shame and of clearcut male/female roles. Her study made a rare contribution by investigating, rather than assuming, ideas and values designated as Greek and relating them to the class background and school experience of Greek–Australian girls.

Georgina Tsolidis (1986) reported on discussions with groups of NESB girls in three Victorian secondary schools (two co-educational, and one single sex), as well as with parents and staff. Tsolidis found these girls to be positive about their cultural mix and flexibility. The girls aspired to university education and did not see careers as incompatible with motherhood. These results were similar to those which emerged from my interviews with Greek–Australian girls in a Sydney school (Bottomley 1983), but I also found the girls comparing their own situations favourably with those of their Anglo-Australian peers, whom they saw as more vulnerable to early pregnancy, rape and male violence. Another difference between these two studies was that Tsolidis's respondents were not particularly confident about their own abilities and believed that they were neglected by their teachers, whereas the girls I interviewed spoke highly of their teachers, particularly those women teachers who made special efforts on their behalf.

The subjects of my studies and those of Isaacs, Strintzos and Tsolidis offered their own views, which the authors have attempted to locate in a more general framework that takes account of ethnic, gender and class perspectives, as well as the cultural concomitants of all three. The views of second generation Greek women were also presented at a workshop held at Monash University in 1988 (see Kunek 1988), where the participants talked about the constraints of sex roles and the double standard for boys and girls, and also, at the same time, about the importance of family life and the need to recognise that Greek women did not have to be judged by the standards of Anglo-Celtic feminists. Because this material was presented with no analysis at all, it may be out of place here, except perhaps as an example of the personal accounts selected by the convenor. The seminar was intended to develop further organisation and discussion, which could well result in the 'ethnospecific studies of women's history' called for by one participant. For our purposes here, the women's comments did indicate that they did not necessarily see themselves as problems, but as somewhat neglected and as people faced with the complexities of conflicting requirements and demands.

A collection of papers on the subject of Greeks in Australia (Kapardis and Tamis 1988) includes little specific information about the second generation, but the chapter by Smolicz discusses the results of surveys of tertiary and secondary students in South Australia, as well as memoirs written by Greek–Australian tertiary students. The studies confirm the importance of Greek language, family ties, customs and celebrations. Although some of the responses are compared with responses from Anglo-Australians, these surveys do not reveal anything of the ambivalence and conflict demonstrated in the more ethnographic studies described—or, indeed, anything of the wider context of beliefs and practices.

Another chapter in the same volume points out that the support for family closeness is, in part, a response to economic hardship and to prejudice and discrimination such as that experienced during the 'Greek' social security scandal of 1978. Of the 50 households interviewed in this study, eighteen had been affected by unemployment, and also by work-related illness. A dilemma brought out in this study is that of parents who would prefer to return to Greece, but whose preference is not shared by their offspring. Despite this dilemma, the obvious hardships faced by these respondents, and the fact that 64 per cent report experience of discrimination in Australia, there are few expressions of dissatisfaction, either from parents or from younger people. The interviewer is Greek and could be seen as more sympathetic than an Anglo-Australian, but responses are generally positive (Bottomley and Georgiou 1988). Nevertheless, the objective circumstances of people's lives are often quite difficult and their own attitudes demonstrate a degree of self-respect that seems to depend heavily on family interaction and what Bourdieu describes as 'cultural capital'.

In a survey of Greek youth in Victoria, also published in *Greeks in Australia* (Kapardis and Tamis 1988), The Victorian Ethnic Affairs Commission listed major issues of concern to Greek youth in the 1980s. Information was gathered from statistical material as well as interviews with young people of Greek background. The focus was heavily problem-oriented, concerned with very real issues such as employment, education and drugs. The questions posed by Cahill and Ewen about the assets of ethnic youth were not raised, nor was the potentially very valuable input of Greek youth into the task of reorienting Anglocentric policy and practice. I believe that this is slowly happening, against considerable odds, but it is worth noting the recommendation of the Australian Greek Welfare Society to the Committee of Review of Australian Studies in Tertiary Education, that Australian studies and *all studies* need to include the perspectives of people from immigrant backgrounds. Although it is undoubtedly true that Australian institutions have still not really faced the task of providing services and opportunities for immigrants and their offspring, those who define policy and practice need a more radical reorientation to take into account the different kinds of cultural capital held by people of non-English speaking background.

The other major body of material that includes the second generation is mainly concerned with families. These studies have been well summarised by Susan Hearst in a publication from the Australian Institute of Family Studies, *Ethnic Family Values in Australia*, edited by Des Storer (1985). Hearst recognises the dangers of constructing stereotypes based on static models of 'traditional Greek values', and orients her discussion to changes in Greek family law and in the Australian context; the diversity of the Greek-speaking population in Australia; techniques such as network analysis that provide some understanding of social processes; and recent information about gender relations, including material from women's networks and refuges. She also notes the need to balance material derived from welfare-oriented research with some understanding of kinship and community networks and the continuing commitment by many of the Australian-born to aspects of Greekness.

Shortage of space has forced me to exclude a number of interesting studies, including Jean Martin's (1975) work on Greek families and bureaucracies and Young, Cox and Daly's (1983) report on Greek and Italian youth employment. Both blend open-ended interviews with information derived from statistics and locate the research within the context of policy-making and the Anglo-Australian social field. They also compare male and female responses and include a class perspective—or, in the employment study, 'employment status'.

This brief overview of some of the sociological writings about second generation Greeks has revealed that there is, in fact, a considerable body of material on the subject. Furthermore, many of these studies include both subjective and objective perspectives and a multi-dimensional approach which enables them to take account of contradictions and complexities that tend to disappear in less nuanced accounts. It is also clear from these studies that 'culture' does not mean 'ethnicity'; that, for example, Anglo-Australian policy creates a particular form of bureaucratic culture, that there is a cultural context to schooling and that socioeconomic status has cultural concomitants. These cultural pressures accompany those structures of necessity, economic and political, which mould preferences and practices into what often becomes, to use another of Bourdieu's terms, 'the choice of the necessary'. Some of these insights have been very well articulated in literary material written by Greek Australians.

Literary works

The editors of a recent collection of 'multicultural women's writing' referred to Barthes' comment that 'literature is what gets taught' (quoted in Gunew and Mahyuddin, 1988:xv). According to this definition, the works discussed here are not literature, since it is unlikely that they are being taught within our determinedly Anglocentric education system. Moreover, George Papaellinas, my main reference here, vehemently rejects the idea of being an ethnic or multicultural writer, a definition he sees as condescending, tokenistic and categorising—a kind of benign racism (Papaellinas 1989).

For our purposes, it is sufficient to say that Papaellinas is an Australian-born writer of Greek background, whose work illuminates many of the intricacies and contradictions that emerge in the sociological studies discussed above. His collection of short stories, *Ikons* (1986) includes a moving account of the memories of an old woman who has transferred her devotion to her dead husband, a merchant, to her young grandson, Petro, her only source of hope in the godless country to which she has migrated. But the boy, more concerned with blending into his Australian environment, has begun to perceive his grandmother as an embarrassment. When she picks him up from school:

> ... the boy would be cold and strange ... She would have to search up and down the asphalt playground and she would find him and seize him by the arm and bend to kiss him and hug him and his smile would be as dry as the kiss he would plant on her cheek. And he walked slightly apart from her in her black, black clothes and the headscarf she wore like a shroud and she would have to prod him and push him and draw him back to her side. All around, the other children would giggle and she would dampen her expression and ask the boy about his day and he would grunt some reply and continue to pretend that he did not understand her language. He would grin a tentative smile back at the smirking children milling around them and he would shy away from her blackness and her pride would silence her and the next day she would wear the same clothes because this was a debt to the merchant. (1986:10)

Papaellinas's stories contain the interplay of status concerns (as Petro learns to speak 'correct' Greek at school) and the limits of necessity (in his stories about factory work and the unending toil of Petro's father and those like him who were brought to Australia to 'work like donkeys'). They also show the strengths of women who not only endure but rise above their circumstances, including the oppressiveness of their menfolk and of their children.

Another Australian-born writer, Zeny Giles (1988), describes, in her story 'Telling Tales', a woman-hating fable gleefully recounted by one Greek man to a group of his compatriots at the local swimming pool. The Australian-born woman listening is horrified by this story—even more so when the narrator threatens to hit his wife and, referring to the fable, to pay with olive oil for her extermination. His male companions are delighted by his display of wit and strength, but:

> His wife continues silent, but as he stands, still threatening, she takes their two towels and hangs them on his upraised arm. She leans across and takes the rest of his belongings from the table and standing as tall as her husband, puts his cloth hat on his head and his packet of cigarettes and his lighter into his bathrobe pocket. 'Come now, Spiro' she says smiling. 'Until you learn to look after yourself, you'd better keep your olive oil for your salad.' (1988:98)

Other Greek–Australian writers, such as Angelo Loukakis and Nikos Papastergiadis, have elaborated on the ambivalence towards things Greek, such as Greek dancing, and the constraints of family life and parental expectations. These themes are similar to those seen in some of the sociological work, but the literary form allows the contradictions to emerge more clearly, rather than being ironed out in an interpretative framework. Elsewhere I have argued that poetry, music and dance can also allow for the kind of multi-dimensional approach I have advocated here (see Bottomley, 1987, 1988). Dance, for example, has frequently been dismissed as trivial and, in the context of migration studies, only of folkloric interest. But dance and music have been important personal and political practices, in opposition to authoritarian people and regimes of various kinds—from Pinochet and Franco at one extreme to the Chinese Red Guard at the other. Jacques Attali's (1985) brilliant study of the political economy of music describes the way in which the ritual use of music and dance was replaced by a mode of representation where the audience submitted to an artificial spectacle of harmony which has, in its turn, been replaced by a deafening syncretic form of music that actually excludes 'man and his body', suppressing differences and ceasing to be a catharsis. In such a context, I have argued, the continuing association of Greek dance and music with familial and other rituals represents a form of non-verbal resistance to the more negative identities—those of unskilled workers, foreigners and so on—accompanying the status of 'immigrant'. The physical communication possible in dance and in music make them powerful embodiments of a form of collective identity which is constantly under threat in the fragmented world of industrial societies (cf.

Bottomley 1987). Similarly, the language used by poets such as Antigone Kefala and Dimitri Tsaloumas bears referents to multiple sources of identity, in other places, other times and other histories.

Connections

I have moved a considerable distance here from a discussion of frames of reference and the breaking down of subject–object dichotomies, through sociological studies, to literary representations. The connecting threads are those of the construction of ways of knowing, the limitations of categories, and the need for interdisciplinary and inclusive frameworks rather than a narrower focus. It is also important to hear conflicting voices and to eschew the search for simple paradigms. This means, for example, avoiding a single-minded emphasis on the necessary priority of one perspective. As some of this material has demonstrated, ethnicists can be advocates of oppressive and limiting practices, and feminist and class-based solidarities can exclude important differences based on other criteria. At another level, a concentration on short-term and welfare-oriented needs can preclude the development of a deeper understanding of the extent and contours of these differences. The subjective accounts that have become so popular can provide a valuable counter to views from afar based on statistical evidence or grand generalisations. But the objective moment is also necessary to locate these subjectivities within a relational framework, to discover something more of the composition of a particular habitus and of its context. This is, after all, the usefulness of such terms as class, ethnicity and gender. These terms signal characteristics that can have a determining influence on people's lives. But the forms and contours, and the relative salience, of those influences can only be demonstrated in context, and are always intertwined.

Earlier in this paper, I suggested a more distrustful approach to such terms and to representations of various kinds. That suggestion included a closer examination of the bases of knowledge as well as the position of the 'knower'. At the same time, I believe that a more multi-dimensional approach can offer a way into the development of a more complete understanding of the diversity of the Australian population. This would not mean a further celebration of the more superficial aspects of multiculturalism, but rather introduce a level of sophistication that could include the multiplicity of Australian identities.

JEANNIE MARTIN

7 Multiculturalism and feminism

Multiculturalism, as a government policy addressed largely (but now not exclusively) to righting the situation of non-English speaking migrant populations in Australia, was first mooted with the election of a Labor government in 1972. From its inception it has proved a highly contentious public policy. The various formulations that underpin policy have vied with each other for centre place on the political stage, and each has been widely challenged from both the Left and the Right. The result has been a political arena marked by shifting and often unlikely political alliances, with each alliance and each stance invariably held contextually, and defensively, against some new onslaught on some new front. For example, the Marxist 'multiculturalism-as-ideology' thesis has shuffled uncomfortably between theoretical rejection of multicultural policy and practical–political support. The same situation has existed in alliances between often-conflicting Left and liberal positions, and between all of these and some conservative positions (ACPEA 1982; Jakubowicz 1984a; Social Alternatives 1983; Martin 1983; Chipman 1978; Blainey 1984).[1]

In the midst of all this activity, the question of 'non-English speaking background (NESB) migrant women' has been widely canvassed, initially by feminists of Left leanings whose main concern was the lot of working class women from disfavoured NESB groups (Italian, Greek, Yugoslav, Turkish, Latin American,

Lebanese, Vietnamese, etc.). It is now well known that the majority of NES migrant women from these groups have come to Australia as wives, mothers or daughters of NESB male labourers, and that these women are disproportionately disadvantaged in work and in the community (Pieri et al. 1980; Martin 1984a,b; 1986). Yet, despite the proliferation of writing on this aspect of the topic, there has been surprisingly little distinctively feminist input to the debate on multiculturalism, or critical attention to the subject matter of multiculturalism within feminism itself.

The reasons for this are twofold. In the first place, the terrain of radical debate has already been colonised by the theoretical preoccupations of a distinctly male Left and male Right, and both have contained all debate with each other, and with the middle ground. Questions about 'migrant women' have tended to be slipped into these positions as a special case of their more general propositions, or added on as an extra 'problem' (empirically, but also sometimes conceptually, as in the class–ethnicity–gender trilogy). Feminist accounts that try to step outside these boundaries are either translated into the language of male theory, or are ignored.

In the second place, there is little help from 'outside'. This male colonisation of the theoretical territory has been compounded by the marginalisation of migrant populations-as-a-whole in 'mainstream' political and social thought. For example, the majority of texts devoted to an analysis of 'Australian society' (sociological, historial, political, etc.) either bracket migrant populations as something other than (outside) the mainstream of Australia life, or mould the 'migrant presence' to a distinctly Anglo form. Unhappily this marginalisation—a telling political act in itself— is echoed in the preoccupations of mainstream (Anglo) feminist thought.

The following discussion is a preliminary exploration of some ambiguities and tensions generated in dialogues between various ethnic theories and ethnic politics, and feminist theories and feminist politics in Australia. The first part of the paper provides a feminist reading of government policies of 'multiculturalism', primarily because a wide range of ethnic positions and politics have been fought out around the multicultural question in Australia. The second part turns the process around to provide a very brief 'multicultural' reading of feminism itself. The reason for

111

including both readings is because a feminist reading of multiculturalism does not suggest a feminist alternative, at least not if
mainstream feminist thought remains aloof from accusations of
ethnocentricism levelled against dominant feminisms by black and
minority-group women. The main focus of both discussions is on
the treatment of the relation between migrant women and their
families.

Multiculturalism: Interest/minority group theories and ethnicist theories

The major intellectual inputs to multicultural policy can be divided into two camps, both of which commence from some
account of NESB migrant inequality, and then advocate some
form of 'pluralism' as part of their solution. In both instances
'pluralism' has a double aspect: a demand for the right to pursue
cultural differences in Australia and a demand for the forms of
political organisation (lobby groups, etc.) necessary for this. The
two camps are interest-group theories (including minority-group
theory) and ethnicist or primordialist theories.

Interest-group minority-group theories

The first approach situates multiculturalism within the broad
parameters of interest-group theory (or minority-group theory)
within liberal thought. As a rule, the majority of interest/minority
group theorists draw on the propositions derived from migration
and ethnic studies in North America, on Weberian-type theories
of class and status and on the propositions of North American
political pluralism. In migration studies in Australia, the major
theorist in this mode was the late Professor Jean Martin, although
the work of other writers, such as Jayasuriya, Encel, Jupp, Price,
and authors associated with the Ecumenical Centre in Melbourne
would fall within the broad parameters of an interest or minority
group approach. The arguments offered by these authors have
both a sociological and a political component.

The sociological component concerns the mode chosen to iso-
late and explain the specific nature of migrant inequality. Put
briefly, the majority of these authors have presented multi-

dimensional analyses of social inequalities. As a rule, the dimensions of inequality are identified along class, status and political lines, and include factors such as race or ethnic background, sometimes sex, and occasionally other factors such as religion, region, age, etc. In the main, interest-group theorists are concerned with the impact of these factors on 'life chances' in a society that promises equal opportunity and political equality irrespective of accidents of birth (e.g. ascribed factors such as class, skin colour, culture, sex, etc.). In brief, they are concerned with inequalities deemed *illegitimate* in terms of the status quo, namely inequalities that arise from ascription rather than achievement, and from social arrangements forged via inherited statuses rather than formal contract. It follows then that in this account social *equality* is generally used in the restricted sense of equality of opportunity, although some authors use the term to include demands for autonomous self-development and institutional (i.e. structural) change.

The main argument here is that non-contractual, ascribed characteristics, such as race or ethnicity, are empirically associated with enduring social inequalities such that the 'life chances' of members of these groups are diminished in comparison with other groups. In the language of political lobbying, this means that members of certain ethnic groups are denied access to the equal opportunities available in Australian society *because* they are members of a particular racial or ethnic group. The language of this argument—phrases and words like discrimination, prejudice, disadvantage, injustice, occasionally capitalism or industrial society, low self-image, rights to participation and self-determination—is well known and need not be reiterated here. Suffice to note that it is the explication of these terms that links the sociological argument to the political argument, and which leads directly to policy.

The political component is concerned with the solution to migrant inequality and is linked to the sociological via the above social and psychological concomitants of migrant inequality. All minority-group multiculturalists argue that the removal of illegitimate inequalities, in a *democratic* society, involves the active *political* organisation of the disadvantaged groups as part of the solution to their disadvantage. In this context, a democratic society is understood as a *pluralist* society representing the diverse interests of the population, and the political system is understood as the arena where differences in social power are battled out. In brief, what is argued is that migrants are excluded from political processes, which compounds migrant inequality and prevents its resolution. Authors arguing in this mode then advocate that migrants be represented as a distinct group in the political process, and in all other significant areas of social life. This argument includes an interventionist role for government: in initiating policies directed towards attitude change; in combatting prejudice and discrimination; in EEO and anti- and positive discrimination policies, and so forth.

The contentious point in this argument is the multiculturalist claim that members of disadvantaged ethnic groups have a legitimate *interest* to pursue, as a group, with claims related to their ascribed status, namely their ethnic *identity*. As should be apparent this claim is based on the argument that members of certain ethnic groups suffer negative prejudice and discrimination because of the traits attributed to the group by the dominant culture. Because prejudice and discrimination are seen as irrational processes by interest-group theorists, they argue that the result is that the negative evaluation of imputed characteristics of migrant groups is reproduced in the personal *identities* of the disadvantaged cultural group itself, for example as negative self-images, low self-esteem, etc. By this account, the combined effects of prejudice and negative identity are to prevent access to the equal opportunities available in Australia for migrants from negatively evaluated groups. Therefore, any resolution of the situation requires political activity directed towards the positive recognition that cultural or ethnic difference is necessary to the positive self-image of ethnic groups, and acts as a counter to anti-migrant prejudice. As the establishment of a positive self-image is seen as a prerequisite to full participation in social and political life, and full participation is regarded as a democratic necessity, then minority-group theorists use these arguments to establish a link between a social/political interests and personal/group identity.

In political terms, all these arguments are summed up in a demand for *cultural* pluralism, that is, a demand that the cultural diversity of the Australian population be expressed in all aspects of social and political life. In the minimal case this means a form of cultural tolerance and political representation which ensures that migrants come on to the social/political stage on the same footing as 'everyone else' (i.e. Anglos), and that the migrant interest has a distinct representation (in politics, in service delivery, in the media, etc.).

Further to this, largely in response to Right-wing and popular resistance to multiculturalism, minority group multiculturalism has produced a radical version, one which pushes the pluralist argument further to demand *structural* pluralism. Put crudely, these writers argue that, in practice, cultural pluralism is no more than a form of benevolent paternalism that leaves Anglo control and Anglo social and political institutions intact. They argue that a fully fledged multiculturalism would demand institutional (i.e. structural) reorganisation, for example, in the areas of law, education, health and national language policy. Some writers demand parallel or plural institutions, for example, plural legal or educational systems, and some push the demand to include autonomous self-management, and even secession (Social Alternatives 1983; Martin 1978).

An important final point is that, in contrast to later accounts, the majority of interest-group theorists are *not* arguing that cultural origin (or 'ethnicity') is a primary concern in social life, or even a primary source of personal identity. Rather, ethnic group membership is posited as one among many, theoretically equal, forms of group affiliation that entail an 'interest' (trade unions, political parties, religious groups, etc.), and ethnic group membership neither excludes not exhausts these. What this means is that writers in this mode draw back from any suggestion that multiculturalism will produce a 'total' solution to migrant inequality: Professor Jean Martin's reservations about the capacity of multiculturalism to address female inequality would be an obvious case in point (Martin 1978). The important point is that, as the theory holds that individuals are constituted via a plethora of group affiliations, none having any necessary personal or political priority, there is clearly room for a distinct 'female' interest in this body of thought. However, as some writers diverge from the 'pure' position in their focus on ethnic affiliation, for example in assumptions about the priority of Anglo domination, this question will be pursued later.

115

Ethnicist/primordialist accounts

In contrast to the previous approach, 'ethnicist' or 'primordialist' approaches posit ethnic differences as the primary source of social identification, and also as a primary source of social divisions and antagonism in liberal democratic societies. This perspective reoriented policy in the 1980s, and the authors involved are often referred to as 'ethnic primordialists' or 'ethnicists'. In the Australian case, the most well known proponents of this position are J. Zubrzycki and J. Smolicz, although their work draws on a range of primarily North American ethnic primordialist literature, and on 'plural society' theses that originated in debates about 'emerging nations' in the post-colonial era (Glazer and Moynihan 1975; Kruper and Smith 1971).

Basically in this form of theorising, ethnic affiliation and the bonds associated with it, enjoy an ontological primacy in accounts of social life. Ethnicity is posited as pre-social, either historically or through the primacy of 'ethnicity' in the socialisation process (bonds, symbols, language, etc.). In these bodies of thought, ethnic affiliation or *ethnicity* is generally identified with *tradition*, that is, with cultural forms of kinship organisation, meanings, language, folkways, worship: in brief, a people's 'way of life' conceived of as a *static* form inherited from the past. The key difference from interest-group accounts is that ethnicist bodies of thought posit no theoretical equality between ethnic affiliation or ethnic identity, and other affiliations or sources of identity: the ethnic is always and necessarily prior. In other words, ethnicist accounts see ethnic affiliation and ethnic identification as an irreducible component of social life, and as an irreducible component of social difference (i.e. ethnicity is primordial).

The main problem for an ethnicist account concerned with ethnic antagonisms and inequities in multi-ethnic societies is that the abstract commitment to the irreducibility of ethnic diversity conflicts with their simultaneous commitment to the necessity of a core of shared values in maintaining social order. The result is that ethnicist theorists are forced, in the terms of their own argument, to consider the possibility that the full expression of primordial sentiments may conflict with civil sentiments and with the maintenance of social order. Predictably, in policy documents informed by ethnicist thought, this dilemma is manifested conservatively, mainly by a preoccupation with the problem of cohesion, and by a call to national unity (ACPEA 1982).

In ethnicist theories that subtend policy, this problem is dealt with by reconceptualising the cause of migrant inequality and its solution, via some speculative propositions about the tension between *unity* and *diversity*, or more appositely, about the resolution of the perceived tension between the two. The purpose of these exercises is to arrive at an argument *for* multiculturalism that takes the necessity of both unity and diversity for granted.

In concrete terms, when this argument is translated into public policies addressing the 'situation of migrants', the authors appear to be arguing that the particular situation suffered by NESB migrants in Australia arise from their designation as 'ethnic' (i.e. different from non-ethnics). As by the ethnicists' own account we are all 'ethnic', their first solution is to point to the error of the ethnic/non-ethnic opposition, entrenched in Australian popular thought and practised as antagonism toward ethnics. In policy terms, at one level, the resolution of the problems consequent to the error is relatively straightforward: public policies should facilitate inter-ethnic tolerance by the positive recognition of *all* ethnic cultures in Australia, including Anglo-Australian (i.e. multiculturalism). In contrast to Right-wing racist anti-multiculturalists, equally committed to the primordiality of ethnicity, the pro-multicultural position argues that a truly democratic society should express the positive 'truth' of ethnicity by facilitating, if not celebrating, cultural pluralism. The expected result is the removal of ethnic antagonisms and the realisation of division as difference.

At this point, however, ethnicist theorists draw back from the ethical relativism threatened in their position. On this point, problematic issues that usually arise concern such things as the relativity of legal codes, marriage practices, male–female relations, etc. The key question facing multiculturalists (posed largely from the Right) is: What are the ethical implications of the proliferation of culturally diverse practices for a democratic society, and for the social order necessary to sustain democracy? Or, put differently, they ask: What degree of cultural relativism is compatible with democratic principles and with the maintenace of a democratic society?

The ethnicist resolution is to rephrase the question as a question about unity versus diversity, and then to privilege 'unity' over 'diversity'. In brief, they argue that 'diversity' can only flourish if founded on a 'unity'. In these writings this unity is a unity that expresses more general human aspirations, such as liberty, freedom, justice, democracy, etc. Predictably, these universal aspirations are identified with 'democracy', in turn identified with some aspects of 'Anglo-Australian' culture and tradition—legal, political, familial—and symbolised in a national character embodied in an Anglo male. In the Australian case this echoes in the unity-in-diversity' theme of recent policy manifestos, and in the refocusing of multicultural policy on the question of national unity. In this context, the argument for pluralism as the definitive condition of a unified democracy is an argument for mutual tolerance of cultural differences within the status quo. There is no reference at this point to inequalities or power relations among the different 'ways of life', as basically this is considered a question of attitude.

Two general comments are called for at this stage. First, it should be noted that one implication of the slippery voyage from universal social givens, such as ethnic difference and ethnicity, to universal social aspirations, such as democracy, 'society', justice and so forth, is an implied distinction between *higher* human aspirations and the *lower* givens of human identification and sociability. In this sense, ethnic claims are given an almost instinctual character, compared with the intellectual character of 'democracy' and democratic values.

Secondly it should be apparent that this account leaves no room for a specific female claim: indeed, a distinct sex-based interest or division is either buried in the ubiquity of the 'ethnic' and 'tradition', or it is buried in the univeral aspirations embodied in the Anglo male. Other authors have pointed to the convenience of this move (Jakubowicz 1984b).

Multiculturalism and women

Overall, women only emerge in these positions in statements about concrete policies, or in taken-for-granted locations within the ethnic community. In the most abstract sense, women are subsumed to the category 'ethnic', and are assumed as parts of families, as the bearers and socialisers of children, with little function outside of these roles. However, there is some empirical recognition that women do other things, (e.g. work) and might suffer disadvantages accordingly. Nevertheless, as there is no attempt to reconcile these conceptions in the multicultural literature, migrant women are usually considered in two separate situations: namely, as members of families, and as a 'particular problem', a subcategory of the general category 'migrant' (or 'ethnic').

Multiculturalism, women and the family

In the most general sense, the language of 'family' is integral to most official accounts of multiculturalism. Initially the 'family' was employed as a metaphor for the form of social organisation envisaged by multiculturalists, for example in Al Grassby's expectation of Australia as a 'family of nations' (Grassby 1973). The appeal to family interaction was intended to evoke a range of sentiments about 'belonging': affective personal ties, tolerance, co-operation, equality, loyalty, reciprocity, duty, obligation, etc. This appeal was an attempt to point to a future where social unity was forged through these sorts of social relations, and not, for example, through impersonal contractual relations. But the family also has a more particular importance in multiculturalism. This is because of the emphasis on 'the family' in family migration policies, and the struggles of migrants to reunite their families, along with their struggles against efforts of the Australian state to fit migrant families to an ideal Anglo-nuclear form (e.g. in family reunion policy) (see de Lepervanche in this volume). Therefore a lot of political debate has focused on migrant families, and it is the family that is the primary location of migrant women in multicultural thought.

Women and the family in the interest-group model

Interest-group *theorists* prefer the language of 'community'—the ethnic community—rather than 'family', to signal sentiments associated with belonging. Within this, the 'family' is generally discussed as an already given *empirical* entity, with persons in particular roles, which has become politicised in the contemporary Australian context. For example, most interest group theorists are aware both of the struggles of migrants as outlined above and the continuing struggles of migrant women against sexual oppression in the family and the workplace, as well as the general feminist critique of 'family life'. Indeed, in contrast to the ethnicist position, one could say that interest-group theorists have at least a minimal awareness that feminism exists, and that there are feminist demands (female lobby groups, etc.).

For these reasons, interest-group theorists have felt compelled to recognise a 'female interest' arising from 'female disadvantage' via familial responsibilities within the ethnic community itself. The result is that, in theory, a space is always left open within this body of thought for the specificity of female disadvantage, or inequality, and a female interest related to a woman's position in family life.

This said, however, it should be stressed that the space is left empty in discussions of multiculturalism. Overall, in interest-group accounts, the family is taken as a self-evident empirical unit in the private sphere, expressed as a unit of analysis, and women do battle from there. Therefore there is little conceptual space for an account of the processes that constitute 'the family', and thus no starting point from a feminist standpoint. The result is that women are 'set' in the remaining feminised, private category of 'family' within the ethnic group, and the theory cannot get them out of it. Professor Jean Martin's constant reservations about the capacity of multiculturalism to address the situation of migrant women along with her own inability to address the question is an illustration of this theoretical bog (Martin 1978; Martin and Encel 1981).

This methodological limitation is compounded by the political purpose of the multicultural argument. The main purpose of the interest-group multiculturalist's work is to argue that, in the context of ethnic domination, a positive *ethnic* self-identity is necessary to the effective conduct of social life, and the above methodology is deployed to this end. Therefore, while women are empirically present as members of families and ethnic communities, this political task overtakes their mode of presence; hence this mode is never scrutinised. The result is that the family remains in the private sphere, as a given unit, whose form alone (rather than construction, etc.) is debated *within* ethnic politics. As it is ethnicity alone that moves into the public sphere (becomes masculinised), this means that, conceptually speaking, any liaising between the family and the outside world is the concern of men.

The family in the ethnicist model

The family as an irreducible unit of social life is at the forefront of the ethnicist model. This is not surprising, given the position of the family in transmitting ethnic 'kin-ness' and reproducing 'tradition'. In 'pure' ethnicist theory, the family is taken for granted as an unproblematic feature of human existence, as is the sexual division of labour inscribed therein. Such issues as male power and female subordination are either not addressed as structured forms of oppression, or are assumed to be part of the natural order of things.

However, as indicated earlier, ethnicists draw back from the implications of pure theory when it comes to public policy. In policy statements informed by ethnicist writers, the commitment to the benevolence of unbridled ethnicity is qualified, often with respect to women, usually as a mode of controlling non-Anglo ethnic diversity while reinforcing family life. The commitment to the existential irreducibility of both ethnicity and the centrality of the family is therefore not qualified, but reasserted by an 'enlightened' sketch of the parameters of traditional family life.

In practice, what this means is that the actual practices of ethnic families with respect to women are weighed against the universal aspirations that are the foundation of the 'good society'. As the 'good society' is captured in substantial aspects of Anglo-Australian culture, and a (male) Anglo-Australian national character, universal aspirations become identical with some unspecified Anglo family norm. The result is that, on the behalf of 'ethnic women', 'foreign' ethnic family practices are closely scrutinised and judged from the position of an ideal Anglo perspective. Control of ethnic family practices is accordingly deemed necessary. What happens then is the familiar, tiresome, one-way, 'pro-female' obsession, shared with Left and Right, with clitoridectomy, child marriage and other 'atavistic' practices, all presented as the limit to diversity in a democratic (socialist, liberal, totalitarian) society. Authors from Fanon onwards have pointed to the deployment of the rhetoric of 'progress' by dominant cultures to justify the colonisation of subordinate cultures and the domination of colonised men. Although the case is not immediately analagous, the project of 'unveiling' by the French authorities in Algeria in the name of progress and democratic liberation is a case in point (Fanon 1967).

What *is* the point is that none of these concerns and interventions have anything to do with the subordination of *women*. It should be apparent that this use of women to spell out the limits of tolerance in a culturally diverse society is not prompted by any interest in female inequality, and certainly not by female oppression itself. The concern is not at all with questions of 'women's liberation'; rather it is overridingly about treating women—wives, mothers, daughters—decently, as a norm of conduct governing the ranking of *men*. In this rhetoric, decent treatment of women is part and parcel of the conduct of democracy—a form of social organisation already immanent in Anglo-Australia and ensconced in enduring aspects of its national character. By implication, Anglo-Australian women are already treated decently, and thus Anglo-Australian family practices are exempt from detailed scrutiny.

On a final note, one curious aspect of the ethnicist account is the manner in which it positions persons in 'Australia'. For example, women continue to be positioned 'out there', beyond society (democracy), in the family and in tradition. Even when they 'come in', for example, to participate in paid work, they come in via the family, which, through the behaviour of other family members, links women to society (democracy, universal aspirations, etc.). Note that, in this imagery, women are positioned as objects of, and never actors in, a democratic society.

Nor are all men actors, or equally actors, in a democratic society. Despite the posited universality of the 'ethnic', it is obvious that some ethnicities more closely approximate (higher) universal aspirations that others, (i.e. are less 'tradition-bound'). It is clear that Anglo-Australian men symbolise democracy more accurately than men from some other groups, and are therefore in 'society' rather than 'tradition'. This imagery produces a sex–ethnic ranking among men, where all women and some men are objects of command. In this scheme of things, if women are located outside society, non-Anglo men are located at the borders: adoption of the universal aspirations embodied in the Anglo male is the cost of a ticket for admission.

Multiculturalism and women

Other discussions of 'the situation of migrant women' are usually pursued independently of the institutional location of women in 'the family', and independently of any concern with family norms. What this means, as pointed out in the previous section, is that the institutional location of women in families is conceptually taken as given, with the result that the processes governing the subordination of women escape scrutiny. This is very much the case in *both* models that underpin multicultural policy. The models do diverge however with respect to pluralism, and the implications of pluralism for women.

With respect to the 'situation of women', both models position women as a 'disadvantaged group' with specific interests or problems related to their femaleness. Here femaleness is separated out either as a particular aspect of the ethnic, one that carries specific non-relational disadvantages, or as a distinct category of disadvantage from the ethnic (i.e. it belongs elsewhere). In the ethnicist argument, the first conception is underscored by a tendency to list 'migrant women' as one of the many problems afflicting ethnic groups—for example, along with health, children, education, unemployment and so forth. In both accounts, female disadvantage is disadvantage predominantly in the public sphere, and therefore the theories tend to favour solutions that ease female forays into the public sphere (e.g. disadvantage at work,: work-related child care; discrimination; language; education; health, etc.). In these cases, female disadvantage is often really about restating the link between women and children, and children's welfare, and is premised on the givenness of the female domestic role.

Neither argument considers female disadvantage in relation to male power, partly because this is outside the brief given in their definition of ethnic politics, but also because of the avoidance of any criss-crossing processes of domination and subordination, except in terms of people's attitudes. Overall, insofar as the literature makes reference to 'oppression' or subordination, the oppression is cultural or ethnic, and is empirically defined in terms of structured relations of domination and subordination among ethnic groups (radical multiculturalists). This holds whether the domination is considered in terms of interests, expressed as an attitude, or as the accidental consequence of a misapprehension.

This problem is writ large in discussions of pluralism. In interest-group discussions of pluralism, the commitment to a multiplicity of criss-crossing interests that meet in the individual is not maintained consistently. For example, what comes through in the interest-group model is that the enduring interest at the level of affective personal identification, prior to achieved relations, is that of the *ethnic* community. In other words, pluralism boils down to *ethnic* pluralism. For females, this means that the claims of women are always secondary to, or a sub-clause of, the ethnic claim: there is no mention of an equivalent female community. The pertinent affective social group for females is the 'ethnic community', within which women are situated in the family. The ethnic group represents women, and the family, and is their bridge to public life. In an important sense, women only achieve the status of a disadvantaged group once this has occurred.

This tendency is underscored in the ethnicist model. Within ethnicist thought, pluralism is exhausted by ethnic pluralism, which represents the fruition of democracy. All other differences and divisions come after this, and are historically specific and transient. These transient historical differences are of secondary existential import, and refer to phenomena such as class. In this analysis women do not constitute even a distinct secondary division. Rather, they are always contained within other divisions, which are led by men.

Comments

A close reading of accounts of 'multiculturalism' with respect to 'women' reveals a surprising inattention to general conditions governing female subordination. To sum up, the main reasons are as follows:

At the most general level, it is obvious that 'women' and 'the family' are constructed in a very complex and shifting manner in discourses of multiculturalism. For example, women are not just immediately situated in the family (although this seems desired), but are so positioned as members of an 'ethnic group'. This positioning is political as well as analytical. In the interest-group model, this is because of the privileging of the 'ethnic' in confronting Anglo domination, and the political importance of maintaining this front. Questions about women thus take second place to the ethnic, or are referred out of the group (out of analysis) to, for example, women's bureaus.[2]

The secondary position of women in ethnicist accounts has a different origin. In the ethnicist account, feminist claims are folded out by the assumption of the ontological priority of 'ethnicity' in the conduct of social life. In this context, the empirical (or natural) location of women in families, which are part of private life, is not seen as a pertinent issue, Rather, it only becomes a matter of concern insofar as the behaviour of (non-Anglo) men transgresses preconceptions about a decent family life.

Feminism multiculturalism, women and family

It is nevertheless apparent that a 'female versus ethnic' opposition is analytically and politically inappropriate for feminism. In Australia, Anglo domination and Anglo ethnocentricism *do* define the lot of NES migrant women, even in their struggles against male domination. For example, it was noted that some discourses of multiculturalism symbolically rank ethnic men under the control of Anglo men, and that 'the situation of migrant women' is deployed to this end. In other words, while women are clearly other than, or a special instance of, the male in multicultrual discourses, ethnic men are also ranked as other than an Anglo-Australian male. It should be self-evident that women are implicated in these processes as oppressors as well as those oppressed. Consequently, each process is also the concern of women.

Therefore, despite the polemic against multiculturalism, the theoretical issue is not at all straightforward. Many of the criticisms of 'multiculturalism' apply equally to other bodies of thought, including 'feminism'. The question of hegemonic ethnocentricism is critical here. The most obvious case is where the analytical and political preoccupations of an ethnically dominant group are falsely universalised and normalised with respect to women from minority and colonised groups, for example, in the hegemonic and imperialistic practices of a White European and North American feminism. It is these features of the hegemonic position of white feminism, normalised, universalised and reproduced in white feminist discourses, which have proved so galling to black feminism, and which make up the core of the black critique of white feminism.

In Australian feminism, one response to these critiques has been to stress the plurality of feminist struggles, to stress autonomy in political organisation and struggle; in other words, to emphasise *differences* among women, and the specificity of the situation of different groups of women. Although, strictly speaking, many of these prescriptions have separate (and occasionally incompatible) intellectual sources, this is the language of contemporary feminism in Australia, particularly regarding black struggles and the struggles of migrant women. In other words, what is stressed in this chain of terms is the political importance of a pluralistic feminism that recognises autonomous, local, etc. struggles, and is informed by regional and non-universalistic, etc., theorising, so that (in the migrant case) all women are not defined, or spoken for, in terms of the preoccupations of a dominant group (Anglo feminists, middle-class feminists, etc.).

In an earlier paper I suggested that, despite the evident desirability of such a feminism, this melange of positions was not without its traps. My main argument was that, given the structural marginality of disfavoured NES migrant groups in Australia, such strategies could merely augment marginality, especially given the structural privilege enjoyed (in this case) by Anglo feminists. In other words, I argued that a commitment to a plurality, etc. of struggles would not *necessarily* resolve questions of the domination of feminism by Anglo feminists; nor would it resolve the exclusion or subordination of the struggles of feminists from culturally powerless groups. Unhappily this has proved to be the case: the majority of migrant feminists continue to struggle unheard on the margins and, apart from occasional ritual gestures, Anglo feminism continues at the centre, as the point of reference for difference, and as what-is-not specific (Martin 1986).

As the question of 'the family' is often controversial in this respect, and as it is also a 'hot' topic in migrant politics in Australia, it seems appropriate to pursue the above comments via a brief consideration of some of the dilemmas surrounding migrant women and families in Australia.

Feminism, migrant women and the family

In Australia, the pitfalls of hegemonic ethnocentrism are well illustrated in many feminist stances towards the 'family', and the 'family and migrant women'. It is well known that feminists involved in migrant struggles around the family face a slippery and kaleidoscopic field of politics. From a feminist perspective, it often seems that feminists struggling in the migrant area hold political positions that are at odds with a feminist enterprise. For example, it is not uncommon for feminists to simultaneously pursue a feminist critique of the family, a demand for liberalised family reunion policies and a defence of 'traditional' family forms.

One common way of coping with totality of these stances in Australia is by reference to political expediency. If one can typify this approach, it is an approach that stresses the *specificity* of migrant struggles, and then provides an analytical accomodation via a class–race–gender trilogy. In brief, on the question of the family, this approach argues that given the *particular* situation of migrant women in Australia, Anglo feminists must support the struggles by migrant women for, for example, family reunion, and reserve judgment on the(ir) families *pro tem*. In this instance, the struggle of migrant women to establish their families is seen as a form of resistance to Anglo domination, and 'explained' in terms of the racist and sexist degradation of (working class) migrant women in this country. From here, one could conclude that the appropriate political strategy is a matter of confronting Anglo hegemony, in this instance via supporting the struggles of migrant women for the families and family customs they wish to maintain (Martin 1984; 1986a,b).

The problem is that this is not all there is to it. It is well known that struggles around family reunion, etc. are not just resistances to Anglo domination, or reactions to an alien and hostile environment. They are also about many women struggling *for* their families or, more accurately, they are many struggles that have neither a necessary nor a univocal political home. In other words, 'the family' is a code word for a multiplicity of struggles, including struggles against ethnic domination, and it is this aspect that can prove uncomfortable for mainstream feminism (see Vasta in this volume).

As a rule, it is at this point that Anglo ethnocentrism often intrudes and, as a consequence, it is at this point that something like an ethnic reading of feminism can be brought into play. Basically, what a polemic from an ethnic position would argue is that the black or 'ethnic' experience of the practices of feminism reveals an unscrutinised ethnocentric centre of domination in European–American mainstream feminism that is anterior to political strategy and theory.

The subtle nature of this process is well illustrated if we follow these misgivings a little further into the practices of feminist politics, particularly, in the Australian case, around migrant women and their families. As the main problem in assessing Anglo feminist stances in this respect lies in the virtual absence of NESB migrant women in mainstream texts (except as obligatory afterwords), the following comments are drawn from the experience of ethnic politics and ethnic feminist politics.

In the world of politics, what we find is two common images of the relationship between migrant women and their families, that lie *behind* analysis and behind the benevolence of accommodation formulae. These images are often stereotypic, and mould many Anglo feminist perceptions of NES migrant women and their struggles. Their function secures the control of the dominant culture over theoretical feminism (as the pivot around which all other 'feminisms' turn) and they often coexist with a politics that 'recognises' that issues defined as key feminist issues by dominant culture feminists may be of secondary importance, or may be differently ranked by women in other cultures or in subordinate cultures. For example, I have found that the 'understanding' of the complex struggles of migrant women around families is usually premised on one or other of the following unformed, and often highly stereotyped, presuppositions:

- NES women 'desire families' because they are locked passively into families by circumstances (usually historical) and traditions beyond their control (i.e. they are backward).
- 'Wanting families' is imagined as an attribute of the 'NESness' of migrant women, that is, as some intrinsic aspect of 'their' difference from 'us'.

Either way, 'wanting families' (sometimes 'wanting men') is equated with *migrant* women, and this phenomenon becomes definitive of 'their' specificity (specific/particular situation). As a rule, the migrant women–family (children–men–sex) image is then presented as a sort of exotic handicap suffered by migrant women— one which requires ('our') special feminist consideration.

This reveals two immediate problems that become evident in the practice of feminist politics. The first is that the general or normative instance is always there, and it is Anglo. In other words, there is a universalised norm that lies behind all specificity formulae and pluralist prescriptions, and that decides what is different or specific, and what is not. The formula is that the struggles of migrant women and colonised women are different *from* the 'main struggle', or are a specific aspect *of* it. Basically, what this reveals is that the question of a universalising or a normalising power inscribed in ethnic domination has not been fully addressed in feminism, and remains anterior to the specific– particular formula *in any current methodological form* (e.g. who speaks for whom; the disavowal of universalistic theories; political prescriptions for pluralism; local struggle, etc.) For example, there is not much talk of the specific situation of Anglo women as situated in hegemonic ethnicity, and no substantial consideration of what this might mean in defining the norms of a radical movement.

The second problem is a detail of the above, one that is illustrative of the general problem at both a political and analytical level and that takes us back to the concerns about the family. As should be apparent from the preceding discussion of migrant women and families, there is a slip in mainstream feminism from talk of the specific circumstances attendant on ethnic domination or oppression to talk of what is particular (peculiar, different) about migrant women themselves. This is an odd slip that occasionally looks like a matter of projection, and which thus adds another dimension to the problem. If the 'family' is taken as an example, it often seems that unresolved issues for feminism— issues that belong to the general—are put outside the mainstream as something 'about migrants' (i.e. 'about them').

Yet this is surely a general problem for feminist theory: it must be obvious that the analytical and political problem about 'family' is not just about 'migrant women and families' or a characteristic of 'ethnic thought', but about a weakness in feminist thought itself. This weakness is twofold. First the concrete family assumed as the locus of oppression in feminist accounts is the privatised bourgeois family of Western capitalism. Theoretically this means that feminist accounts of familial discourses (mothering, reproduction, sexuality, housework, etc.) assume this family, and this family sets the criteria for universal evaluation, despite disclaimers, (Barrett and McIntosh 1982; Chodorow 1978). What happens politically is that the criteria thus set to judge the oppression of women in the family are generalised as the criteria to judge all 'families': all are seen *and compared* as the key site of women's opression. The result is that the terms appropriate to an analysis of the familial oppressions of Western European and North American women are generalised to apply to all women, and conceptual discourse is reduced to typology (types of families; types of people; specific situations, etc.) In this instance, comparison loses its self-referential force, and becomes a ranking of oppressions whose point of reference is a reassertion of the claims of ethnically dominant women. The effect is a consolidation of ethnic privilege and power in feminism.

The second problem is that these issues reveal a further difficulty in the theoretical status of 'the family' within mainstream feminist thought itself. For example, while mainstream feminism can produce polemics on mothering, sexuality, reproduction and so forth, detailed understandings of the ambiguous and contradictory manner in which women are positioned in families, via their implication in and between non-familial discourses, are undeveloped in feminism. It is in this latter sense that 'the family' functions as a code word, as a referent for multiple struggles and resistances whose political locus is not always clear. Perhaps this is the case among all women, and not just women from minority groups, although it is often put out to them. In the Australian case, there have been a couple of attempts to commence work addressing this issue, but they have not been pursued (Curthoys 1988; de Lepervanche in this volume). In essence, the evasion of this question adds more layers of obfuscation to the issues outlined above.

Concluding comments

A critical reading of the social theories that subtend multiculturalism demonstrates the marginalisation or exclusion of the 'female' in multicultural thought. A feminist reading of non-feminist texts, however, does not necessarily produce a feminist alternative. Nor does it exempt feminism from similar scrutiny. For example, it is clear that charges of ethnocentricism levelled against some forms of multiculturalism can equally apply to many propositions and presuppositions of feminist thought. This raises issues for mainstream (dominant) feminism concerning assumptions about the universal (general–normal) female and the particular (specific–deviant, other) female. As Anglo feminists are already situated in a position of ethnic domination, it should be apparent that in-attention to these questions perpetuates, not feminism, but ethnic (or racial) and male domination.

Criticisms are easy, solutions are not: this became clear in the above discussion of 'the family'. Overall the issue seems partly an issue about methodology, at least as it has been discussed in this paper. For example, in the Australian case, methodological 'do-nots' that arise from the foregoing analysis include: do not employ a method that compares oppressions; do not attempt to find out 'about' migrant women, (to pose the question thus immediately positions migrant women 'out there' to be investigated as different from 'us' and calls them to account accordingly); do not pose feminist questions via two-sided formulae (e.g. universal and particular; public and private; women and the family ... and class, and the state, and ...). Rather assume that what is female is situated fluidly, ambiguously and variously in the space between each side, and accept that a feminist account proceeds from here. It could be that some such method would eschew invidious comparisons; would confront dominations among women; would replace aboutness (otherness) with dialogue; and would by-pass concerns with theoretical modes that deploy assumptions about, for example, universal and particular positions in analysis and strategy.

8 The family: In the national interest?

Since white settlement, many learned and not-so-learned men have looked to the family, in its nuclear form as we know it, as *the* crucial institution for peopling this land. The existence of a people already inhabiting the continent was officially denied in various ways from the beginning, so Aboriginals were not included in the many exhortations through two centuries to 'populate or perish'. Aboriginal family forms and family relationships are different from ours and have often been misunderstood if not violated by whites—a point I will return to later.

But our spokesmen have not only been concerned with increasing the (white) population through legitimate childbearing and rearing within the family; they have also given their support to our political masters in their efforts to monitor and control the population through census gathering and surveys; through Royal Commissions of inquiry into the birthrate; through health and welfare measures concerned with child endowment; through legislation pertaining to marriage, divorce and the custody of children; and through policies for restricting the numbers of and introducing more immigrants. In all of these endeavours, the family is referred to quite frequently as if it were a unitary phenomenon marching through history, remaining changeless despite the vicissitudes of the wider social context. Yet, the figures and records tell us that people in Australia live and have lived in a number of different kinds of familial relationships.

Preliminary figures for the 1986 census show that families comprising a couple with dependent children (i.e. the nuclear family) constitute only 35.5 per cent of family types. Families with one parent and dependent children constitute 6 per cent, while 2 per cent of families have one parent, dependent children and an additional family member. The remaining family types include couples, and couples with children and extra family members (ABS 1986; cf. Game and Pringle 1979).

According to other sources, in the decade 1975–85 one-parent families increased by two-thirds to reach 15 per cent of all families with dependent children. Many of these were socially deprived: the majority (90 per cent in the period 1978–79 (Cass 1985:92)) were mother headed and they received minimal support from the absent fathers (Burns 1986:213). The increase in mother-headed families in the period 1975–82 (145 200 to 241 229) was 66 per cent, while the number of two-parent families increased by only 13.9 per cent in the same period (Burns 1986:232). As Bettina Cass comments for the period 1974–83:

> although the rate of all sole parents' dependence on social security increased significantly ... from 65% of women and 10% of men to 84% of women and 22% of men, women remained four times as likely as men to be receiving pensions or benefits, accounting for 96 per cent of all sole parent beneficiaries ...
>
> The disparity between male and female single parents' take-up of pension or benefit demonstrates that it is female gender, rather than single parenthood per se, which affects the job chances of single parents. Women with sole care of dependent children confront a sex-segmented labour market which offers a narrow range of jobs at relatively low rates of pay. In addition, women sole parents are much less likely than their male counterparts to have formal post-school job qualifications, and they are also responsible on average for more and younger children. These barriers to employment are reinforced by an ideology which prescribes dependency for women in a couple relationship and which does not facilitate independent full-time employment when a relationship ends. (Cass 1988:119)

Cass's data show that, in both one-parent and two-parent families, women are more disadvantaged than men. In addition to women's joblessness:

> policies regulating the payment of unemployment benefit (usually paid to the husband as the former breadwinner who is looking for

work, and income-tested on joint married couple income) may ex-
acerbate inequities of income distribution within the family and
create disincentives to women's job seeking (Cass 1988:124).

In any analysis of the family in Australia, therefore, the unequal
access women have to the sex-segmented labour market, and
hence to income and wealth, must always be examined in association with their vulnerability resulting from their dependency and
their unpaid domestic labour (Cass 1988). Moreover, despite
women's general social position as the subordinate gender, it
must be remembered that different types of families characterise
Australian social life. There is no one kind of family out there in
real life, although the invocations to the family usually refer to a
particular kind of domestic group, namely the nuclear family
with a male 'head' supporting a dependent wife and children.
This unit is sanctioned in advertising, in popular discourse and in
our administrative and legislative policies (although some devia-
tions from this 'norm' are recognised in certain welfare measures)
(Baldock and Cass 1983; Bryson 1984; Goodnow and Pateman
1985). It is the quintessential family form of the bourgeoisie.

Against all the anthropological and historical evidence, the
nuclear family is even considered the universal 'natural' domestic
group by many spokesmen and by the sociobiologists (cf. van den
Berghe 1979; Wilson 1978). Some sociologists also consider this
domestic unit and male authority to be the ideal family form. In
writing on the family in multicultural Australia, Zubrzycki refers
to the importance of the primordial ties of the family and of the
family itself as 'the primary functioning agency designed by
nature to care for the young, the sick, and the old' (1978:6).
Woman's role is clearly that of a subordinate provider of services
and, in a thinly veiled attack on women, Zubrzycki argues that
the 'major social problems of the day can be traced to the breakdown of the family': this has been caused by married women
entering the paid workforce, by urbanisation and by 'the widespread dissemination . . . of that trendy antisocial nonsense which
has been given political effect by organisations such as the
Women's Electoral Lobby' (1978:6). This patriarchal rhetoric
is not insignificant: it comes from one of the most influential
advisors on Australia's immigration policy.

How then is it possible to reconcile the differences between real life and the concept of the ideal nuclear family form? There is no reconciliation as such, but what we need to consider is the extent to which the regular promulgation of the ideal affects people's real lives, and how the constant dissemination of this ideal obscures the power relations between family members and between families and the state.

In other words, much of the talk we hear about the family is ideology. Ideology here refers not only to the lack of fit between what exists out there in real life and what our spokesmen and political masters say, but it carries another related meaning, namely the way in which certain beliefs or stated ideals (in this case those of the 'naturalness' of the nuclear family) mask/ disguise the power relations and the relative advantages and disadvantages of those people implicated in family relationships. In this respect, ideology is not simply something to do with ideas that we can dismiss as unimportant. Ideologies are powerful devices in themselves for those in power to control people, keep order and maintain the *status quo*. (Nuclear) family ideology in our society has been and remains enormously powerful, particularly in the control and surveillance of women and children (cf. Ramazanoglu 1989:148). It is to this aspect of power relations, and to some of their implications, that I direct my comments. I am not in favour of destroying families, establishing baby farms or bureaucratised domestic breeding co-operatives. Rather, I tend to agree with an English writer on the family who states:

> Family ideology has been a vital means—the vital means—of holding together and legitimising the existing social, economic, political and gender systems. Challenging the ideology thus means challenging the whole social system, but it would not mean that as a result people ceased living and interacting together in some form of family household. It would mean a radical reappraising of such arrangements. Family households are a vital and integral part of any society in some shape or form. Family ideology is not. There is no ideal family. When politicians articulate a fear that there is a crisis in the family, they are not worried about divorce or rape or incest as such, but rather that the *ideology* is being challenged, and that were this to gain momentum people might start to question the legitimacy of the existing socio-economic, political and patriarchal systems. Without family ideology modern industrial society and its political system might be very different indeed. Without family ideology it would be

possible to reconsider and reconstruct the realities of relationships between men, women and children and to work towards [alternative] ...ways of living and working together. (Gittins, 1985:168)

In the light of that statement of position, I now briefly examine some of the ways in which the ideology of the family has permeated Australian social life. I discuss in passing some of the consequences for women of their serving the 'national interest' in their nuclear family roles.

Governments govern and the majority of those who have exercised this power in Australia have been men, who have tended to come from the more privileged sections of society. Not surprisingly, they have also tended to support family policies and practice which have sustained their position as heads of these units and as the links between the private world of family and the public world of paid work and politics. They were not necessarily consciously conspiring against women in this enterprise: it is, after all, 'natural', the argument goes, for women to be 'protected' in the home where their real talents lie, even if they also work beside their husbands in some family business or outside the home for wages. The ideology of the family states that whatever women do outside the home is secondary to their 'natural' place as wife and mother, caring for husband and children and often for the sick and elderly as well. After all, they do it so well.

Marriage and family is the real career for women, yet one of the contradictions women know is that while:

(their) traditional and paid work efforts may gain unequal recognition on divorce, ... during marriage they gain no legal recognition at all. A woman cannot claim, while the marriage exists, that her work as wife, housewife and mother justifies her ownership of half, or indeed any, of the property bought from her husband's income. (Scutt 1985:131 cf. Poiner 1979; Kingston 1975; Grimshaw and Willett 1981; Cass 1985; Burns 1986)

The sanctioning by the state of the gendered public/private opposition is clearly evident in the notion of the *public* character of the regulation of paid market work (e.g. initially in the family wage for protecting low-income male earners) compared with 'the *private* character of the obligations and relationships surrounding unpaid non-market work' (i.e. domestic labour) (Cass 1985:69). Following the demise of the family wage, and when this notion was transposed to the tax system, it also acquired 'new class connotations' as it was not used to protect low-income male employees, but 'to provide greatest monetary advantage to high-income husbands' (Cass 1985:79). As Cass argues: 'These priorities in the tax/transfer system symbolically represent the rewards that accrue to employed men who have maintained the dependency of their spouse.' (1985:93)

According to family ideology, a man must earn the family living, but that isn't all a bowl of cherries either. Even so, when he needs a wife the powers that be have been ready to help him. The marriage contract itself has traditionally benefited men while providing women with some contradictions to live with. As Carole Pateman argues, the modern liberal democratic state, despite all its reforms, it still anchored in the notion of a fraternal social contract and the status of 'wife' itself, traditionally subordinate to her husband, 'is based on the denial that women are (or can be) "individuals"' in the political sense that men are. To quote her:

> If a woman is to give consent to the status she is to acquire on marriage she must—naturally—have the rights and capacities of an 'individual'. However, it is logically impossible for a 'wife' to possess these attributes because that would be simultaneously to claim that a woman is both naturally free and naturally in subjection. This contradiction is hidden under the fiction of the marriage contract and the mystification of consent; a gloss of free argument is given to the reality of the ceremonial confirmation of the ascribed, patriarchal subjection of wife to husband. (Pateman 1986:179)

The individuals of liberalism belong to the public world of social life. Married women, by comparison, belong to the 'natural' and private institution of the family. In the political theory and practice of liberal democratic states and in their histories, the 'social or public realm was divided from the household, the private sphere where natural inequality held sway, and women were thus also divided from men and placed in subordination to them' (Pateman, 1985:xi; 1986; 1988; 1989).

Modern and even contemporary reforms notwithstanding, the figures for domestic violence demonstrate that husbands still have considerable power over their wives (cf. O'Donnell and Craney 1982; Scutt 1983; SMH 9 March 1988). A random sample study made in Canberra in 1979 estimated that 15 per cent of married women living in the ACT had endured physical abuse from their husbands (Scutt 1983:97). A federal government survey in late 1987 showed that 20 per cent of Australians accepted the use of violence by a man against his female partner and 6 per cent believed that using or threatening to use a weapon could be justified (*SMH* 9 March 1988).

The New South Wales reforms of 1983, through which domestic violence was treated as a criminal offence, certainly 'constituted a major departure from past practice, particularly the treatment of domestic violence under the *Family Law Act* 1975' (L'Orange 1985:6). Traditionally, however, violence in the family has been privatised and regarded even by the state as 'just a domestic' (Burns 1986:212; cf. Scutt 1983:29). The New South Wales reforms acknowledged that women were not prepared to keep violence privately in the family any longer: the social reality of the power structures that women (and children) face is no small terror. According to the New South Wales Bureau of Crime Statistics and Research (in 1986):

> More homicides occur within marriage than in any other single relationship in society. Very nearly one quarter (23.2%) of all homicides in New South Wales occurred between spouses. Women are particularly vulnerable in spouse homicides: almost half (47%) of all female victims were killed by their spouse compared with only 10% of the male victims. Clearly the marital relationship provides the context for some of the most violent encounters in our society. (Wallace 1986:95)

As for children, the majority (95.4%):

> were killed by people known to them: 86.6% were killed by a family member ... Within the family, the child was most vulnerable to attack from a parent: 85.2% of all the children were killed by their father or mother. (Wallace, 1986:125)

These kinds of statistics are more publicly known today, particularly as women have demanded change and law reform. But for generations the family has been regarded as a sacrosanct and private institution, and the state has done its best to help men establish their own family units and to legitimate male dominance within the family as well as in civil society. State policies and programs have repeatedly ignored the power structure within families and the consequences of this for women.

In addition to upholding the institution of marriage itself, the state has assisted the reproduction of women's subordination by introducing female partners for male settlers and by sponsoring brides, especially for non-English speaking immigrants since World War II. Before then, the United Kingdom and Ireland were regarded as source countries for female immigrants. For instance, shortly after the turn of the nineteenth century, in 1821, the first assisted immigrants to New South Wales were 50 women from Ireland who were expected to:

> exert a sobering influence over the moral debauchery held to be rampant in the colony as a result of the excess of single men; they were to become the wives of labouring men and the mothers of their children and they were to provide menial domestic (later factory) labour in the homes and industries of the colonial elite. (Martin, 1984:109)

The independent single female immigrant, (or even the single local woman), on the other hand, was (and is) often suspect. Genteel spinsters might pass muster, as did a good widow who carried on her dead husband's work, provided she behaved in her proper familial role of wife and mother. As the historian of the Irish in Australia comments about one such exemplar:

> The archetypal figure of Mrs O'Hara who ran the Brian Boru [pub] was a feature of the Irish life of many a country town, respected and sought out particularly by single men who needed a sympathetic female ear, thought to be experienced and independent ... These widows—or the wife of mine host—commanded motherly resources: the hotel dining room provided meals to men often denied nutritious cooking otherwise, the bathrooms provided cleanliness, the bar provided contacts for employment, friendship and entertainment, the parlour provided a newspaper, some quiet, the occasional meeting place for organisations. Above all, the Mrs O'Haras provided that female dimension to which the Irish were used ... (O'Farrell 1986:152)

O'Farrell doesn't tell us who cleaned the bathrooms or why the men could not cook their own food. Having reproduced the stereotypical wife and mother in Mrs O'Hara, he then states that among 'the many absurd libels foisted on the Irish by those incapable of understanding them is ... that they dismissed and subjugated women' (1986:153).

Although changes are occurring now and women themselves are rejecting the old stereotypes, working-class women who did not marry, who worked for money whether they wanted to remain independent or not, were often considered whores in the past—if not damned ones (Summers 1975). Some male settlers in the nineteenth century even discouraged their female relatives from emigrating for fear of the 'wicked women' in the colonies. In 1873 a William Martin wrote to his father in Ireland: 'This is a bad country for girls unless the[y] be very wise and steady. Woman is very scerse and the inducements for girls going rong in this Country is something frightfull' (O'Farrell 1986:150).

Fortunately for the poor benighted men, others encouraged their female kin to settle (cf. Grimshaw and Willett 1981:137). However, single women as such still do not constitute an advantaged category in Australian social life. As Cass has pointed out, 'female sex in conjunction with "singleness" connotes such a profound risk of ... deprivation that it is categorised as a "disability" without the addition of other harmful conditions like unemployment, sickness, old age or physical disability' (1984, quoted in Broom 1987:276).

Even married women have not always escaped censure in Australian social life, especially if perceived not to be fulfilling their 'proper' role. A Catholic priest in 1909 complained that 'many outback Catholic women were "ignorant of their faith and totally incapable of either influencing a careless husband or instructing careless children"' (O'Farrell 1986:149). Injunctions to keep husband as well as children in tow might sound quaint in the late twentieth century, but recent warnings of imminent chaos if women neglect their traditional family duties indicate that the ideology of the family remains strongly entrenched in certain quarters. Only a few years ago, in 1985, a professor of philosophy in Brisbane, Hiram Caton, had the following to say:

> It is for women to bear and nurture children; it is for men to provide for and defend kith and kin. In the exercise of this role men feel confident in their actions and justified in their sacrifices; it is the basis of male dignity and stability. Pushed off this keel, males tend to promiscuity, domestic violence, alcoholism, desertion, drifting, opportunism, and indifference to work. Their need for manly exer-

tion cannot find unambiguous objects; they have no definite view of the future; and their awe of women, so important for subduing their grosser impulses, disappears with the contraceptive control of the consequences of the sexual act. (Caton 1985:13)

Then, in 1987, a well known Catholic spokesman, B. A. Santamaria, made his views known. In the midst of the 'long historical crisis' we are in, he said: 'The key to the situation at both ends of life is the presence or the absence of the mother in the home. This constitutes the most important single factor in the functioning of the family as a social institution providing care for the young, the sick and the old.' (1987:40)

The pronouncements of influential men like Caton, Santamaria and, as previously noted, Professor Zubrzyki belong to a long series of exhortations and decrees concerning woman's role, and these have permeated our social life: the state as well as individuals has sought to keep women in their domestic domains, subject to men. Family ideology justifies this subordination and disguises the power structure within the family. Elsewhere (de Lepervanche 1989a, 1989b) I have commented on state support for women's subordination through institutions like the 'family wage', the taxation structure, welfare measures and public policy arising from population inquiries, but here I wish to consider other areas with particular relevance to immigrants since World War II. Immigration policy itself is infected by family ideology— and not always to the advantage of women.

The family reunion plank in our immigration platform endorses the establishment of conventional male-headed nuclear families (and, incidentally, consumption units for capitalist production). The sponsors of new settlers are predominantly men (or a patriarchal government) and most female settlers arrive as dependants of men. Female immigrants themselves are commonly categorised as 'migrant wives' rather than as autonomous people (cf. Simon and Brettell 1986:3), and the transport of women from the Mediterranean and elsewhere has been sanctioned by the state to provide single men with wives (Appleyard and Amera 1986: 215–28; Perez Olleros 1990). Yet, as two researchers note, the men do not always appreciate the women provided: 'Greek male attitudes toward government-nominated girls [sic] who had ventured alone to Australia ... [were] less respectful than their attitudes to personally nominated girls [sic]'. (Appleyard and Amera 1986:222–3)

The good intentions of well meaning governments can at times go very seriously wrong. Following the settlement of many Vietnamese immigrants from the mid-1970s, there was pressure on the Department of Immigration and Ethnic Affairs to redress the pronounced sex imbalance among Vietnamese in Australia. As Viviani notes:

> The Department ... selected a larger number of young single women from the [refugee] camps, but this decision itself had several adverse consequences. Until 1978 most young male refugees selected were ethnic Vietnamese. By 1979, when the young single females were selected, the refugee pool in Malaysian camps had become predominantly ethnic Chinese so that many of those young females entering Australia were Chinese rather than ethnic Vietnamese. In the short term the problem was compounded rather than resolved— numbers of single young Chinese women were now added to the numbers of single young Vietnamese men, but the groups were unlikely to communicate because of ethnic differences. A further effect of selection of young females (on grounds of gender rather than skills) was the refusal to admit their dependant younger siblings who could not qualify under any of the three criteria. Thus the policy helped convert the children of split families into unaccompanied minors remaining in camps, with disastrous effects on these children personally and in terms of their future chances of selection, not to mention the effects on the women entering Australia. (Viviani 1984:121–2)

In addition to bringing in single women and brides for male settlers, the state has also been party to the introduction of female domestic servants for Australians. In the nineteenth and early twentieth centuries, these were English and Irish women (Hamilton 1986; O'Farrell 1986:157). Since World War II, the state has arranged assisted passages for female domestics from Greece, Italy and Spain to work in hospitals, other institutions and in private employment (IAC 1970:15). Both the state and Roman Catholic church have also assisted the recruitment of Spanish domestics for work in the homes of the Anglo-Celtic bourgeoisie (Perez Olleros 1990). As many of these Spanish women subsequently engaged in paid work outside these homes, mostly as cleaners, they have provided domestic service for both the private and public arenas of Australian social life (Perez Olleros 1990; cf. Simon and Bretell 1986:7).

Despite any intention by governments or sponsors to introduce women solely for domestic life, the majority of non-English speaking women who have settled here since World War II have been obliged to work for wages to help provide for themselves and their families. In the workforce they have tended to fill the lower status jobs in manufacturing and service industries: their labour has been cheap and their relatively low wages have often kept them working beyond the home longer than they would have liked. Since 1947, the representation of immigrant women in the workforce has been higher than that for Australian born women. By 1978, for example, the rate for Australian born women was 43 per cent but for Greek women it was 51 per cent and for Yugoslav women 56 per cent (NWAC 1979:17). Among newly arrived women in the decade 1970–80, workforce participation was between 50 and 85 per cent (Martin 1984:112). A very recent study of immigrant women in the workforce indicates that 'there appears to be a great deal of continuity between the experiences and problems of non-English speaking migrant women workers who arrived in Australia in the 1950s and 1960s and those who are arriving now, thirty years later' (Alcorso 1989:90). As Jeannie Martin has pointed out, these women have been expected

> to create nuclear family units that provide an appropriate market for the goods produced by industry, as well as the workforce to produce them. They are to exert a moral and physical control over men through creating dependent family members and provide sexual gratification to their husbands. They are central through this function to the stabilization of male personalities and to industrial effeciency and growth. (Martin 1986b:234)

As Martin also notes, those women are well aware of the extent to which they are expected to fulfil these expectations: their statements reflect this understanding:

> the priests told us that all Australian men were homosexual—the Australian disease they called it. They implore us to go and save our men, to bear their children and keep our people going. (Latin American woman)

143

we were told our future was here ... money, a good kitchen, a future for our children ... if we found the right Greek man. They showed us pictures of this at the immigration place. (Greek woman)

we have to marry ... then there is only the marriage and the children. (Sicilian woman) (Martin 1986b:234)

Initially defined in 1947 to include extended family members (aunts, uncles, nieces, nephews as well as spouses, children and parents—after all, we needed people), the term 'family reunion' has since contracted in meaning. By 1979, it referred to husbands or wives (subject to their satisfactory character and health standards), to unmarried children under 21 who were of the family unit, and to children under 18 years sponsored for adoption (Lippman 1979:39). The category 'special family reunion' applied to additional members of the extended family, admitted only under special circumstances, and to fiance(e)s, provided 'the sponsor has been a resident of Australia for at least one year, is personally known to the fiance(e), and both parties genuinely intend to marry' (Lippman 1979:40). Rejected applicants for family reunion have sometimes been refused permission even to visit relatives in this country on the grounds that they may overstay their visitor's visa and try to change their status while here (Lippman 1979:45). In a statement early in 1986, the Minister for Immigration and Ethnic Affairs made it quite clear that family reunion meant *immediate* family (i.e. spouses, dependent children, fiance(e)s and aged parents). But as a result of lobbying from ethnic community organisations, a new category of 'independent and concessional' from 1 July 1986 permitted extended family members to enter under certain conditions. However, 'only brothers, sisters, nephews, nieces and non-dependent children will be eligible for the concessionary points for sponsorship by an Australian citizen. Sponsors will have to be resident in Australia for at least two years.' (DIEA News Release, April 1986) The Fitzgerald Report on immigration, released in 1988, recommended that 'the Family Immigration Category be expanded to cover grandparents of Australia citizens, 55 years of age or older, that the job offer requirement be dropped for parents 55 years of age and over, and that parents under 55 be processed in the Open category' (Fitzgerald 1988:122). For less well educated or skilled parents, this will mean considerable difficulty in complying with the criteria of the open category, which include labour market skills, entrepreneurship, special talents and language capacity including English as an employability factor (1988:124).

As government policy on family reunion prefers immediate dependants, the state exercises a stricter control over immigrant families than over local ones, ensuring that whenever possible the nuclear family is reproduced (Martin 1984:117). Immigrants and their Australian-born children contributed 59 per cent to population growth in the period 1947–80 (Martin 1986b:233), a contribution which has not always been easy for immigrant women. Upward mobility for many of them, as for some Australian-born women, has been through exploitation of their labour in family businesses. Here they have often been obliged to work for the family enterprise for long hours and without proper wages, although they were also expected to provide 'normal' care for their families. In debates of the 1960s about the danger to children of working mothers, especially immigrant mothers, one liberal expert alluded to the circumstances of a number of these women when he said: 'We must beware of drawing false conclusions about the results of ... employment on the home life and upbringing of immigrant children (because) ... many wives assist ... in running a cafe or small store [so] ... they are therefore "at home" when the children return from school.' (Price 1966: 18–19)

The ideology of the family (with wife and mother at home rearing and caring) notwithstanding, many other immigrant women, like many local women, have had to work for wages to survive. One of the consequences of this imperative to engage in paid work is that non-English speaking women from Southern Europe, the Middle East, South America and Southeast Asia particularly, have 'an acute perception of the tension between production [in wage labour] and social reproduction [in the home]' (Martin 1984:113). Without the customary support of kin and neighbours available in their homelands, many of these women see their lives as being torn between job, home and children. Together with working Australian-born women, they are the victims of grossly inadequate child care. In 1980, for example, while there were at least 600 000 children under school age whose mothers were in paid work, only 62 500 child-care places were available (Power et al. 1984:12). Some Turkish immigrants found the problem of child care in Australia so immense that they sent their children back home to Turkey to stay with kin until they were of school age (Inglis and Manderson 1984). South American immigrants, on the other hand, have sometimes introduced grandparents to help with child minding, but this solution has tended to produce tensions within the household if the older kin members become ill or too aged to care for children. In any case, the younger woman of the household has been the primary carer for the three generations, a burden that has not been easy, particularly if the younger woman has also been working for wages outside the home (Moraes Gorecki 1987; and see contribution to this volume). In circumstances like these, family ties have become strained, if not broken, and the 'triple jeopardy' of ethnicity, class and gender has been acutely felt by the women.

One solution for many immigrant women has been to engage in outwork, and surveys of the labour force have indicated that the 'self-employed' increased by over 50 per cent between 1972 and 1984, when the numbers of wage and salary earners increased by only 14 per cent (Alcorso 1987:10). Southern European and Asian women, particularly, have resorted to this kind of employment and many have been located in the clothing trade which has sought cheap labour to compete with imported goods from even cheaper-labour countries in Asia. Recent surveys of clothing out-workers have revealed that many are non-English speakers and some work for less than others for stitching the same garments (Alcorso 1987:11). As one report 'documenting sweated labour in the 1980s' notes:

> The growth of outwork is a disturbing trend ... It raises many issues related to the labour movement, the status of women and to social and economic policy. Outwork is a result of changing employment patterns which have particular consequences for women, especially migrant women workers. (CWWC, 1986:1)

As another researcher noted: 'the wife/mother/worker is forced to work within the domestic sphere—and is [lowly] paid accordingly ... [This work has] minimum security and maximum exploitation. Immigrant women are well aware of these dimensions of their exploitation.' (Martin 1986b:241) And as one Yugoslav woman said: 'you are not permitted to work and be a mother here ... they make it so you are too tired and have to stop the work, because you cannot stop the mother or you will go to jail. (Martin 1986b:241)

Employers sometimes approach outworkers through kin and community networks. Those who have been disabled by factory work or who cannot find other work are particularly vulnerable to extreme exploitation and even to sexual harassment by middlemen. For employers who have not had to provide leave entitlements and insurance policies, this kind of work is much more profitable than engaging factory labour, as one Asian woman found:

> Quoi had been working in a small, non-unionised factory in the inner city area. She was using a strong smelling glue. She began to have respiratory problems. She took unpaid time off to go to a doctor. Her application for sick leave was refused. When she had to take time off again for treatment, she was refused sick leave and then sacked. She applied for Sickness Benefit, and started doing outwork. (CWWC 1986:9; cf. CATU 1987)

The ideology of the family touches these women, and indeed most women, in another way. Female (paid) workers in general are concentrated in 'feminised' occupations where their jobs as seamstresses, secretaries, nurses, teachers, clerks and saleswomen resonate with their 'proper' familial roles. Figures for August 1989 show that 55.2 per cent of all female employees are in clerical and sales occupations (DEET, October 1989). The immigrant women from Mediterranean countries are especially disadvantaged as they are concentrated in the low-status, low-paid, unskilled jobs with little security or union representation (Martin 1986b:240). In these jobs, women find they are often expected to behave to their male bosses or superiors as daughters, wives or even as sexual game. As a Spanish woman commented: 'it is horrible—they look at our legs and stand too close and we can see them laughing at us'. And a women from Yugoslavia: 'the boss pretends he is our father or husband. He likes us to bring him nice cakes and so forth' (Martin 1986b:241). Indeed, patriarchy expects women to provide selfless service for others in a way never expected of men: 'Secretaries are expected to make their bosses cups of coffee, order their taxis, arrange their social occasions, buy presents for their wives and children, and generally "care" for them as well as work for them' (Gittins 1985:105). The gendered nature of paid work has in many respects been of distinct disadvantage to women (Game and Pringle 1983). Women's work in general is conventionally devalued and the unequal division of labour within the family provides the basis for the division of labour on sex grounds in the workforce. Women therefore become easily exploitable in Australia's labour market, which is segmented by both ethnic identity and gender (Game and Pringle 1979, 1983).

Marriage rates in Australia have been consistently high (Grimshaw and Willett 1981:135). In 1982, the Institute of Family Studies' survey of Australians aged 18–34 found that 52 per cent were married and a further 39 per cent expected to marry or remarry. Only 8 per cent did not expect to marry (Burns 1986: 214). Although the divorce rate has increased over the last quarter of a century (from 0.7 per cent per 1000 population in 1956–60 to 2.8 per cent in the period 1981–85), and approximately 40 per cent of women who marry get divorced (Burns 1986:210), most adult women, whether they engage in paid work or not (and 50 per cent of married women work for wages (Burns 1986:212)) are active participants in (unpaid) domestic labour (i.e. their lives have been/are family centred). In one way or another, then, the ideology and reality of the family is not strange to them.

Yet, in Australia, not all women are, or have been, equal in their endeavours to populate the land in the 'national interest'. In the bearing and rearing of children there has been distinct inequality. Not only the inequalities of class, which advantage the privileged and disadvantage the poor, but differences of ethnic or so-called racial origin have affected the extent to which women have been expected and even permitted to establish and maintain their families. The 'national interest' has indeed been rather selective as far as women and the family are concerned. In the populate or perish business, some have been encouraged to populate while others have been excluded, or literally perished.

For example, colonial and later state and federal policy did not respect Aboriginal families or women. After protests by whites in New South Wales at the increased population of Aboriginal people around newly established townships late last century, the Aboriginal Protection Board was established in 1883. By 1900:

The Board reasoned that if the Aboriginal population characterised in some quarters as a 'wild race of half-castes' was growing, then it would somehow have to be dimished. If the children were to be *de*socialised as Aborigines and *re*socialised as whites, they would have to be removed from their parents ... [That is] ... it was in the interest of the state, as well as of the children themselves, that they be removed from their communities and raised as white. (Edwards and Read 1989:xii)

As the film *Lousy Little Sixpence* documents, in New South Wales from 1909 the *Aborigines Protection Act* permitted the forcible removal of Aboriginal children from their families for the purposes of 'training' them to be hired out as servants and useful workers for whites. From 1909 to 1930, more than one-third of all Aboriginal children in New South Wales suffered this fate (*SMH* 28 October 1983). Right into the 1960s, the Cootamundra home where many were trained sent Aboriginal girls into domestic service for whites (*National Times* 9–15 January 1983). Thousands of children were also fostered and grew up in white families. According to Edwards and Read, writing in the late 1980s, 'there may be one hundred thousand people of Aboriginal descent who do not know their families or communities' (1989:ix). White European society has demeaned Aboriginal families in another way, by pathologising them. These families have been labelled 'unstable' or 'deviant', sometimes for having a female 'head'. Langton, in criticising these representations, comments that the authors:

do not discuss the possibility of the matrifocal family as an accepted or perhaps even desired family form for Aboriginal women and children arising out of particular social conditions; that is those in which Aboriginal men are unable to reside permanently with wives and children because of itinerant labour patterns, unemployment, imprisonment, regulations pertaining to social security benefits for supporting mothers and so on. Aboriginal social and cultural values may also contribute to the incidence of the women-focussed family, in that mothers, grandmothers, aunts and other female relations provide a cultural core, remembering and passing on to their children the knowledge that provides them with an identity in a crowded impersonal urban environment. (Langton 1981:18)

Restrictive legislation, particularly under the White Australia policy, prevented Asian and Melanesian women from joining their menfolk and establishing their families here (de Lepervanche 1984a:56–78; Saunders 1982). In the nineteenth and early twentieth centuries, both the Asian and Island immigrations were predominately male and decidedly not family oriented. Twenty years after the introduction of 'White' Australia in 1901, the Chinese, Japanese and Indian settlers were respectively 93.3 per cent, 92.9 per cent and 94.3 per cent male (Yarwood 1964:163). The proportions for Melanesians were similar. Initially employed as domestic servants or nannies, the few Melanesian women who came were restricted, as their menfolk were, to menial labour in tropical areas of Queensland after legislation was introduced in 1884. If a woman had a baby, she was expected to leave it in her hut all day while she worked. One incident was recorded in 1884 of a Melanesian woman forced to leave her baby in such a place: when she returned from work she found a dog had eaten it. Attempts were made by the authorities to suppress the truth at the time of the incident and the government medical officer who performed the autopsy declared the infant had 'died from exposure alone. It was a very warm afternoon.' (Saunders 1982:25) As late as the 1930s, the tabloid press warned Australians about 'Breeding a colony of clever aliens':

> Scores of Japanese and Chinese in Australia for 'business reasons' are rearing large families and their children, naturally, are not prohibited immigrants ...
> It appeared too that these Orientals when they arrived in Australia showed a tendency to bring with them wives who were expectant mothers. (Sydney, *Truth* 21 August 1932, quoted in Palfreeman 1967:16)

During both the nineteenth and twentieth cenuries it was often said of poor whites that they 'breed too fast', but in other respects, and particularly during the period of 'White' Australia, white women in general were portrayed as virtuous (if rather stupid) and in need of protection particularly from 'Asiatic' men. Politicians vigorously opposed miscegenation in Parliamentary debates on restrictive legislation and condemned instances of Anglo-Asian births (Curthoys 1985:98; Markus 1985:11–13). Both Asian and Aboriginal women were excluded from the 'universalist' maternity allowance of 1912 (Roe 1983:7). Until 1966 it was never as easy for non-Europeans to introduce their relatives as it was for European immigrants (Palfreeman, 1967:58–160). And until 1973 non-European British subjects could not obtain Australian citizenship after twelve months like other British subjects, while non-European aliens could not acquire citizenship after three years' waiting as could other aliens—they had to wait five years. Only in 1973 did amendments to the *Citizenship Act* remove these anomalies (Rivett 1975:44–79). In 1975 the *Racial Discrimination Act* was passed.

Despite the reforms introduced since the 1970s, the ideology of the family has been associated with some very curious contemporary twists which should not be obscured by rhetoric about greater equality for women of all backgrounds. For instance, despite all the talk of expanding population by immigration, family reunion and natural increase, reports have surfaced in the press that some Aboriginal and poorer immigrant women have been administered the controversial contraceptive drug Depo Provera, not always with their informed consent (Melbourne *Age* 27 March 1981; *SMH* 28 February 1981, 7 December 1984; Bottomley 1984a:4). This method of controlling the fertility of certain disadvantaged women provides a marked contrast to the huge sums spent on IVF programs and even on surrogacy, although in Victoria the state has legislated to prohibit commercial surrogacy and it has also denied legal enforcement to informal arrangements (Pateman 1988:210). As Pateman warns, the institution of surrogacy has the potential not only of creating legal wrangles such as the Baby M case in the United States, but also of reinstating patriarchy in its traditional paternal (as distinct from its modern fraternal) sense. As she comments, 'in a spectacular twist of the patriarchal screw, the surrogacy contract enables a man to present his wife with the ultimate gift—a child' (Pateman 1988:214). In her extended commentary on the contracts of the modern liberal democratic state, Pateman argues that:

> The story of the social contract is the greatest story of men giving political birth, but, with the surrogacy contract, modern patriarchy has taken a new turn. Thanks to the power of the creative political medium of contract, men can appropriate physical genesis too. The creative force of the male seed turns the empty property contracted out by an 'individual' [woman] into new human life. Patriarchy in its literal meaning has returned in a new guise. (1988:216–17)

151

Another current practice invoking conventional family ideology and which perhaps requires further investigation is the relatively recent Filipina 'mail-order bride' trade, whereby women from the Philippines marry Australian men in the hope of finding some kind of economic security for themselves and often for members of their families back home. The men in turn hope to acquire docile brides who will fulfil their dreams of a traditional, submissive wife. Not all of them find their ideal, and popular (male) conceptions of Filipina and other Asian women as submissive and obedient have 'continued to undermine the ... [women's] intelligence, resourcefulness and basic human rights' (Boer 1988:7). Such conceptions not only 'excuse' the domination by husbands but also justify 'the exploitation of women by transnational companies, plantation owners, bar and brothel owners and governments. The women are trapped for they desperately need the money and are not in a position to fight for better conditions.' (Boer 1988:7) At the 1986 census, 33 727 Filipinos were in Australia, of whom 23 347 (69 per cent) were women. In the same census there were 15 591 married Filipinas but only 4911 married Filipinos living in Australia. Presumably, the majority of Filipinas arriving in Australia do not marry their own countrymen (Boer 1988:12–13; cf. Watkins 1982).

One study of the Filipinas showed that 59 per cent said their husbands/fiances 'did not allow their wives to work' (quoted in Boer 1988:22). These circumstances for foreign women make them extremely dependent on their menfolk, the more so if the women are disadvantaged by their ignorance of community and legal services available to immigrants. It would appear from television documentaries and some other reports that domestic violence, for example, is not unknown to some of these women but, as an Anglican Church project reported: 'Cultural differences, family pressure, ideologies about the role of men and women, shame and guilt, may mean that a Filipina woman will suffer in silence or accept this violence as normal.' (Boer 1988:23)

A further and ethnocentric nationalistic variation on the theme of traditional family values and kinship appears in Professor Blainey's objections to recent immigration policy. Conflating race, nation and culture, and assuming that, even among those of Anglo-Celtic background, there is cultural homogeneity—an assumption that denies both class and gender differences—Blainey asserts that the 'typical nation practises discrimination against migrants, for the sake of national unity' (1984:52). Australia, by comparison, is not behaving in a typical fashion insofar as it permits entry to so many Asians: the family reunion scheme, according to Blainey, is 'overwhelmingly a racial-reunion scheme' (1984:98) and if the Asian percentage becomes the dominant stream among our immigrants, 'Australia would eventually become an Asian nation' (1984:119). Conceptualising the nation as an (Anglo white) family of 'Old Australians', Blainey complains that recent governments have cut 'the crimson thread' of kinship with Britain and thereby disowned our past (1984:159). In opposition to the advocates of multiculturalism, he sees the attempt to make Australia a 'nation of all nations' as a contradiction of Old Australians' 'present yearning for stability and social cohesion' (1984:153). As I have noted elsewhere (de Lepervanche 1989b:175), Blainey is especially concerned about the women multiculturalism permits entry to under the family reunion scheme. He resents the entry of Filipina brides or recently arrived Middle Eastern women because he sees them being more privileged under multiculturalism than Tasmanian centenarians or:

> a girl [sic] who forty years ago married an American soldier coming to defend Australia, and went to the United States as a war bride and took up American citizenship, [and who] is now seen as having inferior rights to a Lebanese woman who has never seen Australia and whose sponsoring relative has been living here for a mere two years (1984:156).

In his use of family ideology to conceptualise a national unity—in which kinship with Britain overrides all else—Blainey clearly makes some women more acceptable than others in the populate or perish venture. He is frank in admitting his own white British ancestry and his preference for 'our kind of society and most of its ruling values' (1984:17), but these ruling values are those which not only privilege Anglo-conformity but require a subordinate status for all women.

At this stage I wish to reiterate the point that my critical comments are directed to the family as ideology and to the consequences of this. Given the selective attacks by both individuals and states on Aboriginal and some immigrant families, and the greater state control of migrant families, it is important to realise that from the position I occupy—speaking as a privileged white feminist—I need to be wary of criticising the family itself as an institution. Although I may object to the subordinate status women occupy generally, it ill behoves me to neglect the possibility that when all their kind is oppressed, a specific category of people may look to their families first as the most secure foundation from which to resist oppression. This is particularly so when their families are considered 'deviant' in any way by the dominant culture. Working-class women, for example, and women in colonial and neo-colonial situations, have responded to oppression in family-based 'cultures of resistance' (Caulfield 1974; Stack 1974; Langton 1981; Curthoys 1984).

Racist beliefs and practices, both individual and systemic, affect Aboriginal and a number of immigrant groups in Australia, particularly those in the lowest socioeconomic categories. The persistence of these beliefs and practices divides these people from others more privileged. Under such circumstances, the women of the categories discriminated against may well give priority to solidarity with their menfolk and families against both class exploitation and racism (Bottomley 1984b;99; Martin 1986b: 242–5). This strategy highlights the importance of our understanding the relationship between class, ethnicity/race and gender and how these variables operate in Australian social life. As some Aboriginal and migrant women know, Anglo-European women have been their oppressors on both class and ethnic/race grounds, for example, in the relations between mistress and domestic servant (cf. Hamilton 1986; Edwards and Read 1989; Perez Olleros 1990).

Insofar as most rhetoric associated with the family is ideologically loaded and men are allegedly endowed with public instrumental roles and women with private expressive ones, this perpetuates gender divisions focused both on reproduction and on unequal power relations between men and women. As a critique of these common stereotypes and their associated ideology, this paper argues that we need to rethink the extent to which man has socially constructed our genders, our families and emphasised the centrality of biological reproduction even in our grand social theories. All too often we avoid recognising the implications of these social constructions by assuming them to be natural. Indeed, we need to rethink 'the social' and the relations between the family, civil society and the state. More than anyone else, feminists have been doing precisely this.

Rather than homogenise and naturalise the family as a unit marching unchanged through history and through a variety of cultures, or damn it as a 'protection racket' (cf. Laing 1967), feminists from various disciplines have, over the last twenty years, signalled more productive avenues for extending our analysis of the family. Crucial to many of these approaches is the critical questioning of the traditional distinction made between the private, 'natural' unit of family and the public world of civil society and the state. This conventional separation of the family from the wider society (as if the family were not social) simply perpetuates the gendered dichotomies of Western patriarchal thinking and contributes to the reification of the family itself, which has significant consequences for women. By comparison, a focus on power relations within the family instead of the conventional dichotomies makes it apparent that there are continuities between gender relations in the domestic and non-domestic domains (Yeatman 1971; Game and Pringle 1979; Rapp et al. 1979; Burns et al. 1983; Broom 1987).

The conceptual problem is one of relating the family to civil society and the state so that the structure of relations within the family as a kin unit, with its sexual division of labour, and the processes whereby individuals are recruited through this unit to households, genders, classes, ethnic communities, races and nation states are understood. Integral to this enterprise has been the unravelling of the distinction between, firstly, the household as a locus for shared activity and, secondly, the family as a structure of relations and unit of recruitment to household activities which in themselves constitute linkages to the wider society, and which vary according to gender, class, ethnic/race affiliation and even in some respects national type (cf. Rapp et al. 1979:176). Thirdly, feminists distinguish the empirical kin unit (or variety of units) from the notion of the family as an 'ideological shock absorber' (Rapp et al. 1979:178) which the state uses in its surveillance and control of populations, for example, through marriage and divorce law, legislation concerning custody of children, in welfare measures and in immigration policies.

In short, as an analytic category 'the family' is not very useful in the form in which it has been conventionally represented;

however, as an ideological device for patriarchal control and government the notion of the family has been very influential. So far as women are concerned, we need to unmask the relations between the governors and the governed and, in our own interests, examine the links between household, family as kin unit, civil society and the state as they are reproduced or resisted in contest with notions about 'the family'. In this way we can interrogate the 'ideological assumptions of naturalness' (Rapp et al. 1979:179) that subjugate women, colour the conventional literature on the family and which, even in the late twentieth century, continue to characterise state documents and policies, as the statements by Zubrzycki quoted earlier indicate.

As women, we also need to contest the conventional sexual division of labour itself and the marriage contract upon which family life is sanctioned by the state. As Pateman has shown, there is a clear relationship between the fraternal social contract underlying the modern Western liberal democratic state and what she calls the sexual contract, or men's sex-right over women's bodies, which historically has sustained that fraternal contract (e.g. rape in marriage is not universally condemned; women do not have absolute control over their bodies in the matter of abortion; and in the prostitution contract the buyer obtains 'unilateral right of direct sexual use of a woman's body' (Pateman 1988:204)). The gender disadvantages these contracts present for all women in the modern state need to be examined in specific class and ethnic/race contexts. Whatever differences immigrants bring and try to reproduce here as settlers, they, like the Australian-born, encounter the dominant culture and state control. Even so, this meeting is not rigid confrontation or absolute accommodation: in class-structured, gender-divided polyethnic states, cultures including the dominant one are constantly negotiated processes. The way in which 'the family' has been a publicly contested area in the decade of the 1980s provides an illustration of this.

More specifically, at the national level, in attempts by politicians of both Left and Right during the 1980s to influence women voters and sway marginal electorates, Labor focused on the family and social welfare in its health care program, housing policy and assistance plan, while the Right continued to bemoan 'the breakdown of the family' and the erosion of traditional values from kin level to national identity. The Right sought to restrict Asian immigration and, in the interests of cutting government expenditure, also called for the strengthening of traditional family ties with women providing the unpaid domestic welfare work of caring for the young, the sick and the aged. As Marian Sawer comments in opposition to these prescriptions:

> Those of us who are actually family carers can easily be bemused by the antics of politicians who rarely see their families except for photo opportunities. How could political parties which vie to be the most pro-family all agree to abolish what was the only universal form of assistance for mothers of dependent children? How is it that those who praise the value of full-time homemakers believe that if they are single parents these same homemakers are welfare bludgers? Why do those who trumpet the need for more incentives for the individual at the same time espouse policies to increase the dependence of women and other family members on male family heads? (1989:11)

As the decade of the 1990s begins, high interest rates, unemployment levels that are particularly high for some immigrant categories and Aboriginal people, inadequate child care and the incidence of domestic violence all continue to strain or fracture family ties. Yet, opposing this process of apparent disintegration on the domestic front is the ever-widening extension of family networks around the globe. The late twentieth century internationalisation of the division of labour has created polyethnic nation states and, together with the internationalisation of capital which has produced transnational power structures, this has made the interrelation between nation, race, ethnic group, class and gender very complex indeed. Far from being a natural institution, divorced from the social, the family has been central to all these developments. For instance, families have not only provided immigrant workers internationally but have maintained networks for chain migration and international travel: in countries such as Britain, the United States, Canada and Australia, ethnic and race communities have been sites for resistance to class oppression, ethnocentrism and racism. These same communities have also transmitted ethnic/race cultures which in many instances appear to rival class solidarities, although, given the role of migrant labour in the late twentieth century, the relations between class and ethnicity need to be carefully examined (cf. de Lepervanche,

1980). In all these processes, women may have been marginalised by the dominant culture, but they nevertheless remain at the intersections of all these processes as bearers and rearers of children, as 'gatekeepers' of their cultures and in resistance to various forms of oppression (Anthias and Yuval-Davis 1983; Bottomley and de Lepervanche 1984; Stasiulis 1987; Hill 1987).

There are other processes at work too. In resisting their subordinate status within the family, the state and civil society generally, women who might have seen themselves divided by class, race and ethnic background, and whose interests can so easily be divided by ideological stress on their loyalty to family rather than to wider public organisation (cf. Ramazanoglu 1989:148), have increasingly claimed common ground and asserted common interests in struggling for improvements to women's health, women's refuges, rape crisis centres, no-fault divorce, better child care, abortion on demand and state action against domestic violence. Immigrant women have supported these improvements through their own ethnic women's groups (Sgro 1979; Sgro et al. 1980), and they have used these services 'in large numbers, often despite opposition from their men' (Bottomley 1984b:108). Although Aboriginal women have many reasons to criticise whites, perhaps especially white women who have at times had little understanding or sympathy for their black sisters, some of these women are now also expressing common cause with white feminists in supporting campaigns for women as women (e.g. against domestic violence) (Langton 1989). Steps like these present invitations to white feminists to consider more closely the interrelation between domestic violence, poverty, class and race discrimination, and to appreciate the importance of seeing both the connections between all the structures of inequality we are implicated in and the way in which family ideology helps sustain these structures.

ELLIE VASTA

9 Gender, class and ethnic relations: The domestic and work experiences of Italian migrant women in Australia

The aim of this paper is to outline not only the discrimination suffered by migrant women, but also their struggles and resistance against such oppression. The analysis is based on a study of 56 middle-aged and older Southern Italian women (mostly Sicilian) who have lived in Brisbane, Australia for twenty years or more. The paper focuses particularly on the domestic and work experiences of these migrant women in terms of the class, ethnic and gender relations which operate in Australian society (see Vasta 1985 for further information about the research project on which this paper is based).

In the following sections I will outline the workforce experience of the Italian women in the Brisbane sample, as this clearly demonstrates that it was in this area that they had least power to effect any change. Later sections will show that the struggles and strengths of these women lay more in the direction of developing a sense of independence in the family, in their relationship with their children and in resisting Anglo-Australian racism. These are aspects of migrant women's struggles and identities which have too often been ignored.

In her paper to the first Congress of Italo-Australian Women, Franca Arena stated succinctly the effects of the migration process for women generally:

Women throughout the centuries have experienced a kind of 'migration process'. They have for centuries belonged to a patriarchal society which has always expected them to leave their own family to 'migrate' to their husband's new home and family. They have been mobile and invisible; their domestic labour contribution not counted and their paid labour viewed as marginal. (1985:22)

This first migration was indeed the case for the Sicilian women interviewed in Brisbane. Their second migration, to Australia, occured in the 1950s and 1960s and this paper is a substantiation not only of their hardships and struggles, but also of their strengths and successes.

Gender, class and race relations: A brief theoretical overview

At the broad theoretical level, feminist research, whilst revolutionising traditional sociological analysis, has inherited some of the epistemological problems of such traditional analysis. In the analysis of women's subordination, some problems have been inherited from Marxist analysis. Marxist feminism, for example, situates gender inequality in a materialist analysis, whereby women are crucial for the reproduction of labour power through their position in the household, but also crucial in terms of producing exploited labour power in paid employment. A problem arises here when women's oppression in the family is defined universally as functional for the reproduction of the dominant ideology of capitalist exploitation. It falls into a reductionist trap in that women's oppression is generally explained in class terms only. That is, gender relations are reduced to an effect of capital, or class relations (cf. Barrett 1980, Ch. 1).

The same arguments can be applied to some Marxist analyses of race and ethnic relations (cf. Gilroy 1987). Clearly, it is important to outline the position of migrant men and migrant women in terms of Australian labour market segmentation. However, to claim (as many Marxists do) that the ruling class deliberately produces false consciousness among migrant workers is again functionalist. As with the above example, this argument ignores the historical struggles and resistances which have modified capitalist class relations. Thus this Marxist argument claims that race relations and gender relations can be defined in terms of class relations and is therefore also reductionist in nature.

Clearly, the constructions of class, gender and ethnic subjectivities or identities are not analytically distinct from each other. Often they are constructed and defined *within* one another in ambiguous ways, and sometimes they are constructed separately from each other. Gender relations and race relations cannot always be reduced to the effects of class relations. For example, working-class racism and Anglo-Australian women's racism cannot simply be explained away only by class issues. Race and gender subjectivities can at times be constructed separately from class, and at other times their articulation qualifies the very construction of class relations. In other words, it is important to analyse how gender and race relations enter into the very construction of class relations and how class relations enter into the very construction of race and gender relations (Gilroy 1987).

Furthermore, the constructions of these relations have dominant instances which are not always class determined. In other words, in certain historical locations, gender and race can be the determining relation with regard to the effects of the construction of class, gender and race relations. These are not simple categories or divisions which intersect and produce specific effects (Anthias and Yuval-Davis 1983:63). These are in fact identities, subjectivities which are constituted at times separately and at other times within each other; they are constituted through historical experience and political struggle 'through which these identities take on real historical existence' (Less 1986:96). Furthermore, they are constituted through complex and contradictory sets of relations: 'It is one of the facts of human existence that social institutions frequently perform different and conflicting functions: the oppression of women exists alongside and is reproduced by the same institution, that acts as shelter against the hardships of class oppression. (Lees 1986:98) Therefore the relationship between gender, ethnic and class identities and meanings can only be analysed through various forms of action: through the conflicts, struggles and resistances of the subordinate groups. The history of class, gender and race relations is conflict, but many social theorists, in their attempt to document and analyse the oppression of women and migrants, ignore the role of conflict. By allowing analytical primacy to patriarchy and class, as the universal male and capitalist appropriation of social life, they present problems for any notion of human agency and change, via essentialist notions of dominant ideology and false consciousness. Barrett suggests that, instead of concentrating research on such notions as 'false consciousness', we should rather analyse the construction of 'subjectivity and identity' (1980:251) through conflict, struggle and resistance.

There are two important debates on this topic which are basically about primacy and which require some working through. The first concerns the position stated by Sgro et al. (1980), who claim that, in Australia, Italian migrant women's oppression, and hence their political activism, is more connected to their class position than to Italian patriarchy. Bottomley points out that 'this is supported by evidence of the strength of the women's movement in Italy' (1984:99) and that further Australian evidence would be valuable. As the results below demonstrate, the Italian women were exploited with regard to their ethnicity (racism) and their class position. Not only were they exploited in terms of having become deskilled, but they were also discriminated against on the shop floor. They did not, however, engage in any class political activism. Indeed, it was their class position which rendered them most powerless. They were compelled to sell their labour power and it was in that area that they were able to do very little in terms of changing their exploitative conditions.

On the other hand, Sgro et al. (1980:270) maintain that it is not Italian patriarchy which has kept Italian women from participating in community affairs as much as the strain of the forced migration process. My results support their claim in that Italian patriarchy was less of a problem to the women than were the problems of isolation and loneliness caused by the migration experience, in addition to Anglo-Australian and structural racism, and Anglo-Australian structural patriarchy.

Nevertheless, the Sgro et al. paper assumes that Italian women's struggles consist of only class struggles, and they ignore the possibility that Italian migrant women have engaged in struggles against gender and ethnic oppression. Thus, any systematic study of migrant women needs to rest not only on class analysis but must also take account of the interrelationship between class, gender and ethnic relations, and the struggles which reconstitute or modify these relations. In other words, the specificity of migrant women's experience of class exploitation, racism and patriarchy must be accounted for.

The second debate concerns Jeannie Martin's (1984; 1986a

162

and b) position which questions the dominant (hegemonic) construction of migrant women through their ethnicity and class. Helen Andreoni argues that, for Martin, 'gender concerns override those of ethnicity' and further insists that: 'This image of migrant women as the most oppressed and powerless is facile, condescending and finally destructive because it does not permit the establishment of a power base from whence to affect change.' (Andreoni 1986:20)

Several issues need to be disentangled. First, I disagree with Andreoni that the concern about migrant women's gender oppression is 'facile, condescending and finally destructive'. As detailed below, migrant women have been at the bottom of the labour market heap. There is no dispute about this. Secondly, evidence abounds that migrant women's oppression has too often been reproduced in the name of accepting their cultural traditions, for example, as 'dumb peasant-types' (see below). As Martin herself demonstrates, in many ways there has been 'concern with moulding non-English speaking immigrant women to the Australian model'. This position lingers on and is occasionally 'couched in liberationist terms'. For example: 'we need to encourage immigrant mothers to get out of their homes, help in the school canteens, do community work and so forth that Australian women are able to do (migrant welfare worker)' (quoted in Martin 1984:114). The point that Martin is making is that migrant women's oppression is indeed filtered through class and race relations. She clearly suggests that a woman-centred position needs to take analytical precedence but not reject the importance of class and ethnic relations. She simply presents the inadequacies of the latter two positions as hegemonic constructions of the position of migrant women in Australian society.

If, however, migrant women are presented as totally powerless, be it through their position in class, gender or ethnic relations, then Andreoni is absolutely correct to suggest that 'it does not permit the establishment of a power base from whence to effect change' (1986:20). She, in fact, documents the recent development of Italian women's solidarity and networks and suggests that these 'must neither be linked only with disadvantage or powerlessness nor be isloated or stagnant' (1986:20). For too long there has been a tendency by Anglo-Australian women to define their own problems as also being the problems of migrant women, to this is added the migrant experience (cf. Fourth Women and Labour Conference 1984). In fact, such Anglo-centrism has led to viewing migrant women as passive and, by implication, oppressive to themselves, so much so that we often ignore not only the specifity of their often-contradictory experiences, but also their strengths and traditions as well as a battery of strategies for survival and resistance to authority, which these women use in negotiating and manipulating an alien environment to their own advantage.

Italian migrant women and workforce experience

The majority of the 56 women interviewed in Brisbane arrived in Australia between 1949 and 1966, then aged in their 20s and 30s. As is now well recognised, the Australian labour market was then segmented along the axes of ethnicity and gender and remains so today. At the top of the hierarchy there is an over-representation of Anglophone and Northern European males in jobs with higher skills, better pay and conditions. In the next category, non-Anglophone males are over-represented, working in the unskilled, least secure, more difficult and more dangerous jobs; this is followed by a high representation of Anglophone and Northern European women in middle- and low-level white collar jobs; and at the bottom of the ladder are NESB migrant women in manual and manufacturing jobs (Collins 1984:11–12). Aboriginal women and men hardly fit into this scheme of the Australian labour market. Our Brisbane sample slots well into this hierarchy: many Italian women worked long, arduous hours and found their jobs very different from any previous work and very difficult. As Phizacklea (1983) clearly states, the subordinate position of migrant women in economic relations 'warrant(s) the description of a sexually and racially categorised class position' (1983:109).

On arrival, 36 of the women went straight into factory work, including process work in food canneries, on the assembly lines of various manufacturing industries or at sewing machines, piecing together garments; a small number had been involved in outwork. Apart from being aware that they were often the last to be hired and the first to be fired, once they had work they were often maltreated by employers and foremen. Many migrant women and men were recruited into unions throughout the post-war period, though it was not until recently that unions began to take the needs of migrant workers seriously. Mostly, migrant women were kept in the dark not only about wages, but also about conditions. Since many Anglo-Australian workers had taken on the position of a 'labour aristocracy', this was clearly a case of racially constructed class relations. This situation is slowly changing now, due to the organisation of various migrant worker lobbies.

Many women in the Brisbane sample complained that Italians were often given the hardest, dirtiest and heaviest jobs. These women often performed tasks which were repetitious, mentally tedious and monotonous. Storer (1976), in his report on migrant women workers in Melbourne, claimed that employers often suggested that migrant women were well suited to this type of work and even enjoyed it. The class, gender and race exploitation contained in the following employer's statement exemplifies the attitudes and conditions migrant women have had to endure:

> The women are suited to these jobs because they can sit at the machine all day long doing the same thing. If they were more intelligent or better educated they would become bored or go round the bend. But this class of person is suited to the job. These women come from peasant-type backgrounds. (Storer 1976:82)

One of the most significant issues to emerge from the Brisbane project with regard to these working women is that, on arrival, most of the women in the artisan/trade category (seamstresses, lace-makers, etc.) became deskilled. Indeed, of fifteen women in this category, on arrival only four continued their skill in paid work and one woman lost her clerical skills. At the time of the interviews, seven women had reached retirement age and seven were in the paid workforce, with only one woman of the whole sample having become upwardly mobile into the professional category. The remaining 41 continued with home duties, having either withdrawn or been retrenched from the paid workforce.

These figures illustrate a very salient point, especially in light of the recently tabled Fitzgerald Report on Australian immigration Figzgerald, 1988). One of the main recommendations of this report is that selection policy must be oriented more towards skilled migrants. Historically, the skills of migrant women have been ignored, and this report does little to address that problem.

Employers as well as the state have consistently categorised migrant women as dependant wives and mothers, unproductive, illiterate and isolated from the outside world. Often racist and sexist practices are condoned through the construction of 'cultural stereotypes': '[t]hese characteristics are usually attributed to the women's alleged 'cultural backgrounds' and commonly labelled as 'tradition'. Needless to say the stereotype operates for *all* migrant women irrespective of their national and cultural origins. (Morokvasic cited in Phizacklea 1983:13).

Not only did these Italian women feel discriminated against by employers; often they experienced racism from their fellow workers. Some had often felt humiliated either because they had not understood what was being said or they had been called derogatory names. One woman claimed that such treatment had left scars: 'Australians would push us around. I was told to do one job and they'd come up and push me to a dirtier job. They used to pick on us. Call us names. They wouldn't help us because they knew we didn't speak the language. The women were worse. The men were polite.' These results concur with Storer's research on migrant women in Melbourne:

> The most interesting fact about the responses is that the main dislikes about work are not poor wages or even poor conditions. Rather, the main statements criticised work systems which were believed to be unjust and degrading, and criticised social situations created by bosses (foremen, managers) which led women to believe they were being treated unfairly and with little dignity. Many women complained of discrimination and this often took the form of complaints about other women workers and the resultant fears and hostilities that developed between the various social and cultural groupings. (1976:35)

In both these examples, the racism experienced from Anglo–Australian men and women by these migrant women was felt more strongly than was their class exploitation as such. Parmar defines this situation as an example of 'racially constructed gender roles' (1982:237), and it is also a case of racially constructed class exploitation. Nevertheless, any hope for change against racist class oppression and racist gender oppression in the workplace was the least attainable for them because of financial necessity and due to their lack of English language skills, which provided a barrier to dealing with Australian political organisations and institutions.

The family and Italian migrant women's independence

Some of the problems these migrant women have had to endure are the same as those mentioned elsewhere (cf. Bottomley 1984a, c; Martin 1984). Briefly, they include a sense of dislocation and loneliness during the early years of settlement; problems with regard to lack of proficiency in English; problems with spouse and children; and lack of specific programs available for migrant women. In fact, 48 of the women claimed that their most significant problem was the frustration and isolation brought about by the new culture and new language. Furthermore, amongst our sample, almost half (25) of the women felt that their roles had changed in Australia (some positively and some negatively) and, of these nineteen claimed that one major problem was having to work at two jobs, inside and outside the home, which added to their frustration and isolation. It was this situation which rendered them unable to engage in any organised struggle in the public arena. In fact, many of the professional people in the health and welfare areas who were interviewed for the project concurred that the stress from migration had been a much greater problem for these women than Italian patriarchy or marriages which many would consider unsatisfactory.

When asked how they coped with their dual role inside and outside the home, 21 had had some difficulty and a further 23 had experienced a great deal of difficulty. The amount of housework help received from husbands had been minimal, though many women added that it was their job, not a man's job. This of course is not an unusual statement from women of that age group, though some women did add that it was their domain and there they had free reign. This may raise objections from some quarters that power in that sphere (the private) is not 'real' power.

Whilst it is not the place here to debate where real power lies in terms of the public/private dichotomy, suffice it to say that almost two-thirds (30) of the 47 women who answered questions about decision making made major decisions with their husbands, while seven of the women were the major decision makers and only three of the men took the major decisions. Furthermore, because many Italians do adhere to 'la bella figura' (putting on a good face for the public), the Italian wife will often foster the image of the dutiful wife in public. This does not necessarily that she is always submerged within the Italian patriarchal family. The results of a study on Italo-American women suggest that, contrary to popular belief, Italian culture is basically matriarchal: 'The outside world sees the father as the boss, but in reality he's just the p.r. man. It's the mother who is the mover and the shaker and major decision-maker.' (Riotto Sirey: *Staten Island Advance* 10/4/86)

Nevertheless, some women complained that their dual role had left them with very little time to themselves. Indeed, one woman, after returning to her village, noted: 'I could hardly recognise my village. It has become a small town. All the people are very well dressed and the young are well educated ... My friends my age had the chance to go to evening courses.' Similar sentiments were expressed by many of the women. On the other hand, 33 of the women felt that migration to Australia had provided them with the freedom to accomplish their aspirations. These were the aspirations of migrant women, most of whom came from poor backgrounds, often expressed in the following terms: 'I had the aspiration to have a house with all the comforts. I got it. I see my children with a better education and it fulfils my ambitions.' Certainly, in financial terms, through long, hard and monotonous work, they had achieved security and all the women, mostly in partnership with their husbands, owned their own homes. Despite the fact that some felt they had not had the opportunity to train for more satisfying work, some claimed to definitely have achieved greater happiness and freedom in Australia, and many others felt they had gained some freedom in helping the family financially, and that this had provided a degree of independence because of their work in the paid workforce. For these women, who lacked skills for the Australian marketplace and who have therefore lacked certain choices in self-actualisation through paid work, the family remains one of their strongest sources of strength.

To make claims, as many do, that traditional family culture, or in this case Italian patriarchy, is completely oppressive of migrant women cannot be sustained, for these Sicilian women were aware of a larger freedom not to accept intolerable marriages. Many of these women did not feel submissive to their men as is often made out. This does not deny that there are many structural patriarchal practices which they do find oppressive, for example, the dual work roles. As several women stated: 'Here women work and become independent. If there are problems she can easily take off and support herself, so there are more marriage breakups in Australia' and 'There is more scope here not to tolerate bad situations. There, if you had a bad marriage you had to take it. Here you can leave and get help from the government.' Perhaps some of the men's comments were more telling in this regard: 'In Italy I was the man of the house, here my wife became the boss.' and 'My marriage has been broken because here the woman is too protected if she is wrong.'

The above points are not made to suggest that none of these women tolerated unsatisfactory marriages. The point I wish to stress is that, although the Australian women's movement had not reached these women as the women's movement had reached many of their sisters back in Italy, these women found their own strategies and strengths to deal with family problems and other problems. It also must be remembered that 30 years ago, when these women were still in Italy, they had only recently won the right to vote and they did not have the right to careers: 'no equal pay, women's groups or feminist groups were ... heard of. No freedom to go to the pictures on their own, or to go out at night with their boyfriend. No contraception, no sex education, nothing' (FILEF Women's Group 1978:2).

Nevertheless, one Sicilian woman in the sample had left her husband in Italy and migrated with one of her two daughters. For a Sicilian woman in the 1950s, to not only leave her husband but to also emigrate alone was a tremendous act of courage. This woman has not remarried, owns her own home here and returns frequently to Italy to visit her other daughter. Another woman in the sample provided the principal researcher with a recipe for how a woman can have, in terms of gender relations, 'ultimate control if she wants it' and insisted that Italian migrant women have their way of 'trading off' certain points for those that are important to them. This, she insisted, was the practice of many Italian women. She continued, 'Of course there are times when you feel trampled on by both husband and children. And yes, in everything apart from giving birth and bringing up children, men do feel they are smarter and more able than women. But in reality, women are the wiser because they know this is not the case.' Indeed, there were strong indications that many of the Brisbane women did have a relevant, and to them satisfactory, power base. These were migrant Sicilian women, and while migrant women share many problems with their Anglo-Australian sisters, these women had other more pressing issues to deal with: the necessary adaptations brought about by migration with relation to stresses on their marital relationship and their relationships with their children, as well as adaptations to new work conditions and to new social, political and institutional conditions. One doctor who has many Italian migrants as patients claimed that this older generation of Italo-Australians is stable and solid and does not have many marital problems:

> These people have done a lot of adapting in their time and their marriage is one example of such adaptation ... The older Italians did the hard work. They had to succeed to make the trauma of migration worth their while. It is the younger ones, their children, who are having the problems. They are the depressed ones, the ones with marital problems.

Nevertheless, one of the significant achievements of the Italian Welfare Centre in Brisbane was recorded in their 1983 report which claimed a significant 'drop in numbers of women needing psychiatric treatment following depression caused by isolation, alienation and low self-esteem' (1983:6). In fact, among this sample of women there has been a relatively low incidence of depression, though respondents did indicate a higher incidence in the early years of settlement.

The point I wish to stress here is that despite the many problems that Italian migrant women have had to contend with, including a recognition both that they were being exploited in the paid workforce, and that financial constraints left them with very few options, this oppression has not prevented them from finding workable strategies to deal with these problems. As noted earlier, these women have gained more freedom here through paid work, and this freedom has flowed into their family relationships. Indeed, as demonstrated above, the family unit has provided

170

a source of power and strength to the women. The following section helps to emphasise this factor.

Italian migrant women and their children

Overall, the respondents in this sample reported satisfactory relationships with their children. About one-third of the women stated that they had had special problems in the rearing of their children, especially in terms of what is often referred to as 'culture clash', in that the children were growing up with a different language and in a different culture. Part of the problem was that their children wanted more freedom than their parents were prepared to concede. Some children left home at too early an age, others would use the home as a 'crash pad'. The double standard of virginity and honour was still very important and a very strong code of behaviour. Few parents complained that they had been unable to persuade their children to continue with their education.

For migrants who suffer strongly from a sense of loss and separation through the migration experience, an adherence to long-known and trusted values is one way of maintaining certain ties, and also one's sanity. The problem, however, is more complex than simply one of 'cultural differences'. In a country like Australia, as Bottomley states and as I have demonstrated above, 'feminist ideas and practices are widespread ... [They] are often seen by migrant men (and women) as threatening and subversive—as indeed they may be' (Bottomley 1984a:4). Certainly the second generation has confronted both Italian and Anglo-Australian patriarchy far more systematically and structurally than its mothers ever had the wherewithall to do. Nonetheless, these women still found their *own* strategies with which to deal with Italian patriarchy.

One issue of importance, therefore, was the relationship both women and men had with their children. It was not surprising to learn that nearly all the women who answered felt closer to their children than to their husbands, whereas very few of the men felt closer to their children than they did to their wives. As one woman put it, '... my children are my own blood, whereas my husband isn't'. Many women reported that they tended to discuss their problems, including emotional problems with their children, whereas the men confided less in their children. In addition, the women did more activities with their children, and also were helped by their children more than the men.

Whilst it was felt at times that the women were reluctant to be disloyal to their husbands, one Italian doctor claimed from his observations: 'The children are more important to Italian women. Their husband is probably an appendage.' Whilst this latter statement may be extreme, and certainly cannot be supported by my results, it nonetheless alerts us to the autonomy that these women have exercised with regard to their relationship with their husbands and their children.

Furthermore, for these women, the family has also operated as a source of political and cultural resistance to Italian patriarchy, one example being the women's support of their daughters' quests to gain more freedom. Of course, the issue is not that clear cut, for while many Italian migrant mothers still support the patriarchal value of honour and virginity, others have in fact recognised the contradiction of their own female and patriarchal upbringing and are aware of its inherent double standard, which is being reproduced for their daughters. Nevertheless, while struggles continue over this issue within many Italian families, resistance to daughters' quests for freedom continues to break down.

Finally, there are two major ways in which the women in this survey gain their affirmation and sense of self-esteem. Firstly, for Italian migrants of this generation the focal point of their hierarchy of values is the family, from which they gain a strong sense of identity and emotional support. Secondly, the people in this sample, through their extreme hard work, have been able to display a strong sense of achievement by owning their own homes, decorating these and dressing well. This of course is not to say that all Italian migrants have been so materially successful, as evidenced in the Poverty Report (Henderson 1975) and numerous other reports since.

The Italian migrant family and racism

It is useful to begin the discussion of racism with an example of institutional discrimination which migrants have experienced over the years and which continues today. Whilst there has been much official rhetoric about Adult Migrant Education Programs, with particular emphasis on English language acquisition, the majority of migrants have been unable to avail themselves of the meagre services available. In fact, none of the women was able to partake of classes and only four claimed they could speak English adequately, though most of them felt they could get by.

This clearly does not equip them to challenge Australian institutions such as their children's schools or legal institutions. Nor does it permit them to demand on-site language classes, something which continues to be avoided by employers and the state alike. Lack of access to education stifles any chance of contending with and struggling against Australian institutions, which many Italian women and men view with fear and suspicion. The fact that this issue is also a class issue helps to render these migrants powerless in terms of engaging in class political activism.

Racism was experienced by those in the sample at the personal and community level. The Italian migrant family, as described above, was a fundamental social unit for these migrant women, though they were not unaware of the many personal sacrifices they had had to make, as women, in order to 'keep things together'. When they arrived, they all looked towards a brighter future. No one described any apprehension about the possibility of finding the new culture or language difficult to adapt to, nor had they considered that Anglo-Australians might not receive them with at least some measure of acceptance. Their treatment on arrival and the arduous, dirty work, for some, could never have been anticipated.

To begin with, nearly all the sample reported that they now had friendly relationships with Anglo-Australians, referring mostly to their neighbours. Almost all the women, however, stated that they had almost nothing to do with Anglo-Australians. Nearly all claimed they felt a sense of belonging to the Brisbane Italian community because they shared the same language and cultural traditions. In reaction to the racism experienced from Anglo-Australians, it was necessary to define Italian ethnicity in such a way as to ensure that Italian migrant women would find their sense of belonging and self-esteem within the Italian community and especially within the family. Many of the 'cultural

173

practices' froze with them not only because of the need for continuity, but also because Italian migrants were defined as an inferior minority group.

Whilst the majority of the sample found that many Anglo-Australians were 'friendly and kind', a quarter found that Anglo-Australians were 'racist, nasty, spiteful and unkind', thus drawing the following comments:

> They made us feel Italian people came to steal their jobs.

> They thought we ruined their country. We were called dago, wog, macaroni. I thought them rude, stupid and ignorant.

> [Now] I feel more relaxed in their company. They are more liberal now with their affection.

> Some will still let you grasp that they think you are a wog.

For many of these women, the family has operated as a source of political and cultural resistance to racism: they have chosen not to assimilate with their discriminators; they have chosen to have little interaction with Anglo-Australians not only because 'some will still let you grasp that they think you are a wog' but also because Italian migrant women consider their own practices and traditions to be more relevant to them. They guarded the continuation of their language at home, resisted inter marriage and retained their own child-rearing practices. They have, in fact, developed their own forms of resistance as well as forms of accommodation, and often 'rely on their own historical cultural traditions as a means of support' (Parmar 1982:239).

Italian migrant women organise

Italian women in Italy have a history of strong political struggle: working-class and peasant women often struggled together in early socialist and trade union movements. In 1925, for example, the tobacco women workers of Puglia staged a general strike and many women were involved in the Resistance movement during World War II. According to Sgro et al., '[w]omen in the south have borne the brunt of the migration of their men, the survival of their families and their communities being left to their struggle for dignity and life' (1980:3). During the post-war years, many of these women have been at the forefront of land reforms in the south.

For reasons mentioned above, migrant women's structural disadvantages often prevented them from organising against specific class, patriarchal and racist exploitative practices. The inevitable failure of assimilation policy has led to an increase in services under the rubric of multiculturalism. The availability of Italian-speaking professionals and the grant-in-aid and welfare workers at the Italian Welfare Centre have provided some respite compared with the policy of assimilationism which dominated the first few decades of the post-war years, even though such services are far from adequate.

The Australian women's movement has had a belated effect on migrant women. Anglo-Australian women either ignored migrant women or defined migrant women's needs and identities through Anglocentric constructs. While there have been migrant women's organisations since the 1970s, it was not until the 1984 Women and Labour Conference that migrant and Aboriginal women began to voice their protests over this issue.

More recently, a number of Italian migrant women's organisations have been formed, one being the Italo-Australian Women's Association, which held its first conference in Sydney and Melbourne in 1985. This group has been organised to develop solidarity, share information and set up networks. Earlier, in the mid-1970s, the FILEF (Federazione Italiana Lavoratori Emigrati e Famiglie) Women's Group was inaugurated in order to deal with migrant women's issues at work and in the community generally. It is this women's group which has made significant advances. Phizacklea suggests that '[s]elf-organisation and activity may have been forced on migrant women in the workplace but self-organisation is in itself a prerequisite for migrant women's struggle against their triple oppression' (1983:111).

It is useful to note that in the mid-1970s, as many as 45 per cent of Italian women were working as labourers, production or process workers (Storer 1976). With the decline in manufacturing in the 1980s, many migrant women lost their jobs, which resulted in a significant increase in outwork. This represents one of the most exploitative work conditions possible, with low rates of pay, working in isolation at home and no security or control over work conditions. Training and retraining schemes to facilitate re-entry into the workforce are still minimal.

Nonetheless, migrant women continue to struggle. At the Third Australian Conference on Italian Culture and Italy Today in 1986, Vera Zaccari from FILEF, Sydney outlined some of the advances made by the FILEF Women's Group in the course of its struggles. I will mention just two of the projects in which Italian women have been involved. One project began in the early 1980s in North Coburg, an industrial area of Melbourne, and was concerned with establishing child-care services in the area. The FILEF Women's Group formed a working party which included representatives from unions, the local council, FILEF and migrant women workers. The Coburg Council supported the project by providing land near the Government Clothing Factory, which was selected because of the large numbers of migrant women who worked there and because it was a publicly owned factory. Zaccari goes on to say:

> Even though there was much support for the project, over 18 months of struggle were necessary to secure funding from State and Federal Governments. During this time the Liberal Minister for Finance announced his intentions to sell or lease the factory for private firms. Filef organised factory meetings, lobbied government and sought the support of unions. The women working in the factory fought the privatisation proposal for over 18 months until, in 1983, the decision was revoked by the newly elected Labor government and ... announced that it would provide funding for maintainance and running of the centre. (Zaccari 1986:3)

Another major victory for migrant women has been the agreement forged between Fenner Fashions and the New South Wales Clothing and Allied Trades Union (C&ATU). In this case the employer contributes $10 000 towards the women's wages for language classes on the job. Furthermore, there are now eight elected migrant women officers and three women industrial officers in the C&ATU (Zaccari 1986:4,7).

Conclusions

To return to the issue raised earlier in this paper, about whether class, ethnicity or gender should take centre stage in understanding the struggles of Italian migrant women, what needs to be remembered in any analysis of migrant women is that they occupy multiple subject positions. In other words, they do not have a single identity, but multiple identities. They are working women, Italo-Australian women, wives, mothers, etc. who do not retain static identities but who struggle and resist daily, wherever and whenever possible, hegemonic constructions of them. This is one reason why we cannot reify 'the public' as the one area which contains most explanatory weight in terms of power. In her analysis of Asian women in Britain, Parmar rejects the passive status often accorded migrant women:

> A picture is painted whereby they appear totally helpless, oppressing themselves and their families with their onerous traditions and cultures, illiterates who must be helped to develop a 'critical faculty' and who remain totally passive in the face of changes imposed on them. In short, wide-eyed peasant women, finding it extremely difficult to negotiate their way around the big, bad concrete metropolis. (Parmar 1982:252)

Thus the effects of class position, racism and patriarchy cannot be defined as unitary categories. The important issue is that it is necessary to look at the mechanisms of power which constitute migrant women and which have a historical and non-essentialist, non-universalising trajectory of differentiation, contradiction, etc. Thus, as Martin (1986a:245) correctly suggests, for many migrant women, while aware that 'the family is the site of female oppression, it is an extraordinarily ambiguous and contradictory site' where historical, political and cultural perspectives must be taken into account. Furthermore, it is the ambiguity and contradictions within these sites which make struggle and resistance possible. So whilst these women have had as little formal education as their husbands, whilst their knowledge of the English language is even less adequate than their husbands', while they have been exploited on the shop floor like their husbands but also because of their gender, and whilst they may serve their husbands at home, they have struggled against these limited choices, they have modified many practices, contradictory as they are, and have secured their own power base which in itself is not fixed.

10 Domesticity and Latin American women in Australia

Among Latin American immigrants, the relations between the conventional construction of gender types and the circulation of market commodities have interacted in such a way as to enhance female subordination in traditional household practices. In economic and practical terms, immigrant women have found that the acquisition of modern household appliances has helped to emphasise rather than reduce their so-called feminine domestic tasks. In the material below, I examine two interwoven processes reinforcing conservative socio-cultural practices with respect to gender relations. Secondly, I argue that these constraining and exploitative practices have been largely shaped by a combination of historical developments in industrial capitalism. Within this overall context, the relations of most Latin American immigrant women to the main axes of the Australian economy have become characterised by sexual oppression and class exploitation. From the consumption viewpoint, the women are also enmeshed in a process involving the feminisation of white goods and other electrical appliances which has generated a cultural context in which they receive a symbolic reward for the housewife's domestic work, a reward which I call 'the fatal gift'.

Within traditional households, and Latin American migrant families in Australia are no exception to this, budgeting and patterns of consumption are part of the woman's managerial activities. These arrangements are related to gender identity and the sexual division of labour in the domestic sphere. Most commonly, the family's welfare depends heavily on the woman's ability to adjust and perform her domestic tasks, including cooking, ironing and all other menial services. In her job as a housekeeper, her administrative capabilities are at stake in the allocation of money for food, clothing and leisure (picnics, pleasure trips, overseas travel and so on). These various levels of activity are the responsibility of the housewife and her competence in these areas is believed by all family members to be a prerequisite for the smooth operation of the family's daily life.

In addition to this, and within the context of nuclear families, child rearing and children's education are also activities which men tend to consider as being part of the woman's responsibility. In extended family situations (i.e. households composed of three generations), the older woman is also expected to participate in and contribute to the domestic work, in particular to child minding. However, as one could expect, there are many cases where, through old age or physical disability, older women are not in a position to perform household chores or care for the children at all. In these circumstances, and irrespective of the elderly relative's sex and kin relationships to the housewife (the older person might be her mother or mother-in-law, father or father-in-law), the care of the aged is always seen as part of the younger woman's kinship obligations arising from the social contract of marriage.

Such family commitments usually entail reciprocity, and Latin American religious beliefs buttress the notion of filial devotion towards aged parents and in particular aged widowed mothers. Thus conventions emphasising family solidarity reinforce the traditional cultural practice that the care of the aged is first and foremost the responsibility of their offspring. But family reciprocity also places a strong emphasis on the relationship between grandparents and their grandchildren; the grandmother, for example, is usually seen as an educator, a minder and a protectress; that is, a person whom a child can trust and count upon. Immigrants' traditional customs do not cease after emigration, even if difficulties arise. People do all they can to ensure that these customs are upheld in Australia.

It is these cultural traditions which are the major elements contributing to the formation of vertical extended migrant families in this country. Three-generation households are mostly composed of an elderly woman (who may be widowed, divorced, separated or a single mother), a married couple who are themselves parents, and their unmarried children. Less frequently there are households composed of an elderly couple (the grandparents) and their married daughter/son and grandchildren. In only a few households is the elderly person a single man (widowed, divorced) living with his child's family. The overall trend in my field experience indicated that elderly family members, and particularly aged women, more frequently live with daughters than sons. Within these households, the domestic domain is the realm of the housewife/mother (Moraes Gorecki 1987).

The immigrant housewife is not necessarily solely engaged in non-paid housekeeping. She often works for wages and therefore undertakes a double shift. I found that the large majority of Latin American migrant women fall into the category which is popularly known as 'working mothers' and, I would add, 'working grandmothers'. The younger woman is either employed outside the home or engaged in home-based paid work production. The working grandmother, if not ill or disabled, provides home comforts and child minding services. This allows the young couple to go out to work and also secures the reproduction of women's domesticity in submission to the established patriarchal order.

With regard to employment, Collins' general scheme concerning the segments of the Australian labour force, arranged according to sex and ethnicity axes, helps to explain the incorporation of migrant women in the employment market (Collins 1984:11–13). Collins defines the third segment of the labour market as being composed of Australian-born or Anglophone migrant women who earn less than is paid to men in similar or even less skilled employment. Those Latin American women represented in this third segment are primarily community workers for migrant social welfare services, secretaries and nurses, together with a few professionals and school teachers.

However, the large majority of these migrant women, like other non-Anglophone migrant women in Australia, are at the bottom of what Collins calls the fourth segment. They are to be found among women employed in the manufacturing or service sectors. Connell and Irving (1980) point out that between the world wars in Australia, clothing and footwear industries mostly used native-born female workers. Later, with the absorption of Australian women into clerical work and white-collar jobs in other industries, employers used the most recent waves of immigrant women as labourers (also cf. Game and Pringle 1983). Latin American migrant women, like many Southern Europeans, were no exception to this, and went predominantly into industries such as clothing, footwear and textiles. In Australia, and also overseas, these industries are traditionally seen as 'a woman's field'. Their pay is low and the jobs are not secure.

Among these new factory workers, many had come to this country with higher skills and work experience in the secondary sectors of their own economies. This pattern of downward occupational mobility is not unrelated to the needs of the Australian market economy, however (cf. Collins 1978), and the types of employment which these migrant women entered were structured by gender divisions and also by the allocation of certain work in Australia to immigrants regardless of their qualifications. In this context, non-English speaking migrant women's employment reflected the demand for labour to fill industrial occupational vacancies in unskilled/semi-skilled factory work. This is not a new trend; rather, it has recurred throughout the history of Australian immigration (Connell and Irving 1980; Collins 1978, 1984; de Lepervanche 1975, 1980; Lever Tracy 1981).

The challenges these women face do not only arise from the type of work available, but also from a lack of child-care facilities, after-school care and care for their elderly. For instance, in October 1984, 600 000 Australian children under school age had mothers in paid employment, yet there were only 62 500 child-care places for them (Power et al. 1984). With respect to the elderly, immigration inevitably tends to make grandparents economically redundant or, at least, increasingly dependent on their children for financial support. Often language difficulties constitute a cruel barrier between aged immigrants and the host society, and this leads the extended immigrant family into a cluster of social and economic difficulties as well as problems between kin.

Kinship obligations notwithstanding, in Western industrial societies, kinship as a social and economic regulatory agency has to some extent been replaced by the state with its child-care centres, community health services, pensions and nursing homes, however inadequate they may be (Haviland 1975:192). But because the welfare state has not totally appropriated these functions in Australia, pioneer immigrant families face an ambiguous situation. Their aged parents generally arrive without any financial means, either in the form of pension or savings. Even where there is a pension paid by the country of origin, financial constraints are not relieved because of the small amount of money involved. Often when newcomers have some investment prior to immigration, for example, owning a house, this is no longer the case after emigration. Many of the elderly have sold their houses to pay for their airfares and other expenses. Therefore, in most cases, the cost of providing for older immigrant parents becomes the responsibility of their children, especially their daughters (Moraes Gorecki 1987).

Another problem arises from the particular kind of integration into the household structure whereby the aged parents become subordinates/dependents of their children. This situation is exceptional in the homeland. In Latin America, old parents are heads of families: their married children may live under their parental roof until they can afford a neolocal residence and become independent or, alternatively, the children may provide for the aged parents' household, but the elders retain their autonomy and authority. In Australia, however, people discover rapidly that a three-generation household is not always synonymous with harmony.

For the recently arrived aged migrants, old age very often becomes equal to poverty, as the host welfare state makes no provision for at least ten years involved in receiving and caring for these people; usually the country of origin cancels their pensions, if any, on the grounds of their emigrant status. So, for a period of ten years, both countries deny the presence and almost the existence of the elderly's needs, leaving them totally the responsibility of their children, especially daughters, as the women of the household inherit the caring obligations. Non-productive old people without financial means are therefore marginalised and adult migrant women are given an extra burden.

These circumstances induce immigrant women to look for alternative ways in which to earn an income and at the same time keep up with their increased domestic work of child and aged care. If they do not get a paid job outside the home, the most viable ways of earning a living are the home-based services such as child-minding, sewing for factories, boutiques or patrons (i.e. dressmaking), engaging in take-away food production or hairdressing at home. Even so, it is not uncommon to find these women facing periods without work. Thus there is the predicament of home-based work unemployment, which is far from what immigrants expect fo find in Australia.

The social consequences arising from this state of affairs are tremendous:

1 Women are isolated in their homes.
2 Their economic subordination to their husbands increases.
3 They become victims of highly exploitative relations with the market, being faced with a choice between engaging in home-based services, which are grossly underpaid and low in social status, or no paid work at all.

Such circumstances do not develop from the husband's (sometimes known as the 'breadwinner's') incompetence or unwillingness to provide economic support for the family, but from the low income of the large majority of immigrant male wage earners. A single income is usually insufficient to meet minimal levels of expenses and necessities required for an extended family household. This has unfortunate repercussions on the men themselves as, for many Latin American males, the maintenance of a wife at home is a symbol of fulfilment and achievement as well as a way of attaining a higher social status among their peers. In practice, however, the assertion of these established (male) cultural notions often leads to grievances between spouses, and the inability to live up to expected custom may produce a sense of failure on the man's part. The emphasis on a 'wife at home' also underlines the ideological strategies used to depress and erode both the advancement of women's 'degrees of freedom' and the women's ability to make choices about their lives. It accentuates the fixed horizons between the public world of paid work and the private world of unpaid domestic labour which conveniently neglect women's contribution to economic production and inhibit the possibilities for structural change in this society. Even so, in addition to their domestic responsibilities, the large majority of Latin American migrant women in Australia are compelled to augment and contribute to the 'family income'.

Women, like men, are producers and consumers of commodities and services, and I now turn to a discussion of how the major features of the immigrant household's financial arrangements—budgeting and consumption—are related to gender identity and to the sexual division of labour. As I have already mentioned, within the Latin American household, budgeting and patterns of consumption are part of the woman's managerial activities; the domestic domain is also the realm of the housewife. However, a recent manifestation of male power is apparent in that development, whereby expenses which are perceived to be beyond the domestic sphere, though related to it, are actually identified as the man's responsibility. That is, purchases of large expensive household goods such as washing machines, vacuum cleaners, refrigerators, freezers, stoves, colour televisions and numerous other electrical appliances are under men's control, even though the payment of instalments or otherwise for these items may be partly or entirely drawn from the women's wages. Two related mechanisms which are deeply rooted in this custom of male domination contribute to women's acceptance of male authority in decisions of this kind. First, there is the way the dichotomies woman/man, private/public relate to the operation of household finances. Second, there is the relationship between the housewife's domestic work and her symbolic reward—the 'fatal gift' which I discuss below.

The fatal gift

Many of the women I met while conducting my research were unfamiliar with the use of the Australian credit card system. This was not a result of their lack of knowledge of any required mathematical calculations; rather it was due to the fact that, for them, business transactions were activities linked to the alleged superior entrepreneurial skills of their men. As the use of credit cards involved legal and financial procedures of a rather public nature, the women tended to use cash for all purchases and kept their cards, if they had any, in a drawer at home. Thus the acquisition of costly domestic appliances, usually purchased by credit instalments, remained under men's control. For the more educated women this behaviour was recognised as discriminatory.

However, even here they were conditioned to submit to male authority because not only did the women pool their income in the 'family' home budget, as there was an obligation to do so, but the majority followed 'the husband's' decisions on how to spend or save the combined finances.

The traditional view that money spent within the household sphere is part of the woman's managerial role, while money allocated to transactions which have a business character is under the man's administration, reflects the way gendered economic roles are socially constructed (Moraes Gorecki 1988). Another related aspect is that traditionally a 'woman', seen from the point of view of a man's constructed stereotype, is the one 'to attend to her husband's plans and creative dreams, while sturdily struggling to keep the house together, give the family a sense of stability and bring up [the] generations [to come]' (Schipper 1985:224). Behind this idea is the woman's economic subordination to her husband in both the domestic (or private) and public spheres of their lives. This form of man's domination over the domestic space is further intensified by the way in which industrial domestic commodities are commercially advertised and subsequently introduced to the household: washing machines, vacuum cleaners and a range of other domestic appliances are personalised and linked to feminine 'nature' (i.e. to the mother/housewife). One of the consequences of this among the Latin American immigrants is that many women take pride in commenting that 'the washing machine was given to me on mother's day', or 'on the occasion of our wedding anniversary' or 'for my birthday': such expressions of gratitude for the 'fatal gift' belong to everyday language.

Reinforcing the ties between the woman and her domestic commodities is the male's resistance, if not objection, to engaging in any interaction with these 'feminine objects'. To aggravate this state of affairs, a man's sharing and participating in the house-work is popularly seen as merely 'helping his wife'. This assertion then denies any acknowledgment that in reality he could be democratically 'doing his bit' (i.e. a denial that he is contributing to the daily domestic services required to run a household).

I suggest that for the Latin American, and possibly other, housewives in Australia, the giving and receiving of household appliances help to emphasise that the so-called feminine domestic tasks are in economic and practical terms conditioned by female subordination to men. It can even be said that the washing machine almost has a quality inherent in it which justifies and legitimises men's uneasiness in using or even touching it. Such a machine, in a metaphorical sense, is the wife's fatal gift, which undermines the housewife's 'liberation' in terms of housework sharing. It constitutes an emotional weapon which serves her as a symbolic reward.

To conclude, I would argue that the fatal gift retains its symbolic significance in offering to the housewife a 'reward' for her double shift—for the work she does in her paid employment as well as her fulfilment of kinship obligations. In this way, emotional ties within the family are strengthened and help disguise the reality of discrimination against women (in their domestic/public existence) which in turn ultimately hinders their participation and incorporation in the democratic process of this society.

11 Racism, sexism and sociology

Dominant representations of minority women are frequently both racist and sexist in their construction (cf. Hull et al. 1982; Carby, in CCCS 1982: Amos and Parmar 1984). This is due in part to the unreconstructed nature of much sociological and some feminist analysis, and in part to the absence or marginalised presence of Aboriginal women and women of non-English speaking backgrounds within academe. It also reflects the difficulties in representing and theorising multiple oppression.

As other chapters in this book demonstrate, 'Aborigines' and 'migrants' are frequently ungendered categories in Aboriginal studies, multicultural studies and sociology; and 'women' often turn out to be white in women's studies. Once minority women's absence is noticed, they may be added in, in a guest lecture or book chapter on Aboriginal women or on women from non-English speaking backgrounds. Such containment of minority women may allow the overall structure of study to remain unaffected. On the other hand, any serious attempt to 'add in' other women will soon encounter serious analytic difficulties, and unsettle central concepts and categories in both sociology and feminism. The challenge then becomes one of finding ways to theorise the connections between different forms of oppression, and to represent the experiences of those who, like Aboriginal women and women from non-English speaking backgrounds, are subject to both racism and sexism simultaneously.

187

Those who argue for the primacy of gender oppression may, for example, seek to include the experiences of minority women in their recognition of the changing nature of patriarchy over time and place. Others may seek to prioritise oppressions in specific situations, to ask whether race or class or gender is most significant. Racism, for instance, may be the primary oppression currently facing Aboriginal women. Or researchers may use an alternative model of oppression which has different sections or focii on blacks, on the working class and on women, despite the fact that half the blacks and rather more than half the poor are women; and of course women also come from different class and ethnic backgrounds. In this kind of representation, minority women are again rendered invisible, as they slip between the category cracks (Christian 1989:19).

One attempted solution is an additive model, which posits that race plus class plus gender equals the black women's position of triple jeopardy; or race plus culture plus class plus gender equals quadruple jeopardy and so on. While recognising the multi-faceted nature of social inequality, this model still does not account for the dynamic interaction between different forms of oppression, or the ways in which each is experienced in and through the other (King 1988). Thus Aboriginal women experience racism differently from Aboriginal men and differently among themselves, depending on age, class, disability and place of residence. And Aboriginal women experience gender differently from white women, through the impact of colonisation and ongoing racism upon them.

One way to approach the complexities of multiple oppression is through an analysis of the social construction of race and ethnic categories and collectivities. Another is to recognise and analyse oppositional representations of the 'victims' themselves, as they engage in 'the struggle to come to representation' (Hall 1988b:27).

Race and ethnicity are not 'natural', even though they are often represented as if they were. Their boundaries are not fixed, nor is their membership uncontested. Race and ethnic groups, like nations, are imagined communities (Anderson 1983). They are ideological entities, made and changed in struggle. They are discursive formations, signalling a language through which differences which are accorded social significance may be named and explained. They also carry with them material consequences for those who are included within, or excluded from, them.

Thus racism, for example, is both discursive and systemic. It is an ideology, a field of language and images and assumptions about 'race' (Goldberg 1987:60). It is also a set of practices which, over time, produces and reproduces unequally structured social relations (CCCS 1982; Hall 1988a).

Race and ethnicity are constructed through, and help construct, relations of domination and subordination. Those in a position of power in a society can validate and impose their own definitions of normality, and define boundaries for the purpose of excluding, enclosing or exploiting others (Pettman 1988a:27). These definitions carry with them particular notions of value and entitlement, and so defend privilege either directly or through the operation of codes, norms and rules which may appeal to universalism, but which actually represent the social interests of dominant groups.

In the so-called 'Protection' period in Australia through the first half of this century, for example, those defined as Aboriginal were subject to state-ward status, to insititutionalisation and to exclusion from citizenship. They were also made vulnerable to brutal exploitation, including sexual exploitation and the abuse of women (Markus, in de Lepervanche and Bottomley 1988; Evans 1982). The ideology which represented Aboriginal people as children, as dependent upon the more civilised and knowledgeable whites, also provided a rationalisation for their dispossession and control. Until the 1970s, Australia's immigration selection policy was also racially exclusive, and even today definitions of who is a desirable migrant, of who is assimilable and who is inevitably 'other', inform the so-called Asian immigration debate and related disputes about multiculturalism (Jakubowicz 1985).

These and other arguments about race and ethnicity are not only about 'them'. They are also about 'us'. They are part of the politics of boundary-making. They play a refractive role (Prager 1987:68), for they are fundamentally about what is fair, about the good society, about who is Australian and about what that should mean (Pettman 1988a).

One kind of identity is imposed upon minority groups from the outside, with the state playing an active constituting role. The media and the ac/knowledge makers are also part of the process

INTERSEXIONS

of constituting racialised subjects and national, racial and ethnic collectivities (Hall 1988a). In this process, the race and ethnicity of the dominant groups is naturalised and becomes the norm, against which the 'others' are represented through difference and deviance, if they are represented at all.

But race and ethnicity are not only imposed. Nor are subordinate groups only victims. They resist, subvert, use and collude in their own interests. They may 'seize the category', claim it for their own and invert it, attaching positive value where before it was negative. They seek to use the common experiences of those so labelled to organise, mobilise and claim against dominant groups and the (their) state. This can at times lead to a strange convergence in the language of the racist right and of black or ethnic nationalists, as both infuse the race or ethnic category with essentialist, and supposedly naturally inherited, characteristics (Gilroy 1987:66).

Here it becomes clear that race and ethnicity are political resources (Yuval-Davis and Anthias, 1989), used by both dominant and subordinate groups for the purposes of legitimising and furthering their own social identities and social interests. In this contest, nothing—not boundaries, or criteria for allocating or withholding membership, or the consequences that flow from membership—is unchanging.

Race and ethnicity are about difference. Sites of difference are also sites of power (Barrett and McIntosh 1985:35). Dominant representations of difference function to exclude and/or exploit, and to justify unequal access and valuing. Subordinate groups, on the other hand, may use difference to mystify, to deny knowledge of themselves to the dominant groups and to confuse and neutralise those who attempt to control or 'help' them. They may use difference to stress their own separateness and to authorise their own representations. They may seek to legitimise their definitions of cultural differences, including those against others from within their own collectivity. Here, powerlessness is a comparative and relational concept, for 'the weak' often have spaces within which they can act and some choices about how they play their roles, no matter how small (Carroll 1972). But some groups are more powerful than others, and some 'ethnic' communities, or rather their spokespeople (usually spokesmen), *do* have considerable social and political influence (Jupp et al. 1989).

So identity is not simply imposed. It is also chosen, and actively used, albeit within particular social contexts and constraints. Against dominant representations of 'others', there is resistance. Within structures of dominance, there is agency. Analysing resistance and agency re-politicises relations between collectivities and draws attention to the central constituting factor of power in social relations.

But it is possible to overemphasise resistance; to validate others through valorising the lives of the colonised and exploited. Thus Reynolds' significant rewriting of Aboriginal history as resistance and adaptation has been criticised for representations which are in some ways militaristic and masculinist, again rendering Aboriginal women invisible or politically unimportant.

Sociology writings against the grain do recognise resistance. Thus Hall (1988a:67) and Gilroy (1987), for example, analyse black culture in Britain as oppositional culture, belonging not so much to 'them' as a birthright, as forged in their location within, and resistance to, state, systemic and popular racism.

While recognising the political and personal realities and energies beyond the depressing victim/problem couplet representation (Gilroy 1987:39), the concept of oppositional culture needs to be used carefully, in order to avoid romanticising the oppressed. Moreover, some forms of oppositional behaviour generated by racism and poverty are not, nor should they be, represented as collective political action (Cowlishaw 1988). Rather, like heavy drinking and fighting, they may be highly destructive both to their participants and to those closest to them, and may have the effect of further disrupting and immobilising the powerless (cf. Langton 1988b). Valorising resistance may also have the unintended effect of belittling the enormous costs exacted in situations of unequal power, exclusion and discrimination (Larbalestier 1980).

Race and ethnic categories function both to create false differences and to mask real ones (Bannerji 1987). Thus categories like 'Aboriginal women' or 'migrant women' disguise differences among women so categorised, including those relating to class, age, sexuality, type of household, place of residence, religion and ideology. This is especially true of the 'migrant' category, for even ignoring the many migrant women who come from Britain, for example, it still lumps together an older Greek-born woman, initially a factory worker and now as a result of industrial injury and/or the restructuring of industry doing outwork, with a younger Indian-born female academic.

Likewise, stressing race and ethnic differences can obscure the experiences and interests that women may share as women. The state does act on gendered subjects (Pateman 1988), and for a range of purposes the state directs its attention to women qua women. State legislation and policy affect women disproportionately, as single parents or as primary carers for children and aged people, for example (Edwards 1988). Women also share locality and interest activities, like women's learning centres or health centres or bingo, thus building links and friendships across racial and ethnic boundaries.

We therefore need to ask: Who is constructing the categories and defining the boundaries? Who is resisting these constructions and definitions? What are the consequences of being written into or out of particular categories? What happens when subordinate groups seek to mobilise along boundaries drawn for the purposes of domination? What happens to individuals whose multiple identities may be fractured and segmented by category politics? (Bannerji 1987:12).

Here we need to recognise the very different uses of categories for analytic, or alternatively for political, purposes. Some may seek to deconstruct and demystify categories, to reveal the politics behind their making and remakings. Others, or else the same people in different contexts, may seek to use the category as a resource. Identity politics can be powerful, as rallying calls and bases for solidarity, as 'sisterhood', or 'black is beautiful' demonstrate (Barrett and McIntosh 1985:27).

Political legitimacy, gaining access or a hearing, may depend on being able to 'call up' a constituency and authorise representations through appeals to authenticity, as 'excluding insiders', who 'know' by virtue of their experience as members of the category (Said 1985:15). Identity politics may then take on a kind of moralism which again disguises the interests involved. There is, after all, nothing essentially or inevitably good or radical about being black or being a woman (Gilroy 1987:149; Sivanandan 1988). A critical sociologist or feminist may thus challenge dominant representations, despite being white and of English-speaking background. Alternatively, an 'ethnic' politician may utilise oppositional or conservative representations of ethnic families and the role of women to reinforce his own power base. Hence it is necessary to ask who is representating whom; who can speak for, or even about, others? And it is also important to analyse what they are actually saying (cf. chapters by Jolly, Larbalestier and Bottomley in this volume).

Thus Hall, analysing the 'extraordinary diversity of objective positions, social experiences and cultural identities which compose the category 'black', goes on to argue for 'a recognition that we all speak from a particular place, out of a particular history, out of a particular experience, a particular culture, without being contained by that position' (1988b:28–9). What we seek, then, is to reflect upon the implications of each of us being ethnically located, including those whose membership of dominant groups naturalises and disguises that location. We seek, too, ways to pursue a critical engagement, both with others and with the materials and concepts with which we work.

The different political projects around race, ethnicity and gender can be revealed through an analysis of the representation of 'the black family', and especially through the stereotype of the black matriarch.

The black family is frequently represented in sociological literature as pathological, deviant or damaged as a result of slavery, colonisation or migration. Two rather different models are used to 'explain' the black family. The first, cultural deprivation, is also associated with the cycle of poverty. It is seen as applying especially to those who experienced slavery or colonisation, namely to Afro-Caribbeans, Afro-Americans and Aborigines. Here the family is viewed as damaged by those who cite as evidence the number of single mothers, female heads of households and presumed low educational achievement and social problems of the children (Carby 1982). The second, a 'culture' model, is applied especially to recent immigrants of non-English speaking backgrounds. This model focuses on presumed repressive family structures, on conflicts between generations and on a lack of opportunities for girls (Amos and Parmar 1984). The norm against which these different family forms are judged is the conventional nuclear family, which is itself a particular cultural and class form, and one which is increasingly unrepresentative even of those from that culture and class which generated it.

Black women writers and some critical sociologists and feminists are challenging these representations of the black family, to suggest other explanations for supposedly 'deviant' family forms. Thus Langton criticises white social scientists' studies of Aboriginal families and urban communities. She raises:

> the possibility of the matrifocal family as an accepted or perhaps even desired family form for Aboriginal women and children arising out of particular social conditions, that is those in which Aboriginal men are unable to reside permanently with wives and children because of itinerant labour patterns, unemployment, imprisonment, regulations pertaining to social security benefits for supporting mothers and so on.

She continues:

> The anomie and signs of marginality that have been observed in poor, urban Aboriginal populations may be responses to racism, the denial of housing and services, the insensitive intrusion of social workers, the image of the poor, both black and white, as criminal, the diminution of particularly male roles where Aboriginal men are forced into menial employment positions, or worse into unemployment, and the range of half-truths and myths about 'part-Aborigines'. (1981:18–19)

Collmann (1988) has documented the experiences of Aboriginal 'fringe-dwellers' in their interactions with, and resistance to, welfare authorities. Especially before 1967, welfare agents could legally restrict Aboriginal people's movements, and they intervened extensively in Aboriginal families, even removing their children from them (Edwards and Read 1989). Aboriginal men usually had to move to find jobs, and welfare regulations made it impossible for Aboriginal women to at the same time accompany their husbands and be seen as good mothers (Collmann 1988).

Studies of contemporary Aboriginal families confirm the ongoing vulnerability of those families to welfare intervention, especially with respect to the placement of Aboriginal children in 'care' (Gale and Wurdersitz 1986; Tomlinson 1986). Moreover, in the face of high unemployment or sporadic, seasonal or unreliable employment for Aboriginal men, Aboriginal women may be better off financially as single mothers on supporting parent pensions. Thus, while Aboriginal family forms do exhibit cultural characteristics, including attachment to a home place and to extended kin, they also reflect the effects of, and attempts at mutual support in the face of, generations of state intervention and ongoing poverty and racism.

Aboriginal women share many experiences with other black women in Britain and in the United States. Where they are welfare-dependent, for example, they are subject to surveillance and intervention concerning their sexual relationships, household membership and control of children. Where they do find paid work, it is frequently in the worst-paid and most vulnerable sectors. Against appalling odds, they find themselves portrayed as 'black matriarchs', represented as dominant, as part of the problem. They are berated for their very survival and capacity to cope. They are blamed for children's difficulties and youth's delinquency, for emasculating 'their' men and usurping male roles in the family.

Here it becomes clear that the 'black matriarch' is an ideological construction which is both racist and sexist. Some white discourses associate black men's masculinity with property, productivity and authority, in true patriarchal mode, and label black women as deviant for assuming the very roles and responsibilities that good, strong men are supposed to exhibit (Scott in Hull et al. 1982:87). Thus:

> women are called matriarchs when the power they exercise relative to men in their group is in some respect greater than that defined as appropriate by the dominant culture. Given this standard, women need not be the equals of men, much less men's superiors, in order to qualify as matriarchs. The acquisition by women of just one commonly masculine prerogative will do, and hence it becomes possible to attach matriarchal power to some of society's most disadvantaged people. (Lesbock 1983:147)

So black women are not praised for their adaptability, courage and resilience in the face of grim odds. Instead, they are stigmatised for failing to conform to conventional feminine stereotypes. Further, they are blamed for supposedly harming those closest to them when in fact they are rarely able to protect either themselves or their loved ones from the destructive consequences of poverty and racism. Their presumed deviance also attracts the attention of patriarchal and racist state policy-makers and welfare agencies. The enormous cost to black women in both physical and mental health problems and near-epidemic exhaustion and anxiety is rarely noted (Higginbotham in Hull et al. 1982:94; Larbalestier 1980). Their vulnerability outside the home may also be duplicated within it. The frustration and anger of some black men is turned against those closest to them, rather than against the system or its powerful representations and agents (Bell 1986:7).

However, black mothers are not necessarily alone in their struggles. Some still have communal support, including female extended kin. Others share locality and community centres, and women's organisations. The existence of wider support networks, and other women as neighbours and friends, is frequently overlooked in mainstream writing about the black family (Phoenix 1985:55; Smith 1983), yet this support is frequently documented and celebrated in many black women's writings (Christian 1985; Evans 1985; Willis 1985).

Black women have long defended their family forms and variety of household arrangements against misrepresentation by social scientists, social workers and the media. They may agree that black families (like other families) can be repressive and/or violent. But they reject some white feminist representations of 'the' family as the primary site of oppression, arguing that the black family has frequently been a site of resistance and relative freedom.

In Australia, the production of academic knowledge about Aboriginal people remains largely in white hands, with exceptions like social scientist Marcia Langton (1983, 1988) and historian Jackie Huggins (1987/88). Debates continue regarding Aboriginal women's traditional roles, the impact of colonisation and ongoing racism upon them, and their place in the welfare system and in their communities (Larbalestier 1980; Gale 1983; Ryan 1986a; Hamilton 1986; Merlan 1988). Meanwhile, Aboriginal women themselves are recording their own experiences, as Jan Larbalestier's chapter in this volume demonstrates.

Aboriginal women's writing usually take the form of autobiography and family history (Ryan 1986b), and their stories are also increasingly available through the recording of oral histories (for example in Aboriginal history: Huggins 1987/88) and conference proceedings (for example, Gale 1983), and through autobiographies (for example, Langford 1988; Morgan 1987) and interviews (White et al. 1985). The Report of the Aboriginal

Women's Taskforce, which undertook the first (and only) national consultation with Aboriginal women, produced information on a wide range of issues (*Women's Business* 1986). These various sources stress the strengths of Aboriginal women and the resilience and comfort of Aboriginal families against enormous odds: poverty, racism and state surveillance and control. But some of them also tell of violence within families, and of damage where the victims are usually women and children, as they are in other families under stress.

Here we come to further difficulties and dangers in representing black families. Celebrating the black family gives it its due as a place of safety and pleasure for many people and counteracts negative representation through recognition of the strengths and variety of family forms. But romantic and uncritical representations of it can be equally false. Alternatively, naming problems and troubles which face many black families carries the risk of reinforcing popular and racist representations.

Efforts to defend the black family may obscure the fact that family politics and gender relations are constructed through and as power relations. Traditions or relations which give strength can also oppress (Rapp 1979:511; Hamilton 1986:8). Extended families can be warm and loving; they can mobilise material and emotional resources far beyound the capacity of an individual or couple; they can provide a safe and congenial retreat from a threatening world. But they can also be repressive, manipulative, highly demanding and downright dangerous.

Analysing black families—indeed, any families—includes tackling the painful topics and even more painful realities of rape, domestic violence and child abuse. These topics are potentially inflammatory politically where their naming plays upon popular perceptions of black violence and criminality (Walker 1982). Here the interplay of race and gender, racism and sexism again becomes clear.

Historically, in colonial situations and in the United States, black masculinity was constructed as bestial and as a threat to white womanhood. Simultaneously, black women's sexuality was constructed as loose and wanton, so black women were devalued and vulnerable to abuse (Sykes 1975; Evans 1982; Carby 1986). In these circumstances, white women rarely recognised black women as sisters or acted in their defence. White women were

themselves socially dependent on white men for status and livelihood, and often directed their anger at white men's abuse of
black women against those same women.

In colonial situations, white women were frequently blamed for
deteriorating race relations, for reinforcing caste lines, and for
causing the sexual abandonment or discrete exploitation of black
women. Such a myth disguises and romanticises the 'maleness'
and violence of the frontier and the grossly unequal power relations between white men and black women, even in those (probably rare) cases of mutual affection and loyalty. White women
were themselves confined and controlled within the different
gender boundaries drawn in patriarchal racism, even where they
also acted as values carriers and boundary police. Thus it was
not white women alone so much as the patriarchal use made of
white women's supposed vulnerability, and the mobilisation of
myths around male black sexuality, which determined gender-
in-race relations (Inglis 1974; Knapman 1986; Ware 1983/84).

This was evident in Australia and in Australia's sphere of
influence in the Pacific. Thus 'rape' was used as a way to police
and intimidate black men in colonial Queensland, while Aboriginal women were left totally vulnerable to sexual abuse from
white men (Evans 1982; Harris 1982; O'Shane 1976a; Sykes
1975).

Racism construes difference as danger, and rape is central to
this construction. Rape is not a sexual act but a violent crime and
a political–power act. Historically, 'rape' was used to signal moral
panic, and for the purpose of controlling white women's, black
men's and black women's bodies, movements and relationships
(Carby 1986; Inglis 1974). White men protected 'their' women
while simultaneously controlling them and monopolising sexual
access to them. They stigmatised and intimidated black men,
while maintaining their access to and abuse of black women.
Thus enclosing, excluding boundaries were drawn around black
men and around white women, while white men were free to
'transgress' racial boundaries, without assuming responsibility
either for black women or for their own children born to those
women.

These boundaries are still potent in Australia today. Dominant
representations of Aboriginal women as 'available', and of Aboriginal men as drunk and violent, endanger them. Aboriginal vic-

tims of racist violence and Aboriginal women subject to racist and sexist attack often go unrecognised and unsupported (Sykes 1975; Burgmann 1984). Relations between Aboriginal people and the police are bitter and hostile. In this situation, calls for more effective policing of the streets, for example, may permit further police intervention and harrassment against those they label as troublemakers.

These associations make it especially difficult to analyse issues of domestic violence, rape and child abuse in families and communities which are already stigmatised as criminal or violent. Failing to speak out may be taken as colluding with violence and leaving black women undefended as they have been so often historically (Bell and Naparrala Nelson 1989). Yet speaking out may activate racist and sexist representations imposed on black communities (Marshment 1983; see also Walker 1982). Assuming a black man's guilt when media, police and courts are frequently anti-black may reinforce racism and deny the possibility of a just outcome. With the added horror of the high rates of black deaths in custody, Aboriginal women, for example, may well be reluctant to involve white agencies in assisting them to cope with the devastation wreaked by generations of colonisation, racism and poverty.

Some of these issues were dramatically demonstrated in Australia in the trial of Alwyn Peter for the murder of his girlfriend (Wilson 1982; see also David Bradbury's film *State of Shock*). Peter was acquitted on evidence of the systematic damage done to Aboriginal men and of the horrifically high rates of serious assault, homicide and self-mutilation on Queensland reserves. Meanwhile, families continue to bear the brunt of structural as well as personal violence.

Women have long had to absorb the anger of powerless, victimised or otherwise damaged men, often at their own cost. Such displacement is, of course, not restricted to black men. Black sexuality and sexism cannot be analysed in terms of gender relations within black communities alone or even, perhaps, primarily (Higginbotham, in Hull et al. 1982:96; Dill 1983:136). Rather, it is the interplay between race and gender and class which locates black women in relation to black men, and to white women and white men.

Analysing racism and sexism means recognising that the sexual politics of communities cannot be separated from sexual politics in the wider society. Nor can they be validated as if they were simply cultural givens. Sexual politics are always politics constructed in and through power relations.

The politics of family roles and women's status can be seen, too, through analysis of the effects of the migration process. Many women from overseas rural backgrounds, for example, lived, worked and cared for children largely in the company of, and supported by, other women. Yet some women felt constrained within these supports, and differences between a young wife and a mother-in-law, for example, could generate much insecurity and strife for the younger, less powerful woman. This also reminds us that there is no automatic sisterhood amongst women. Solidarity needs to be built through collective feminist or womanist political action (Walker 1983). Moreover, even where women's spaces did exist, they were usually defined within gender relations which were strongly patriarchal and unequal (Hamilton 1986).

The process of migration frequently split extended families, although in some cases women moved to already established families and communities which eased the hardship of resettlement. Others came alone, or in unfamiliar immediate family groupings, and were forced to make their own ways through a strange new world. Migrant women tell of their anxiety about family members left behind, about their children at the mercy of an alien school system or in unsatisfactory child care, and about the awful tiredness of multiple tasking in a new and troublesome place. But some also tell of new opportunities, of choices, of feelings of exhilaration and freedom when first earning their own wages or getting their driving licence (Martin 1986; Bottomley 1984c). These contradictions again raise questions about how to recognise the variety, the complexity, the specificity of women's experiences.

Representing minority women's experiences through writing and teaching is problematic. While women's studies courses are usually taught by and use materials largely written by (white) women, Aboriginal studies, multicultural studies and the sociology of race relations remain largely in 'white' hands. This is not to say that only Aboriginal women can teach about or research

Aboriginal women, for example, but there is something wrong when only non-Aboriginal people do so.

Aboriginal women and women from non-English speaking backgrounds are even more drastically under-represented in the academy than are white Australian-born women. Where they are employed it is often within 'special' programs, for example, as Aboriginal support or liaison staff in Aboriginal education programs. Their Aboriginality may be recognised as a qualification, but it also contains them, as white colleagues tend to assume that their competence lies only in areas of 'Aboriginal affairs' in which they are frequently expected to be all-knowing (Pettman 1990).

There are problems here about authenticity and also about representativeness. Those Aboriginal women and women of non-English speaking backgrounds who do come to occupy 'knowledgeable' positions, as academics, teachers, administrators or advisers, may find themselves caught between the institutional culture in which they work and the community/ies with which they may have strong personal, social and political links. Yet their working position indicates educational and class experiences and interests which are not typical of their background. They may feel reluctant to speak for other women, even of their own group.

How, then, do white, English-speaking background academics go about researching and teaching about 'others'? Here we enter a minefield of political, ethical and professional issues, associated with equal opportunity as an industrial issue, and with the production and dissemination of academic knowledge. It is essential, however, for those employed to devise strategies and programs to recruit and support academics from minority backgrounds. It is also essential for those employed to scrutinise course offerings, materials, perspectives and entry procedures, to eliminate racism and sexism (Pettman 1990).

Minority women's lack of representation in public knowledge-making reflects their exclusion from power, including ideational power. Yet these women are producing knowledge about themselves, theorising and analysing, albeit often within their own homes, groups and communities, and in ways not accessible to outsiders or even in some instances to each other (Christian 1989; Smith 1983). Now, however, there are growing numbers of writings about and by Aboriginal women. There are also 'migrant' women's writings and the beginnings of literary criticisms of them (Gunew and Mahyuddin 1988). As Jan Larbalestier and Gill Bottomley demonstrate in their respective chapters, these works add to the resources available to us in teaching and learning.

The use of these writings raises fascinating questions about the nature of evidence in the social sciences and the status of these more personalised accounts of women's lives (Gunew and Mahyuddin). And sociology, including the business of constructing and filling social categories, can also be fictive or imaginative (McHoul 1988).

As the writers in this book indicate, we need to find ways to represent the specificity and variety of women's experiences and social identities, and to locate those experiences and identities within structures of domination and resistance, and within the politics of category and identity-making. We must also problematise 'experience' (Barrett 1987:32; Gunew and Mahyuddin 1988), for while personal accounts and stories give us crucial insights into women's lives, theoretical work needs to be done to politicise our readings and to plot the emerging patterns and connections.

Thus racial and ethnic categories are not givens, but are social constructions whose making and contesting require analysis. They also require gendering, and the further recognition of the diversity of social interest and experience within them. The 'culture' attached to them is not a fixed, apolitical tradition but rather a terrain of politics in which sexual politics, including the roles, status and representation of women, is central.

Notes

Chapter 1 Moving in from the margins
1 Significant aspects of the argument of this paper are developed in my forthcoming book in far greater detail than is possible here: *Mukkuvar Women: The Sexual Contradictions in a South India Fishing Community* Sydney: Allen and Unwin, in press.

Chapter 2 Ethno-religious communities and gender divisions
in Bangladesh
1 Doria and Palashi are pseudonyms for the village and the local union where I have conducted my fieldwork. Pseudonyms have also been used for the persons referred to in the paper.
2 The word 'Bengali' has been used to refer both to the people of Bangladesh and to their language and culture. It is to emphasise their cultural rather than political identity that 'Bengalis' instead of 'Bangladeshis' has been used to refer to the people of Bangladesh.
3 *Parda*, literally meaning curtain, refers to the practice of female seclusion. In the strictest sense, *parda* involves keeping women confined within the home and covering them in veils whenever they venture out of the home. In a wider context, *parda* refers to women's modesty and restrictions on their interactions with males who do not fall in the specified categories with whom contact is permitted (Papanek 1982; Jahan 1975 Alamgir 1977).
4 The ideology of 'community' does not have any predetermined meaning. It may be used to refer to a village, a religious group, a

203

racial group, a caste, or to a nation, depending on the political or cultural context (Chatterjee 1982; Anderson 1983; Rozario 1988b). In this paper, Christians, who cut across several villages, have been referred to as a 'community', the political significance of which should be clear from the paper itself.

5   Mission *samity* consists of one or two Christian leaders from each of the fourteen villages within the mission and is headed by the mission priest. It is responsible for organising, managing and resolving secular aspects of church matters. There are no women in the *samity*.

Chapter 4   The politics of difference: feminism, colonialism and decolonisation in Vanuatu

1   Here I am alluding to difference between women rather than to difference as a way of conceiving woman versus man. This has been as influential strand of ferminist philosophy, emanating mainly from France but with many Australian proponents, which challenges the adequacy of ideas of equality, on the basis that this means homologisation to male values (Eisenstein 1984; Grosz 1989; Marks and Courtrivon 1981). I think it is a debatable point whether either feminist philosphers of equality or of difference have so far dealt adequately with ethnic and racial differences between women.

2   Sykes (1975) and O'Shane (1976) early challenged the relevance of the Australian women's movement for Aboriginal women and in 1975 many Aboriginal women decided not to participate in International Women's Year activities on the grounds that racism not sexism was pre-eminent in their lives. Our demands for sexual freedom sounded inappropriate to Aboriginal women long stereotyped as promiscuous 'gins' and subject to white male sexual abuse and rape. Grimshaw (1981) compared white and black families in Australia in attempting to explain Aboriginal women's attitude to sexism, and Larbalestier (1980) suggested affinities between Aboriginal women and those in poor white families. Burgmann (1984) in her superb study of the views of urban Aboriginal women, emphasised the fact that they were often better educated and employed than their male counterparts, and that they were often central not just to family life but to political struggle. In the last ten years or so there have been several excellent life histories, personal testaments and autobiographies

published (Clare 1978; Gale 1983; Huffer and Roughsey 1980; Mum Shirl with Sykes 1981; Roughsey and Labumore 1984; West 1984; White 1985).

Johnston in her thesis on 'the government women' of Papua New Guinea (1984a) and in a related article (1984b), sees the position taken by many such women, namely denying the relevance of feminism, as a defence of their class position and their class identity with their husbands. There is no doubt that proclamations about the harmonious state of gender relations on the part of women such as Nahau Rooney, fit uneasily with the perceptions of many poor rural and urban women. Rural women involved in movements such as *work meri* in the Highlands perceive real conflicts with their menfolk, intensified by the new demands of coffee cultivation (e.g. Sexton 1986). However these kinds of reports from villages by anthropologists are continually dismissed by Rooney and other women politicians and bureaucrats. For example in the *Post-Courier* early this year Rooney claimed that 'there is no information regarding a genuine status of women in traditional PNG' (1989:37). The voluminous writings of anthropologists and sociologists are dismissed because they are by foreigners whose sole purpose in writing is academic achievement. Moreover she suggests that their interpretations are reflective of their own prejudices 'reflecting the patriarchal nature of their capitalist countries back home' She suggests that if PNG women accept this portrait of themselves as mere shadows they have only themselves to blame.

3   In an interview with Jill Emberson, broadcast on Radio National on 10th September 1988, Molisa was more positive about Melanesian values. Speaking to an Australian journalist and to a predominantly Australian audience, she stressed the diversity in the indigenous situation of ni-Vanuatu women and in particular the greater influence of women in matrilineal societies in north Vanuatu. But she was also strongly critical of male politicians de-emphasising women's issues for strategic reasons and of ni-Vanuatu women themselves for not fighting their subordination, for colluding in their 'colonization' by men.

4   A third volume of poetry, *Black Stone II* was published in 1989, but is not considered here. It is worth noting that proceeds from the sale of *Colonised People* helped to finance Hilda Lini's political campaign in 1987 (Grace Mera Molisa, personal communication).

Chapter 7 Multiculturalism and feminism

1 Note that I am only referring to federal government policy in this paper. I am not including the initiatives of the various state-based Ethnic Affairs Commissions. The activities and intentions of these latter institutions are often more radical, and certainly more contested, and they often enter into debate with the federal policies covered in this paper.

2 Again I should stress that this paper is only concerned with the two major theoretical positions that subtend federal policy. It is not concerned with the many feminist initiatives set in place under the auspices of 'multiculturalism' mainly because these have been the result of the actions of individual migrant feminists and other groups struggling in these areas. The point is that any feminist initiatives in the area have been battled for, and won, in a number of government instrumentalities, but they are not inscribed in policy itself.

Bibliography

Abu-Lughod, L. (1986) *Veiled sentiments: Honor and Poetry in a Beduin Society* Berkeley, Los Angeles and London: University of California Press

Abustam, Idrus M. (1975) *Tukang Sepatu Toraja di Ujung Pandang* Laporan Penelihan Pusat Latihan Penelihan Ilmu Ilmu Sosial, Ujung Pandang

Adam-Smith, P. (1984) *Australian Women at War* Melbourne: Nelson

Alamgir, S. F. (1977) *Profile of Bangladeshi Women: Selected Aspects of Women's Roles and Status in Bangladesh* Dhaka: USAID

Alcorso, C. (1987) 'Outwork and Migrant Women: Some Responses' *Migration Action* 9, 3, pp. 10–13

—— (1989) *Newly Arrived Immigrant Women in the Workforce* A Report for the Office of Multicultural Affairs, Wollongong: The University of Wollongong Centre for Multicultural Studies

Allen, M. (1982) 'The Hindi View of Women' in M. Allen and S. Mukherjee (eds) *Women in India and Nepal* Australian National University, Canberra: ANU Printing, pp. 1–20

Allen, M. and Mukherjee, S. (eds) (1982) *Women in India and Nepal*, ANU monographs on South Asia, 8, Canberra: ANU

Amos, V. and Parmar, P. (1984) 'Challenging Imperial Feminism' *Feminist Review* 17, pp. 3–20

Anderson, B. (1983) *Imagined Communities: Reflections on the Origin and Spread of Nationalism* London: Verso

Andreoni, H. (1986) 'Italian Women in Multicultural Australia' un-published paper

Anthias, F. and Yuval-Davis, N. (1983) 'Contextualizing Feminism —gender, ethnic and class divisions' *Feminist Review* 15, pp. 62–75

Appleyard, R. and Amera, A. (1986) 'Postwar Immigration of Greek Women to Australia: A Longitudinal Study' in R. J. Simon and C. B. Brettel (eds) *International Migration: The Female Experience* New Jersey: Rowman and Allanheld

Arena, F. (1985) 'The Contribution of Italian-Australian women to Australian Society: an Overview' in *Noi Donne Italo-Australiane*, Proceedings of the First Congress of Italo-Australian Women, Sydney

Ariss, R. (1988) 'Writing Blacks: The construction of an Aboriginal discourse' in Beckett, J. (ed.) *Past and Present: The Construction of Aboriginality* Canberra: Aboriginal Studies Press, pp. 131–46

'Asterisk' [Fletcher, R. J.] (1923) in Lynch (ed.) *Isles of Illusion: Letters from the South Seas* London: Constable and Co.

Attali, J. (1985) *Noise: A Political Economy of Music* Minnesota: University of Minnesota Press

Australian Bureau of Statistics (ABS) *Census 1986* (selected figures) Canberra: AGPS

Australian Council on Population and Ethnic Affairs (ACPEA) (1982) *Multiculturalism for all Australians: Our developing nationhood* Canberra: AGPS

Australian Government Commission of Inquiry into Poverty (1975) *Welfare of Migrants* Canberra: AGPS

Australian Population and Immigration Council (APIC) (1977) *Immigration Policies and Australia's Population* Canberra: AGPS

Baker-Reynolds, M. (1978) To keep the *tali* strong: women's rituals in Tamil Nadu, PhD thesis, Madison: University of Wisconsin

Baldock, C. V. and Cass, B. (eds) (1983) *Women, Social Welfare and the State* Sydney: Allen & Unwin

Bannerji, H. (1987) 'Introducing Racism: Notes Towards an Anti-Racist Feminism' *Resources for Feminist Research* 16, 1, pp. 10–12.

Barrett, M. (1980 and 1988) *Women's Oppression Today* London: Verso

—— (1987) 'The concept of "difference"' *Feminist Review* 26, pp. 26–41

Barrett, M. and McIntosh, M. (1982) *The Anti-Social Family* London: Verso

—— (1985) 'Ethnocentrism and Socialist Feminist Theory' *Feminist Review* 20, pp. 24–47

Bayly, S. (1981) 'A Christian caste in Hindu society' *Modern Asian Studies*, 15, 2, pp. 203–34

Beasant, J. (1984) *The Santo Rebellion: An Imperial Reckoning* Honolulu and Richmond: University of Hawaii Press and Heinemann Publishers, Australia

Beck, B. (1974) 'The kin nucleus in Tamil folklore' in T. Trautmann (ed.) *Kinship and history in South Asia* Michigan Papers on South and South East Asia, 7, Ann Arbor: University of Michigan, pp. 1–28

Beckett, J. (1988) 'The past in the present; the present in the past: Constructing a national Aboriginality' in Beckett, J. (ed.) *Past and Present: the Construction of Aboriginality* Canberra: Aboriginal Studies Press for the AIAS, pp. 191–217

Bell, D. (1983) *Daughters of the Dreaming* Melbourne: McPhee Gribble/Allen & Unwin

Bell, D. and Naparrala Nelson, T. (1989) 'Speaking About Rape is Everyone's Business' *Women's Studies International Forum* 14, 1, pp. 403–16

Bell, J. (1986) interview in *Hecate* xxii, 1–2, pp. 64–75

Berger, J. (with Mohr, J.) (1975) *A Seventh Man* London: Penguin

Berger, P. and Luckmann, T. (1969) *The social construction of reality* Harmondsworth: Allen and Lane

Berita Buana (1988a) 'Pasaran Tenaga Kerjadi Saudi arkup besar harus dimanfaatkan' 3, 5 May

—— (1988b) '300 Tenaga Kerja Indonesia Dikirim ke Arab Saudi' 3, 19 August

—— (1988c) 'Tenaga kerja Indonesia di Arab Saudi dekati 100,000 orang' 1, 7, 22 September

Bhavnani, K.-K. and Coulson, M. (1986) 'Transforming Socialist-Feminism: The Challenge of Racism' *Feminist Review* 23, pp. 81–92

Binnion, J. (1984) Review of 'An Aboriginal mother tells of the old and the new by Elsie Roughsey' in *Aboriginal Studies* 2

Birrell, R. and Birrell, T. (1981) *An Issue of People* Melbourne: Longman Cheshire

Bishop, M. and Wigglesworth, A. (1982) *A Touch of Australian Enterprise: The Vanuatu Experience* Fitzroy, Melbourne: International Development Action

Blainey, G. (1984) *All for Australia* Sydney: Methuen Haynes

Blanchet, T. (1984) *Women, Pollution and Marginality: Meanings and Rituals of Birth in Rural Bangladesh* Dhaka: The University Press

Boer, C. (1988) 'Are You Looking For a Filipino Wife?', A Study of Filipina–Australian Marriages. A Research Project of the Anglican General Synod Social Responsibilities Commission and The International Affairs Commission. Sydney, General Synod Office

Bonnemaison, J. (1984) 'Social and Cultural Aspects of Land Tenure' in P. Larmour (ed.) *Land Tenure in Vanuatu* Suva: University of South Pacific, Institute of Pacific Studies and USP Extension Centre, Port Vila

Boserup, E. (1970) *Women's Role in Economic Development* London: Allen & Unwin

Bottomley, G. (1979) *After the Odyssey: A Study of Greek Australians* St Lucia: University of Queensland Press

—— (1981) 'Class, gender and ethnicity' unpublished paper presented to Ethnicity and Class Conference, Wollongong, August

—— (1983) 'Eurydice in the Underworld: Mediterranean women in Australia' in A. Burns, G. Bottomley and P. Jools (eds) *Family in the Modern World* Sydney: Allen & Unwin

—— (1984a) 'Women on the move: migration and feminism' in G. Bottomley and M. de Lepervanche (eds) *Ethnicity, Class and Gender in Australia* Studies in Society 24, Sydney: Allen & Unwin, pp. 98–108

—— (1984b) *Export of people: Emigration from and return migration to Greece* Wollongong: Centre for Multicultural Studies

—— (1984c) 'Mediterranean women in Australia: an overview' in *Multicultural Australia Paper No. 35* Melbourne: Clearing House on Migration Issues

—— (1985) 'Perpetuation de la dot chez les Grecs d'Australie: transformation et re-negociation des pratiques traditionnelles', in C. Piault (ed.) *Familles et Biens en Grece et a Chypre* Paris: h'Harmattan, pp. 145–64

—— (1986) 'A world divided? Studies of gender relations in modern Greece' *Mankind* 16, 3, December, pp. 181–9

—— (1987) 'Cultures, multiculturalism and the politics of representation' *Journal of Intercultural Studies* 8, 2, pp. 1–10

—— (1989) 'Ethnicity, Race and Nationalism in Australia: Some Critical Perspectives' *Australia Journal of Social Issues* 23, 3, pp. 169–83

—— (1990) 'Identity, difference and inequalities: gender, ethnicity and class in Australia', in Academy of the Social Sciences in

Australia, *Australian National Identity* Canberra (forthcoming publication).

Bottomley, G. and de Lepervanche, M. (eds) (1984) *Ethnicity, Class and Gender in Australia* Sydney: Allen & Unwin

Bottomley, G. and Georgiou, V. (1988) 'Multiculturalism in practice: A study of Greek Australian families in Sydney' in A. Tamis and A. Kapardis (eds) *Greeks in Australia* Melbourne: River Seine Publications

Bourdieu, P. (1977) *Outline of a theory of practice* Cambridge: Cambridge University Press

—— (1986) *Distinction: A Social Critique of the Judgment of Taste* London: Routledge and Kegan Paul

—— (1987) *Choses Dites* Paris: Editions de Minuit

Bourne, J. (1983) 'Towards an anti-racist feminism' *Race and Class* 25, 1, pp. 1–22

Boyle, H. (1983) 'The conflicting role of Aboriginal women in today's society' in F. Gale (ed.) *We Are Bosses Ourselves: The status and role of Aboriginal women today*, Canberra: AIAS

Briscoe, G. (1989) 'Class "welfare" and capitalism: The role Aborigines have played in the State-building processes in Northern Territory history' in R. Kennedy (ed.) *Australian Welfare* Melbourne: Macmillan

Broom, D. (1987) 'Another Tribe: Gender and Inequality' in C. Jennett and R. G. Stewart (eds) *Three Worlds of Inequality* Melbourne: Macmillan, pp. 264–81

Bropho, R. (1980) *Fringedweller* Sydney: Alternative Publishing Co-operative Ltd

Bryson, L. (1984) 'The Australian Patriarchal Family' in S. Encel and L. Bryson (eds) *Australian Society* 4th edn, Melbourne: Longman Cheshire, pp. 113–69

Burgmann, M. (1984) 'Black Sisterhood: The Situation of Urban Aboriginal Women and their Relationship to the White Women's Movement' in G. Simms (ed.) *Australian Women and the Political System*, Melbourne: Longman Cheshire

Burnley, I., Encel, S. and McCall, G. (1985). *Immigration and Ethnicity in the 1980s* Melbourne: Longman Cheshire

Burns, A. (1986) 'Why Do Women Continue to Marry?' in N. Grieve and A. Burns (eds) *Australian Women: New Feminist Perspectives* Melbourne: Oxford University Press, pp. 210–32

Burns, A., Bottomley, G. and Jools, P. (eds) (1983) *The Family in the Modern World* Sydney: Allen & Unwin

211

Cahill, D. and Ewen, J. (1987) *Ethnic youth: Their assets and aspiration* Canberra: Department of the Prime Minister

Caine, B., Grosz, E. A. and de Lepervanche, M. (eds) (1988) *Crossing Boundaries* Sydney: Allen & Unwin

Callaway, H. (1987) *Gender, Culture and Empire: European Women in Colonial Nigeria* Oxford: St Anthony's College and Macmillan Press

Calvino, I. (1982) *The Uses of Literature* San Diego: Harcourt Brace Jovanovich

Carby, H. (1982) 'White Women Listen! Black Feminism and the Boundaries of Sisterhood' in Centre for Contemporary Cultural Studies *The Empire Strikes Back: Race and Racism in 70s Britain* London: Hutchinson

—— (1986) 'Lynching, Empire and Sexuality in Black Feminist Theory' in H. Gates (ed.) *Race, Writing and Difference* Chicago: University of Chicago Press

Carroll, B. (1972) 'Peace Research: The Cult of Power' *Conflict Resolution* xvi, 4, pp. 591–616

Cass, B. (1983) 'Population, Policies and Family Policies: State Construction of Domestic Life' in C. V. Baldock and B. Cass (eds) *Women, Social Welfare and the State* Sydney: Allen & Unwin

—— (1985) 'Rewards for Women's Work' in J. Goodnow and C. Pateman (eds) *Women, Social Science and Public Policy* Sydney: Allen & Unwin, pp. 110–28

—— (1988) 'The Feminisation of Poverty' in B. Caine, E. Grosz and M. de Lepervanche (eds) *Crossing Boundaries* Sydney: Allen & Unwin, pp. 110–28

Castan, C. (1988) 'The Greeks and Australian Literature' in A. Kapardis and A. Tamis (eds) *Greeks in Australia* Melbourne: River Seine Press

Castles, S., Booth, H. and Wallace, T. (1984) *Here for Good: Western Europe's New Ethnic Minorities* London: Pluto Press

Castles, S., Lewis D., Morrissey, M. and Black, J. D. (1986) *Patterns of Disadvantage among the overseas born and their children* Wollongong: Centre for Multicultural Studies

Castles, S., Kalantzis M., Cope, B. and Morrissey, M. (1988) *Mistaken Identity: Multiculturalism and the demise of nationalism in Australia* Sydney: Pluto Press

Caton, H. (1985) 'Feminism and the Family' Queensland: The Council for Free Australia

Caulfield, M. D. (1974) 'Imperialism, the Family and Cultures of Resistance' *Socialist Revolution* 20 (October)

Centre for Contemporary Cultural Studies (CCCS) (1982) *The Empire Strikes Back: Race and Racism in 70s Britain* London: Hutchinson

Centre for Working Women Co-operative (CWWC) (1986) *Women Outworkers: A Report documenting sweated labour in the 1980s* Footscray, Centre for Working Women Co-operative

Chatterjee, P. (1982) 'Agrarian Relations and Communalism in Bengal, 1926–1935' in R. Guha (ed.) *Subaltern Studies I: Writings on South Asian History and Society* Delhi: Oxford University Press, pp. 9–38

Chipman, L. (1978) 'Multicultural Myth' *Quadrant* 128, XXII, 3

—— (1980) 'The Menace of Multiculturalism' *Quadrant* 158, XXIV, 10

Chodorow, N. (1978) *The Reproduction of Mothering: Psychoanalysis and the Sociology of Gender* Berkeley: University of California Press

Christian, B. (1985) *Black Feminist Criticism: Perspectives on Black Women Writers* New York: Pergamon Press

—— (1989) 'But Who Do You Really Belong To—Black Studies or Women's Studies' *Women's Studies* 17, 1, pp. 17–24

Clare, M. (1978) *Karoban, the story of an Aboriginal Girl* Chippendale, Sydney: Alternative Publishing

Clothing and Allied Trades Union (1987) *Outwork and the Australian Clothing Industry* Sydney: Clothing and Allied Trades Union of Australia

Cock, J. (1980) *Maids and Madams: A study in the Politics of Exploitation* Johannesburg: Ravan Press

Cohen, A. P. (1985) *The Symbolic Construction of Community* London and New York: Tavistock Publications

Collins, J. (1975) 'The Political Economy of Post-War Immigration' in E. L. Wheelwright and K. Buckley (eds) *Essays in the Political Economy of Australian Capitalism* 1, pp. 105–29, Sydney: ANZ Book Company

—— (1978) 'Fragmentation of the Working Class' in E. L. Wheelwright and K. Buckley (eds) *Essays in Political Economy of Australian Capitalism* 3, Sydney: ANZ Book Company

—— (1984) 'Immigration and class: The Australian experience' in G. Bottomley and M. de Lepervanche (eds) *Ethnicity, Class and Gender in Australia* Sydney: Allen & Unwin

Collmann, G. (1988) '"I'm Proper No. 1 Fighter, Me": Aborigines, Gender and Bureaucracy in Central Australia' *Gender and Society* 2, 1, pp. 9–23

Committee to Advise on Australia's Immigration Policy (CAAIP) (1988) *Immigration: A Commitment to Australia* Canberra: AGPS

Connell, R. W. and Irving, T. H. (1980) *Class Structure in Australian History* Melbourne: Longman Cheshire

Couani, A. (1989) 'Writing from a non-Anglo perspective' in *The Age Monthly Review* September, p. 16

Cowlishaw, G. (1986) 'Aborigines and Anthropologists' *Australian Aboriginal Studies* 1, pp. 2–12

—— (1988) *Black, White or Brindle: Race in Rural Australia* New York and Melbourne: Cambridge University Press

Cremer, G. (1988) 'Deployment of Indonesian migrants in the Middle East: Present situation and prospects' *Bulletin of Indonesian Economic Studies* 24, 3, pp. 73–86

Cuneen, C. and Robb, T. (1987) *Criminal Justice in North-West New South Wales* Sydney: NSW Bureau of Crime Statistics and Research

Curthoys, A. (1984) 'Ann Curthoys' in R. Rowland (ed.) *Women who do and Women who don't join the Women's Movement* London: Routledge and Kegan Paul, pp. 56–62

—— (1985) 'Racism and Class in the Nineteenth-Century Immigration Debate' in Markus, A. and Ricklefs, M. C. (eds) *Surrender Australia?* Sydney: Allen & Unwin, pp. 94–100

—— (1988) *For and against feminism* Sydney: Allen & Unwin

D'Costa, J. (ed.) (1981) *The Catholic Directory of Bangladesh* Archbishop's House, Dhaka, Bangladesh

de Lepervanche, M. (1975) 'Australian Immigrants, 1788–1940' in E. L. Wheelwright and K. Buckley (eds) *Essays in the Political Economy of Australian Capitalism* 1, Sydney: ANZ Book Company, pp. 72–104

—— (1980) 'From Race to Ethnicity' *Australia and New Zealand Journal of Sociology* 16, 1, pp. 24–37

—— (1984a) *Indians in a White Australia* Sydney: Allen & Unwin

—— (1984b) 'Immigrants and Ethnic Groups' in S. Encel and L. Bryson (eds) *Australian Society* 4th edn, Melbourne: Longman Cheshire

—— (1988) 'Racism and sexism in Australian national life' in M. de Lepervanche and G. Bottomley (eds) *The cultural construction of race* Sydney: University of Sydney

—— (1989a) 'Women, Nation and the State in Australia' in N.

Yuval-Davis and F. Anthias (eds) *Women–Nation–State* London: Macmillan, pp. 46–57

—— (1989b) 'Breeders for Australia: A National Identity for Women?' *Australian Journal of Social Issues* 24, 3

—— (1990) 'Holding it all together: Multiculturalism, Nationalism, Women and the State in Australia'. Paper presented to XIIth World Congress of Sociology, Madrid

de Lepervanche, M. and Bottomley, G. (eds) (1988) *The Cultural Construction of Race* Sydney: Association for the Study of Society and Culture

Daniels, K. and Murnane, M. (eds) (1980) *Uphill All the Way: A Documentary History of Women in Australia* St Lucia: University of Queensland Press

Davis, A. (1971) 'Reflections on the Black Women's Role in the Community of Slaves' *Black Scholar* 2, p. 15

—— (1982) *Women, Race and Class* London: Women's Press

Davis, John (1973) *Land and Family in Pisticci* London: Athlone Press

Davis, J. (1985) 'Aboriginal Writing: a personal view' in J. Davis and B. Hodge (eds) *Aboriginal Writing Today* Canberra: AIAS, pp. 11–19

Davis, J. and Hodge, B. (1985) 'Introduction' in J. Davis and B. Hodge (eds) *Aboriginal Writing Today* Canberra: AIAS, pp. 1–6 pp. 1–6

Denoon, L. (1989) 'The Denoons Pass on the Torch' in *Broadside*, Newsletter of the National Foundation for Australian Women 1, 1, p. 7

Dill, B. T. (1983) 'Prospects for an All-Inclusive Sisterhood' *Feminist Studies* 9, 1, pp. 131–50

Dirks, N. B. (1987) *The Hollow Crown: Ethnohistory of an Indian Kingdom* Cambridge University Press: Cambridge

Dixson, M. (1976) *The real Matilda: Women and identity in Australia* Ringwood Victoria: Penguin; rev. edn 1984

Douglas, M. (1966) *Purity and Danger: An analysis of the concepts of pollution and taboo* London, Boston and Henley: Routledge and Kegan Paul

Dumont, L. (1972) *Homo Hierarchicus: The caste system and its implications* London: Paladin

—— (1980) (revised edition) Chicago and London: University of Chicago Press

Edgar, D. (1981) 'Reagan's hidden agenda: racism and the new American Right' *Race and Class* XXII, 3

Edwards, A. (1988) *Regulation and Repression* Sydney: Allen & Unwin, Ch. 7

Edwards, C. and Read, P. (eds) (1989) *The Lost Children* Sydney: Doubleday

Eisenstein, H. (1984) *Contemporary Feminist Thought* London and Sydney: Unwin Paperbacks

Eisenstein, Z. (ed.) (1979) *Capitalist Patriarchy and the case for Socialist Feminism* New York and London: Monthly Review Press

Eliadis, M. et al. (1989) 'Issues for Non English Speaking Background Women' Office of Multicultural Affairs, Canberra: AGPS

El Saadawi, N. (1980) *The Hidden Face of Eve: Women in the Arab World* London: Zed Press

Ethnic Affairs Commission of New South Wales (1978) *Participation* Report to the Premier, Sydney

Evans, A. (1982) '"Don't You Remember Black Alive, Sam Holt?" Aboriginal Women in Queensland History' *Hecate* VIII, 2, pp. 7–21

Evans, M. (ed.) (1983) *Black Women Writers* London: Pluto Press

Fahey, S. (1988) 'From "Women in Development" to "Gender in development": A fundamental shift' in D. Goldsworthy (ed.) *Development Studies in Australia: Themes and Issues* Melbourne: Monash Development Studies Centre Monograph No. 1

Fanon, F. (1965) *A Dying Colonialism* New York: Grove Press

—— (1967) *Black Skin, White Masks* New York: Grove Press

FILEF Women's Group Conference Circular 26 June 1978

Fitzgerald, S. (1988) *Immigration: A Commitment to Australia* Report of the Committee to advise on Australia's Immigration Policies, Canberra: AGPS

Foley, Matthew (1984) 'Aborigines and the Police' in P. Hanks and B. Keon-Cohen, *Aborigines and the Law* Sydney: Allen & Unwin

Fourth Women and Labour Conference, The (1984) Proceedings from the Conference, Brisbane

Fraser, N. and Nicholson, L. (1988) 'Social criticism without philosophy: an encounter between feminism and post-modernism' *Theory Culture & Society* 5, 2–3, June, pp. 373–394

Fruzzetti, L. M. (1982) *The Gift of a Virgin: Women, Marriage and Ritual in a Bengali Society* New Jersey: Rutgers University Press

Gaitskell, D. (1982) 'Are Servants Ever Sisters?' *Hecate* 8, 1, pp. 102–12

Galbally Report on Migrant Services and Programmes (1978) Canberra: AGPS

Gale, F. (ed.) (1983) *We Are Bosses Ourselves: The Status and Role of Aboriginal Women Today* Canberra: Australian Institute of Aboriginal Studies

Gale, F. and Wundersitz, J. (1986) 'Aboriginal Visability in the "System"' *Australian Social Work* 39, 1, pp. 21–6

Game, A. and Pringle, R. (1979) 'The Making of the Australian Family' *Intervention* 12, pp. 63–83

—— (1983) *Gender at Work* Sydney: Allen & Unwin

Geertz, H. (1963) 'Indonesian cultures and communities' in R. McVey *Indonesia* Ithaca N.J.: Cornell University Press

Giddens, A. (1987) *Social Theory and Modern Sociology* Cambridge: Polity Press

Giddings, P. (1985) *When and Where I Enter* New York: Bantam Books

Gilbert, K. (1977) *Living Black* Melbourne: Allan Lane, Penguin

Giles, Z. (1988) 'Telling Tales' in S. Gunew and J. Mahyuddin (eds) *Beyond the Echo: Multicultural Women's Writing* St Lucia: University of Queensland Press

Gilroy, P. (1987) *There Ain't No Black in the Union Jack* London: Hutchinson

—— (1988/89) 'Cruciality and the Frog's Perspective' *Third Text* 5, Winter, pp. 33–44

Gittins, D. (1985) *The Family in Question* London: Macmillan

Glazer, N. and Moynihan, D. (1975) *Ethnicity: Theory and Experience* Cambridge, Mass.: Harvard University Press

Goddard, V. (1987) 'Honour and shame: The control of women's sexuality and group identity in Naples' in P. Caplan (ed.) *The cultural construction of sexuality* London and New York: Tavistock

Goldberg, D. (1987) 'Raking the Field of the Discourse of Racism' *Journal of Black Studies* 18, 1, pp. 58–77

Goodnow, J. and Pateman, C. (eds) (1985) *Women, Social Science and Public Policy* Sydney: Allen & Unwin

Gorelick, S. (1989) 'Review article: Ethnic Feminism: Beyond the Pseudo-Pluralists' *Feminist Review* 32, Summer

Grassby, A. (1973) *A multi-cultural Society for the future* Immigration Reference Paper, Department of Immigration, Canberra: AGPS

Grimshaw, P. (1981) 'Aboriginal women: A study of culture contact' in N. Grieve and P. Grimshaw (eds) *Australian Women:*

217

Feminist Perspectives Melbourne: Oxford University Press

Grimshaw, P. and Willett, G. (1981) 'Women's History and Family History' in N. Grieve and P. Grimshaw (eds) *Australian Women: Feminist Perspectives* Melbourne: Oxford University Press

Grosz, E. (1989) *Sexual Subversions: Three French Feminists* Sydney: Allen & Unwin

Gunew, S. (1983) 'Migrant Women Writers: Who's on Whose Margins?' *Meanjin* 42, 1, pp. 16–26

—— (1985a) 'Framing Marginality: Distinguishing the textual politics of the marginal voice' *Southern Review* 18, 2

—— (1985b) 'Migrant women Writers: Who's on whose Margins?' in C. Ferrier (ed.) *Gender, Politics and Fiction* St Lucia: University of Queensland Press

—— (1988) 'Authenticity and The Writing Cure' in S. Sheridan (ed.) *Grafts: Feminist Cultural Criticism* London: Verso, pp. 111–23

Gunew, S. and Mahyuddin, J. (eds) (1988) *Beyond the Echo: Multicultural Women's Writing* St Lucia: University of Queensland Press

Hall, J. D. (1984) 'Women, Rape, and Racial Violence' in A. Snitow et al. (eds) *Desire: The Politics of Sexuality* London: Virago, pp. 339–60

Hall, S. (1980) 'Race, Articulation and Societies Structured in Dominance' in *Sociological Theories: Race and Colonialism* Paris: Verso

—— (1988a) 'The Toad in the Garden: Thatcherism Among the Theorists' in C. Nelson and L. Grossberg (eds) *Marxism and the Interpretation of Culture* London: MacMillan

—— (1988b) 'New Ethnicities' in ICA Document 7, Black Film: British Cinema, pp. 27–31

Hamilton, A. (1989) 'Bond Slaves of Satan: Aboriginal Women and the missionary dilemma' in M. Jolly and M. Macintyre (eds) *Family and Gender in the Pacific: Domestic Contradictions and Colonial Impact* Cambridge: Cambridge University Press

Hamilton, Paula (1986) 'A Better Type of Girl: The Training of British migrant women for Australia in the 1920s' Australian and New Zealand History of Education Society Conference (Adelaide), programme and abstracts, pp. 1–29

Hampel, B. (1987) *Class, Gender, Culture and Sicilian Australians* unpublished PhD thesis, Macquarie University

Hantrakul, Sukanya (1988) 'Prostitution in Thailand in development and displacement: Women in Southeast Asia' in G. Chandler, N. Sullivan and J. Branson (eds) *Monash Papers on South East Asia* No. 18, Melbourne: Monash University

—— (1989) in N. Sullivan and J. Branson (eds) *Asian Women, Victims of Development?* Melbourne: Monash University Centre for Development Studies

Harding, S. (ed.) (1987) *Feminism and Methodology* London: Open University Press

Harris, C. (1982) 'The "Terror of the Law" As Applied to Black Rapists in Colonial Queensland' *Hecate* VIII, 2, pp. 22–48

Harris, K. (1984) *Sex, Ideology and Religion: The Representation of Women in the Bible* New Jersey: Barnes and Noble Books

Harroway, D. (1988) 'Situated knowledges: The science question in feminism and the privilege of partial perspective' *Feminist Studies* 14, 3

Hart, G. (1975) 'Ancient Tamil literature: Its scholarly past and future' in B. Stein (ed.) *Essays on South India* Hawaii: University Press of Hawaii

Hau'ofa, E. (1987) 'The New South Pacific Society: Integration and Independence' in A. Hooper et al. (eds) *Class and Culture in the South Pacific* Auckland: Centre for Pacific Studies; Suva: Institute of Pacific Studies, University of the South Pacific

Haviland, W. A. (1975) *Cultural Anthropology* New York: Holt, Rinehart and Winston, Inc.

Hearst, S. (1985) 'Greek Families' in D. Storer (ed.) *Ethnic Family Values in Australia* Melbourne: Prentice Hall

Hecate (1986) Special Double Issue on 'Black women, racism, multiculturalism, black oppression and resistance' XII, 1/2

Henderson, R. (1975) *Poverty in Australia* Canberra: Australian Government Printer

Hill, H. (1987) 'Gender and Inequality in the South: The Gender Variable in Development Politics ...' in C. Jennett and R. G. Stewart (eds) *Three Worlds of Inequality: Race Class and Gender* Melbourne: Macmillan, pp. 340–60

Hooks, B. (1982) *Ain't I a Woman? Black Women and Feminism* London: Pluto Press

Huffer, V. (1980) with E. Roughsey *The Sweetness of the Fig: Aboriginal Women in Transition* Sydney: NSW University Press

Huggins, J. (1987) 'Black Women and Women's Liberation' in *Hecate* XIII, 1, pp. 77–82

—— (1987/88) '"Firing on in the Mind": Aboriginal Women

Domestic Servants in the Interwar Years' *Hecate* 13, 2, pp. 5–23

Hugo, G. J., Hull, T. H., Hull, V. J. and Jones, G. W. (1987) *The Demographic Dimension in Indonesian Development* Singapore: Oxford University Press

Hull, G. T., Scott, P. B. and Smith, B. (eds) (1982) *All the Women Are White, All the Blacks Are Men, But Some of Us Are Brave* New York: Feminist Press

Humphrey, Michael (1984) 'Religion, law and family disputes in a Lebanese Muslim Community in Sydney' in G. Bottomley and M. de Lepervanche (eds) *Ethnicity, Class and Gender in Australia* Sydney: Allen & Unwin

Immigration Advisory Council (IAC) (1970) *Immigration and the Balance of the Sexes in Australia* Report to the Minister of State for Immigration, Canberra: AGPS

Inglis, A. (1974) 'Not a White Woman Safe' *Sexual Anxiety and Politics in Port Moresby, 1920–1934* Canberra: ANU Press

Inglis, C. and Manderson, L. (1984) 'Patterns of Childcare amongst Women in the Sydney Turkish Community' *Australian Journal of Social Issues* 19, 2, pp. 113–24

Isaacs, E. (1976) *Greek children in Sydney* Canberra: Australian National University Press

Italian Welfare Centre (1983) *Annual Report* Brisbane

Iyer, A. K. (1981) *The Tribes and Castes of Cochin* Vol. 1, [1909] Cosmo Publications

Jahan, R. (1975) 'Women in Bangladesh' in *Women for women: Bangladesh* Dhaka: University Press Ltd

Jakubowicz, A. (1984a) 'State and Ideology: Multiculturalism as Ideology' in J. Jupp (ed.) *Ethnic Politics in Australia* Sydney: Allen & Unwin

—— (1984b) 'Ethnicity, multiculturalism and neo-conservatism' in G. Bottomley and M. de Lepervanche (eds) *Ethnicity, Class and Gender in Australia* Sydney: Allen & Unwin

—— (1985) 'Racism, Multiculturalism and the Migration debate in Australia' *Sage Race Relations Abstracts* 10, 3, pp. 1–15

Jameson, F. (1981) *The Political Unconscious: Narrative as a socially symbolic act* Cornell University Press, London: Methuen

Jelin, E. (1977) 'Migration and labour force participation of Latin American women: The Domestic servants in the cities' *Signs: A Journal of Women in Culture and Society* pp. 129–41

Jennette, C., Cole, R. and Stewart, R. (eds) (1987) *Three Worlds of Inequality Race, Class and Gender* London: Methuen

Johnson, C. (1985) 'White forms, Aboriginal content' in J. Davis and B. Hodge (eds) *Aboriginal Writing Today* Canberra: AIAS
—— (1987) 'Captured Discourse, Captured Lives' *Aboriginal History* 11
Johnson, D. (1984a) *The Government Women: Gender and Structural Contradiction in Papua New Guinea* PhD thesis, University of Sydney
—— (1984b) 'Gender and Ideology: Women in the Papua New Guinea Bureaucracy' *Refractory Girl* May, pp. 34–6
Johnson, P. (1988) 'Feminism and Difference: The Dilemmas of Luce Irigaray' *Australian Feminist Studies* No. 6, Autumn
Jolly, M. (1987) 'The Forgotten Women: A History of Migrant Labour and Gender Relations in Vanuatu' *Oceania* 58, 2, pp. 119–39
—— (n.d.a.) 'To Save the Girls for Brighter and Better Lives' *The Journal of Pacific History* (forthcoming)
—— (n.d.b.) 'Engendering Colonialism: Women and the History of Vanuatu' unpublished thesis
—— (n.d.c.) 'Spouses and Siblings in Sa Stories' *Oceania* (forthcoming)
—— (n.s.s.) '"Ill-Natured Comparisons": Racism and Relativism in European Representations of ni-Vanuatu from Cook's Second voyage' *History and Anthropology* (forthcoming)
Jolly, M. and Macintyre, M. (eds) (1989) *Family and Gender in the Pacific: Domestic Contradictions and Colonial Impact* Cambridge: Cambridge University Press
Jupp, J., York, B. and McRobbie, A. (1989) *The Political Participation of Ethnic Minorities in Australia* Canberra: AGPS
Juteau-Lee, D. and Roberts, B. (1981) 'Ethnicity and femininity: (d') apres nos experiences' *Canadian Ethnic Studies* XIII, 1
Kalantzis, M. and Cope, B. (1988) 'Why we need multicultural education: a review of the "ethnic disadvantage" debate' *Journal of Intercultural Studies* 9, 2, pp. 39–57
Kalowski, J. (1986) 'Women in a Multicultural Society' *Migration Action* viii, 1, pp. 10–14
Kanarakis, G. (1987) *Greek Voices in Australia* Sydney: ANU Press
Kapardis, A. and Tamis, A. (eds) (1988) *Greeks in Australia* Melbourne: River Seine Press
Keesing, R. (1988) *Colonial Discourse and Codes of Discrimination in Pacific* Paris: UNESCO Division of Human Rights and Peace
Kennedy, M. (1985) *Born a half-Caste* Canberra: AIAS

Kenneth, D. and Silas, H. (1986) 'Vanuatu: Traditional diversity and modern uniformity' *Land Rights of Pacific Women* Suva: Institute of Pacific Studies, University of South Pacific

King, D. (1988) 'Multiple Jeopardy, Multiple Consciousness' *Signs* 14, 1, pp. 42–71

Kingston, B. (1975) *My Wife, My Daughter and Poor Mary Ann* Melbourne: Nelson

Knapman, C. (1986) *White Women in Fiji 1835–1930. The Ruin of Empire?* Sydney: Allen & Unwin

Knopfelmacher, F. (1982) 'The case against multiculturalism' in R. Manne (ed.) *The New Conservatism in Australia* London and Melbourne: Oxford University Press

Kompas (1984) Musalmer TKW Indonesia di Arab Saudi, Kalau Memang Tahu Datanya, Laporkan ke KBRI, 1, 9, 12 Mei

Kruper, L. and Smith, M. G. (1971) *Pluralism in Africa* California and London: University of California Press

Krygier, J. (1982) 'Caste and Female Pollution' in Allen, N. and Mukherjee, S. N. (eds) *Women in India and Nepal* Canberra: Australian National University

Kunek, S. (convenor) (1988) *Women of the Mediterranean Greek–Australian Women's Workshops* Clayton: Monash University

L'Orange, H. (chairperson) (1985) *Report of the New South Wales Domestic Violence Committee* to the Premier of New South Wales, Sydney: Premier's Department

Labumore, E. Roughsey (1984) *An Aboriginal Mother Tells of the Old and the New* Fitzroy, Victoria: McPhee Gribble/Penguin Books

Laing, R. D. (1967) *The Politics of Experience* Harmondsworth: Penguin

Langford, R. (1988) *Don't Take Your Love to Town* Australia: Penguin

Langton, M. (1981) 'Urbanizing Aborigines: The Social Scientists' Great Deception' *Social Alternatives* 2, 2, pp. 16–22

—— (1988a) *Being Black: Aboriginal Cultures in 'Settled' Australia* Canberra: AIAS

—— (1988b) 'The Getting of Power' *Australian Feminist Studies* No. 6, Autumn pp. 1–5

—— (1989) 'Feminism: What Do Aboriginal Women Gain?' *Broadside*, Newsletter of the National Foundation of Australian Women 1, 1, p. 3

Larbalestier, J. (1977) 'Black Women in Colonial Australia' *Refractory Girl* March, pp. 13–14

—— (1980) 'Feminism as Myth: Aboriginal Women and the Feminist Encounter' *Refractory Girl* October, pp. 31–41

—— (1988) *A World After Its Own Image* PhD thesis, Macquarie University, Sydney

Lazreg, M. (1988) 'Feminism and Difference' *Feminist Studies* 14, 1

Lees, S. (1986) 'Sex, Race and Culture: Feminism and the Limits of Cultural Pluralism' *Feminist Review* 22, Spring, pp. 92–102

Lesbock, S. (1983) 'Free Black Women And The Question of Matriarchy' in J. Newton et al. (eds) *Sex and Class in Women's History* London: Routledge and Kegan Paul

Lever Tracy, C. (1981) 'Post War Immigrants in Australia and Western Europe in Reserve or Centre Forward', paper presented to Ethnicity and Class Conference, University of Wollongong

Lineton, J. (1975) '"Pasompe" ugi: Bugis migrants and wanderers' *Archipel* 10, pp. 173–201

Lini, Hilda (1982) 'Pacific feminism', The Pacific Women's Resource Bureau Viewpoint. Noumea: South Pacific Commission

—— (1987) 'Pacific development strategies' in V. Griffen (ed.) Women, Development & Empowerment: A Pacific Feminist Perspective. Report on Pacific Women's Workshop, Fiji, 1987, pp. 68–71

Lippman, W. (1979) 'Family Reunion and the Refugee Crisis' in R. Birnell et al. (eds) *Refugees, Resources, Reunions: Australia's Immigration Dilemmas* Melbourne: VCTA Publishing

Lipton, M. (1977) *Why Poor People Stay Poor: Urban Bias in World Development* Cambridge Mass.: Harvard University Press

Lloyd, G. (1984) *The Man of Reason* London: Methuen

McClancy, J. (1981) 'From the New Hebrides to Vanuatu 1979–80' *The Journal of Pacific History* 7, pp. 92–104

McGrath, A. (1987) '*Born in the cattle*' Sydney: Allen & Unwin

McHoul, A. (1988) 'Sociology and Literature: The Voice of Fact and The Writing of Fiction' *Australian and New Zealand Journal of Sociology* 24, 2, pp. 208–25

Mama, A. (1984) 'Black women, the economic crisis and the British State' *Feminist Review* 17

—— (1989) 'Violence against Black women: gender, race and State responses' *Feminist Review* 32, Summer

Manonni, O. (1956) *Prospero and Caliban: The Psychology of Colonization* trans. by P. Powesland, London: Methuen

Marks, E. and de Courtrivon, I. (eds) (1981) *New French Feminisms* Brighton: Harvester Press

Markus, A. (1985) '1984 or 1901? Immigration and some lessons of Australian History' in A. Markus and M. C. Ricklefs (eds) *Surrender Australia* Sydney: Allen & Unwin

Marshment, M. (1983) Review of Alice Walker *Race and Class* XXV, 2, pp. 91–4

Martin, J. A. (1983) 'The development of multiculturalism' in Cass, M. (chairman) *Report to the Minister for Immigration and Ethnic Affairs* vol. 2, pp. 120–160, Canberra: Australian Government Printer

—— (1984 and 1986a) 'Non-English-speaking women: Production and social reproduction' in G. Bottomley and M. de Lepervanche (eds) *Ethnicity, Class and Gender in Australia* Sydney: Allen & Unwin

—— (1986b) 'Non-English-Speaking Women: in Australia' in N. Grieve and A. Burns (eds) *Australian Women: New Feminist Perspectives* Melbourne: Oxford University Press

Martin, J. I. (1975) 'Family and Bureaucracy' in C. Price (ed.) *Greeks in Australian* Canberra: Australian National University Press

—— (1978) *The Migrant Presence* Sydney: Allen & Unwin

Martin, J. I. and Encel, S. (1981) *The Ethnic Dimension* Sydney: Allen & Unwin

Melbourne Age, March 27, 1981

Mera Molisa, G. (1978) Speech to the First Conference of Vanuaaku Women, Efate, Ts (translation)

—— (1983) *Black Stone* Suva: Mana Publication

—— (1987) *Colonised People* Port Vila: Black Stone Publications

Merlan, F. (1988) 'Gender in Aboriginal Life: A Review' in R. M. Berndt and R. Tonkinson (eds) *Social Anthropology and Australian Aboriginal Studies* Canberra: Australian Institute of Aboriginal Affairs pp. 17–76

Mernissi, F. (1975) *Beyond the Veil: Male–female dynamics in a modern Muslim society* Cambridge, Mass.: Schenkman Publishing Co.

—— (1982) 'Virginity and Patriarchy' in Azizah Al-Hibri (ed.) *Women and Islam* Sydney and Oxford: Pergamon Press

Miles, R. (1987) *Capitalism and Unfree Labour: Anomaly or Necessity* London and New York: Tavistock

Mines, M. (1984) *The Warrior Merchants: Textiles, trade and territory in South India* Cambridge: Cambridge University Press

Moffat, M. (1979) *An untouchable community in South India: Structure and consensus* Princeton, NJ: Princeton University Press

Molisa, Grace Mera (see Mera Molisa)

Moore, H. (1988) *Feminism and Anthropology* Oxford: Polity Press and Basil Blackwell

Moraes-Gorecki, V. (1987) Family Migration and South American Women in Australia, PhD thesis, University of Sydney

—— (1988) 'Cultural Variations on Gender: Latin American Marianismo/Machismo in Australia' *Mankind* 18, 1, pp. 26–35

Moraga, C. and Anzaldua, G. (eds) (1983) *This Bridge called my back* New York: Kitchen Table

Morgan, S. (1987) *My Place* Fremantle: Fremantle Arts Centre Press

Morokvasic, M. (1983) 'Women in Migration: Beyond the Reductionist Outlook' in A. Phizacklea (ed.) *One Way Ticket* London: Routledge and Kegan Paul

Mum Shirl, with the assistance of B. Sykes (1981) *Mum Shirl: An Autobiography* Richmond, Melbourne: Heinemann Educational

Narogin, Mudrooroo (1990) *Writing from the Fringe* Melbourne: Hyland House Publishing

National Times, January 9–15, 1983

National Women's Advisory Council (1979) (NWAC) *Migrant Women Speak* A Report to the Commonwealth Government by the NWAC Canberra: AGPS

Newton, J. and Rosenfelt, D. (1985) *Feminist Criticism and Social Change: Sex, Class and Race in Literature and Culture* New York and London: Methuen

Ngcobo, Lauretta (1988) *Let it be told* London: Virago Press

Nkweto Simmonds, F. (1988) 'She's Gotta Have It: The Representation of Black Female Sexuality on Film' in *Feminist Review* 29, pp. 10–22

O'Donnell, C. and Craney, J. (1982) *Family Violence in Australia* Melbourne: Longman Cheshire

O'Farrell, P. (1986) *The Irish in Australia* Sydney: New South Wales University Press

O'Shane, P. (1976a) 'Is there any Relevance in the Women's Movement for Aboriginal Women?' *Refractory Girl* 12, September, pp. 31–4

—— (1976b) in J. Mitchell (ed.) *Tall Poppies* Richmond: Penguin

Omalade, B. (1980) 'Black women and Feminism' in H. Eisenstein and A. Jardine (eds) *The future of Difference* Boston: G. K. Hall

Ortner, S. B. and Whitehead, H. (eds) (1981) *Sexual Meanings: The Cultural Construction of Gender and Sexuality* Cambridge: Cambridge University Press

Palabrica-Costello, M. (1984) 'Female domestic servants in Cagayan de Oro, Philippines: Social and economic implications of employment in a "premodern" occupation' in G. Jones (ed.) *Women in the Urban and Industrial Workforce: South east and East Asia* Canberra: Development Studies Centre

Palfreeman, A. C. (1967) *The Administration of the White Australia Policy* Melbourne: Melbourne University Press

Papaellinas, G. (1986a) *Ikons* Australia: Penguin Books

—— (1986b) *Ethnos* 56, Sydney: Ethnic Affairs Commission of NSW

Papanek, H. (1982) 'Purdah: Separate Worlds and Symbolic Shelter' in H. Papanek, and G. Minault (eds) *Separate Worlds and Studies of Purdah in South Asia* New Delhi: Chanakya Publications

Parmar, P. (1982) 'Gender, race and class: Asian women in resistance' in Centre for Contemporary Cultural Studies (eds) *The Empire Strikes Back* London: Hutchinson

—— (1989) 'Other kinds of dreams' *Feminist Review* 31, Spring (Special Issue) pp. 55–65

Pastner, C. McC. (1974) 'Accommodations to Purdah: The Female Perspective' *Journal of Marriage and the Family* 36, 2, pp. 408–14

Pateman, C. (1985) Introduction to J. Goodnow and C. Pateman (eds) *Women, Social Science and Public Policy* Sydney: Allen & Unwin

—— (1986) 'The Marriage Contract' in N. Grieve and A. Burns, (eds) *Australian Women: New Feminist Perspectives* Melbourne: Oxford University Press, pp. 172–81

—— (1988) *The Sexual Contract* Oxford: Polity Press and Basil Blackwell

—— (1989) *The Disorder of Women* Cambridge: Polity Press

Pateman, C. and Gross, E. (eds) (1986) *Feminist Challenges: Social and Political Theory* Sydney: Allen & Unwin

Perez Olleros, A. (1990) 'So Far. The October 1961 Spanish Women's Expedition to Australia and their Process of Adjustment in a New Country' MA (Hons) thesis, University of Sydney

Peristiany, J. G. (ed.) (1965) *Honour and Shame: The Values of Mediterranean Society* Chicago/London: University of Chicago Press

Pettman, J. (1988a) 'Whose Country Is It Anyway? Cultural Politics, Racism and the Construction of Being Australian' *Journal of Intercultural Studies* 9, 1, pp. 1–24

—— (1988b) 'The Politics of Race' Peace Research Centre Working Paper No. 54, Canberra: Australian National University

—— (1988c) '"All the Women are White, All the Blacks are Men": Racism, Sexism and Sociology', paper presented to SAANZ Conference, Canberra, November (forthcoming 1990 *Australian Feminist Studies*)

—— (1990) 'Racism and Sexism in Tertiary Education' Working Paper SACAE: Aboriginal Studies and Teacher Education Centre (forthcoming)

Phizacklea, A. (1983) 'In the Front Line' in A. Phizacklea (ed.) *One Way Ticket* London: Routledge and Kegan Paul

Phoenix, A. (1985) 'Theories of Gender and Black Families' in G. Weiner (ed.) *Just a Bunch of Girls* London: Open University Press pp. 50–63

Pieri, S., Risk, M. and Sgro, A. (1980) 'Italian migrant women, participation and the women's movement' paper delivered to the second *Women and Labour Conference* Melbourne

Pitt-Rivers, J. (1965) 'Honour and Social Status' in J. G. Peristiany (ed.) *Honour and Shame: The Values of Mediterranean Society* Chicago/London: University of Chicago Press

—— (1977) *The Fate of Shechem: or the Politics of Sex: Essays in the Anthropology of the Mediterranean* Cambridge: Cambridge University Press

Poiner, G. (1979) 'Country Wives' in *Australian and New Zealand Journal of Sociology* 15, 2

Pongpavichit, Pasuk (1984) 'The Bangkok masseuses: Origins, status and prospects' in G. Jones (ed.) *Women in the Urban and Industrial Workforce* Canberra: Development Studies Centre Monograph no. 33

Power, M., Outhwaite, S. and Rosewarne, S. (1984) 'Writing Women Out of the Economy', paper presented to 'From Margin to Mainstream', a National Conference about Women and Employment, Melbourne, 16 October 1984

Prager, J. (1987) 'American Political Culture and the Shifting Language of Race' *Ethnic and Racial Studies* 10, 1, pp. 62–81

Price, C. A. (1966) 'Post-war Migration: Demographic Background' in A. Stoller (ed.) *New Faces: Immigration and Family Life in Australia* Melbourne: Cheshire

Pringle, R. (1973) 'Octavius Beale and the Royal Commissions of Enquiry into Birth Control' *Refractory Girl* 3

Ramazanoglu, C. (1989) *Feminimism and the contradictions of oppression* London and New York: Routledge and Kegan Paul

Rapp, R. (1979) 'Anthropology: Review Essay' *Signs* 4, 3, pp. 498–513

Rapp, R., Ross, E. and Bridenthal, R. (1979) 'Examining Family History' *Feminist Studies* 5, 1, pp. 174–200

Rarua Lini, K. (1982) 'Some comments on the experience of women in Vanuatu', *Journal of Pacific Studies* 8, pp. 70–82

Rarua, K. 'Vanuatu' (1986) in T. Tongamoa (ed.) *Pacific Women: Roles and Status of Women in Pacific Societies* Suva: Institute of Pacific Studies, University of the South Pacific

Reid, A. (ed.) (1983) *Slavery, Bondage and Dependence in Southeast Asia* St Lucia: University of Queensland Press

Reiger, K. (1982) 'Women's Labour Redefined: Child-bearing and Rearing Advice in Australia 1880–1930s' in M. Bevege et al. (eds) *Worth Her Salt* Sydney: Hale and Iremonger, pp. 72–83

Riotto Sirey, A. (1986) Interview with *Staten Island Advance*, New York, 10 April 1986

Rivett, K. (1975) *Australia and the Non-White Migrant* Melbourne: Melbourne University Press

Robinson, K. M. (1986) *Stepchildren of Progress: The Political Economy of Development in an Indonesian Mining Town* Albany NY: State University of New York Press

Roche, P. (1984) *The fishermen of the Coromandel: The social study of the Paravas of the Coromandel* New Delhi: Manohar

Roe, J. (1983) 'The End is Where We start From: Women and Welfare Since 1901' in C. Baldock and B. Cass (eds) *Women, Social Welfare and the State* Sydney: Allen & Unwin, pp. 1–19

Rooney, N. (1989) 'Where are the women of PNG today?' *Post-Courier* September 14, Independence Supplement, p. 37

Rozario, S. (1988a) *Sexual Purity and Communal Boundaries: Domination and Social Change in a Bangladeshi Village* PhD thesis, University of New South Wales

—— (1988b) 'Legitimation and the re-discovery of ritual: Inter-communal and class relationships in a Bangladeshi village' *Mankind* 18, 3, pp. 133–45

Ryan, E. and Conlon, A. (1975) *Gentle Invaders: Australian Women at Work 1788–1974* Melbourne: Nelson

Ryan, L. (1986a) 'Aboriginal Women and Agency in the Process of Conquest: A Review of Some Recent Work' in *Australian Feminist Studies* 2, pp. 37–44

—— (1986b) 'Reading Aboriginal Histories' *Meanjin* 45, 1, pp. 49–57

Said, E. (1978) *Orientalism* Harmondsworth: Penguin

—— (1985 and 1986) 'Orientalism Reconsidered' *Cultural Critique* 1, Fall, pp. 89–107, and *Race and Class* 27, 2, pp. 1–15

Santamaria, B. A. (1987) *Australia at the Crossroads* Melbourne: Melbourne University Press

Saunders, K. (1982) 'Pacific Islander Women in Queensland 1863–1907' in M. Bevege et al., (eds) *Worth Her Salt* Sydney: Hale and Iremonger, pp. 16–32

Sawer, M. (1989) 'The Battle for the Family' *Australian Society* August, pp. 10–11

Schipper, M. (ed.) (1985) *Women and Literature in Africa, the Arab World, Asia, the Caribbean and Latin America* London: Allison and Busby

Schneider, J. (1971) 'Of vigilance and virgins: Honor, shame and access to resources in Mediterranean societies' *Ethnology* X, 1, pp. 1–24

Scutt, J. (1983) *Even in the Best of Homes* Ringwood: Penguin

—— (1985) 'In Pursuit of Equality: Women and Legal Thought 1788–1984' in J. Goodnow and C. Pateman (eds) *Women, Social Science and Public Policy* Sydney: Allen & Unwin, pp. 116–39

Sexton, L. (1986) *Mothers of Money, Daughters of Coffee: the Wok Meri Movement* Studies in Cultural Anthropology 10, Ann Arbor, Michigan: UMI Research Press

Sgro, A. (1979) 'Not a special group . . . Italian women in Australia' *Migration Today* 24, pp. 8–9

Sgro, A., Pieri, A. and Risk, M. (1980) 'Italian migrant women: Participation in the women's movement' paper delivered to *Second Women and Labour Conference*, Melbourne

Shoemaker, A. (1989) *Black Words White Page* St Lucia: University of Queensland Press

Simon, R. J. and Brettell, C. (eds) (1986) *International Migration: The Female Experience* New Jersey: Rowman and Allanheld

Sinar, H. (1984) '93 tenaga keya wanita ke Arab Saudi' 11 May

Sivanandan, A. (1988) 'No Such Thing as Anti-Racist Ideology' *New Statement* 27 May

Smith, B. (1960) *European Vision in the South Pacific 1768–1850: A Study in the History of Art and Ideas* London: Oxford University Press

Smith, M. L. (1973) 'Domestic service as a channel of upward mobility for the lower-class woman: The Lima case' in A. Pescatello (ed.) *Female and Male in Latin America: Essays* Pittsburgh: University of Pittsburgh Press

—— (1981) *Home Girls: A Black Feminist Anthology* New York: Kitchen Table

Smolicz, J. (1974) 'The concept of tradition' *Australian and New Zealand Journal of Sociology* 10, 2

—— (1981) 'Core values and cultural identity' *Ethnic and Racial Studies* 4, 1

—— (1988) 'Tradition, core values and cultural change among Greek Australians' in A. Kapardis and A. Tamis (eds) (1988) *Greeks in Australia* Melbourne: River Seine Press

Social Alternatives (1983) *Multiculturalism* 3, 3, July

Sope, B. N. B. (1975) *Land and politics in the New Hebrides* Suva: South Pacific Social Sciences Association

Spivak, G. C. (1981) 'French feminism in an international frame' in *Yale French Studies* 62

—— (1982) ' "Darupadi" by Mahjazveta' in E. Abel (ed.) *Writing and Sexual Difference* Chicago: University of Chicago Press

—— (1986) 'Three Women's texts and a critique of Imperialism' in H. L. Gates *"Race", writing and difference* Chicago: University of Chicago Press

—— (1988a) *In Other Worlds: Essays in Cultural Politics* London and New York: Methuen

—— (1988b) 'Can the Subaltern Speak?' in G. Nelson and L. Grossberg (eds) *Marxism and the Interpretation of Culture* Urbana: University of Illinois Press

Stack, C. B. (1974) *All our Kin: Strategies for Survival in a Black Community* New York: Harper and Row

Stasiulis, D. K. (1987) 'Rainbow Feminism: Perspectives on Minority Women in Canada' in *Resources for Feminist Research* 16, 1, pp. 5–9

—— (1990) 'Theorizing Connections: Gender, Race, Ethnicity and Class' in P. S. Li (ed.) *Race and Ethnic Relations in Canada* Toronto: Oxford University Press

Stoler, A. L. (1985) *Capitalism and Confrontation in Sumatra's Plantation Belt* New Haven and London: Yale University Press

Storer, D. (1975) *Ethnic Rights, Power and Participation: towards a multicultural Australia* Monograph 2, Melbourne: CHOMI

—— (1976) *But I wouldn't want my wife to work here* A study of migrant women in Melbourne Industry, Fitzroy, Victoria: CURA

Strintzos, M. (1984) 'To be Greek is to be good' in *Cultural Politics* Melbourne: Working Papers Series 5 (Dept. of Education, University of Melbourne)

Summers, A. (1975) *Damned Whores and God's Policy: The Colonization of Women in Australia* Victoria, New York: Penguin Books

Sydney Morning Herald, 28 February 1981, 28 October 1983, 7 December 1984

Sydney Morning Herald report on domestic violence survey, 9 March 1988

Sykes, B. (1975) 'Black Women in Australia: A History' in J. Mercer (ed.) *The Other Half: Women in Australian Society* Ringwood Victoria: Penguin

—— (1989) *Black Majority* Melbourne: Hudson Publishing

Taylor, J. G. (1983) *The Social World of Batavia: European and Eurasian in Dutch Asia* Madison: University of Wisconsin Press

Thomas, N. (1989) 'The Force of Ethnology: Origins and Significance of the Melanesia/Polynesia Division' *Current Anthropology* 30, pp. 27–42

Thompson, R. C. (1980) *Australian Imperialism in the Pacific: The Expansionist Era 1820–1920* Melbourne: Melbourne University Press

Thornton Dill, B. (1983) 'Race, Class and Gender: Prospects for an All-inclusive Sisterhood' *Feminist Studies* 9, 1, pp. 131–50

Threadgold, T. (1990) 'Introduction' in T. Threadgold and A. Cranny-Francis (eds) *Feminine/Masculine and Representation* Sydney: Allen & Unwin, pp. 1–35

Threadgold, T. and Cranny Francis, A. (eds) (1990) *Feminine/Masculine and Representation* Sydney: Allen & Unwin

Tomlinson, J. (1986) 'Aboriginalising Child Care' *Australian Social Worker* 39, 1, pp. 25–30

Tsolidis, G. (1986) *Educating Voula: A Report on non-English-speaking background girls and education* Melbourne: Victorian Ministerial Advisory Committee on Multicultural and Migrant Education

Turner, B. S. (1984) *The Body and Society: Explorations in Social Theory* Oxford: Basil Blackwell

van den Berghe, P. (1978) 'Race and ethnicity: a sociobiological perspective' *Ethnic and Racial Studies* 1, 4

—— (1979) *Human Family Systems* New York: Elsevier

Vasta, E. (1985) '*If you had your time again, would you migrate to Australia?': A study of long-settled Italo-Australians in Brisbane* Canberra: DIEA Report

Viviani, N. (1984) *The Long Journey: Vietnamese Migration and Settlement in Australia* Melbourne: Melbourne University Press

231

Volkkman, T. A. (1985) *Feasts of Honour Ritual and Change in the Toraja Highlands* Urbana and Chicago: University of Illinois Press

Walker, A. (1982) 'Advancing Luna—and the Ida D. Wells' in Walker, A. *You Can't Keep a Good Woman Down* London: The Women's Press

Wallace, A. (1986) *Homicide: The Social Reality* New South Wales Bureau of Crime Statistics and Research, Attorney General's Department, Sydney

Ward, G. (1987) *Wandering Girl* Broome, WA: Magbala

Ware, V. (1983/84) 'Imperialism, Racism and Violence Against Women' *Emergency* 1, pp. 25–30

Warner, M. (1976) *Alone of all her sex: The myth and cult of the Virgin Mary* Great Britain: Weidenfield and Nicolson

Warren, J. F. (1981) *The Sulu Zone 1765–1898: The Dynamics of External Trade, Slavery and Ethnicity in the Transformation of a Southeast Asian Maritime State* Singapore: Singapore University Press

Washington, M. H. (1989) *Invented Lives: Narratives of Black Women 1860–1960* London: Virago Press

Watkins, D. (1982) 'Filipino Brides: Slaves or Marriage Partners' *Australian Journal of Social Issues* 17, 1, pp. 73–84

West, I. (1984) *Pride Against Prejudice: Reminiscences of a Tasmanian Aborigine* Canberra: Australian Institute of Aboriginal Studies

White, I., Barwick, D. and Meehan, B. (eds) (1985) *Fighters and Singers: The Lives of Some Aboriginal Women* Sydney: Allen & Unwin

White, G. M. and Lindstrom, L. (eds) (1989) *The Pacific Theater: Island Representations of World War II* Pacific Islands Monograph Series 8, Honolulu: University of Hawaii Press and Center for Pacific Islands Studies

Williams, R. (1977) *Marxism and Literature* Oxford: Oxford University Press

Willis, S. (1985) 'Black Women Writers' in Greene, G. and Kahn, C. (eds) *Making a Difference: Feminist Literary Criticism* London: Routledge & Kegan Paul

Wilson, E. O. (1978) *On Human Nature* Mass.: Harvard University Press

Wilson, P. (1982) *Black Death, White Hands* Sydney: Allen & Unwin

Wolf, D. L. (1984) 'Making the bread and bringing it home: Female factory workers and the family economy in rural Java' in G. Jones (ed.) *Women in the Urban and Industrial Workforce: Southeast and East Asia* Canberra: Development Studies Centre

Women's Business: Report of the Aboriginal Women's Task Force, (1986) Canberra: AGPS

Worsley, P. (1984) *The Three Worlds: Culture and World Development* London: Weidenfeld and Nicolson

Yalman, N. (1963) 'On the purity of women in the castes of Ceylon and Malabar' in *Journal of the Royal Anthropological Institute* 93, pp. 25–58

Yarwood, A. T. (1964) *Asian Migration to Australia* Melbourne: Melbourne University Press

Yeatman, A. (1971) 'The Marriage–Family Institution' *Australian Left Review* December 1970–January 1971, pp. 21–37

Young, C., Cox, D. and Daly, A. (1983) *Report of the Greek and Italian Youth Employment Study* Canberra: Department of Immigration and Ethnic Affairs

Young, M. (n.d.) '"Gone Native" in the "Isles of Illusion": in Search of Asterisk in Epi', forthcoming in J. Carrier (ed.) *Reconsidering Anthropology in Melanesia* Berkeley: University of California Press

Yuval-Davis, N. and Anthias, F. (eds) (1989) *Women–Nation–State* London: Macmillan

Zaccari, V. (1986) 'Filef, Italian Migrant Women and Australian Trade Unions' *Multicultural Australia Papers* Melbourne: CHOMI

Zubrzycki, J. (1977) 'Towards a multicultural Australia' in M. Bowen (ed.) *Australia 2000: the ethnic impact* Armidale: University of New England

—— (1978) 'Immigration and the Family in a Multicultural Australia' Meredith Memorial Lecture, Melbourne: La Trobe University

Index

Aboriginal cultural identity, 76–7
Aboriginal family, demeaning of,
149; family forms denied, 132;
studies of, 194–5
Aboriginal identity, 75–91
*Aboriginal mother tells of the old
and new, An* (Labumore [Elsie
Roughsey]), 75, 78–83
Aboriginal Protection Board,
abduction of Aboriginal children,
148–9
Aboriginal women, academy, in,
201; administration of
DepoProvera, 54, 151;
experiences, 195–6; exploitation,
as domestic servants, 88, sexual,
88-9; racism and sexism, subject
to, 187, 188; representations of,
197; and white feminists, 56–7,
76; women's movement,
challenges to, 55; writings of,
75–91, 196, 201
Aboriginal Women's Taskforce,
Report (1986), 196–7
Aboriginal workers, in labour
market hierarchy, 164
Aboriginal writings, 75–91, 196,
201

Aboriginals, Australian society, in,
90, 91; protection of, 189; social
relations, inequality, 91
Aborigines Protection Act, 149
abortion on demand, 53–4
Adult Migrant Education Programs,
173
aged care, extended family, in, 179;
migrant families, in, 182
aged migrants, problems, 182
Algeria, 'unveiling', 122
Allawah, Aboriginal hostel, 87
Ambae, 68
Aneityum, 69
Anglocentrism, in education, 101
Anthias, Floya, 92–3
anti-colonialist discourse,
exclusivism, 93
appliances, household, feminisation
of, 178, 184–6
assimilation policy, Australian,
failure of, 175
Attali, Jacques, 107
Australian Citizenship Act 1948
(Cmwlth), 151
Australian family, 1975–85
statistics, family types, 133;
inequality of women, 134; nuclear

234

population census and surveys,
Australian, 132, 133
population growth, white,
Australian, 132
post-colonial state, gender issues,
58; male dominance, 59–60, 66
poverty, exploitation and, women
service industry workers, 50–1
Poverty Report, and Italian migrant
women, 172
primordialist approach, to
multiculturalism, 116–18
prostitution, Thailand, 47, 51
'purity', sexual, Bangladeshi
Christian women, 19–21, 26
'purity/pollution' ideologies in
Bangladesh, 14–18 *passim*

Quiros, Pedro Fernandez de, 67

race, ideological entity, 188–9;
nature of, 189–90
race categories, effect of, 191–3
race relations, class and gender,
feminist research, Marxist
influences on, 160–4
Racial Discrimination Act 1975
(Cmwlth), 151
racism, 101; and Aboriginal women,
187, 188; Anglo–Australian, and
Italian migrant women, 173–4;
institutional discrimination, and
Italian migrants, 172–4; and
sexism, 187–202 *passim*
Red Guards, China, 107
representation, Aboriginal women,
197–9; black family, 193–4,
195–6, 197, 199; issues of, x;
minority women, experiences,
200–1
resistance, to ethnicity, 191
Roughsey, Dick (Goobalathaldin),
78
Roughsey, Elsie (Labumore), 75, 76,
78–83, 90, 91

Royal Commissions of Inquiry, into
birthrate, 132

St Vincent de Paul Society, 24, 30
Santamaria, B.A., 141
Santo, 68
Saudi Arabia, migrant workers in,
47–51
second generation migrants,
disadvantage, patterns of, 100–1;
families, 104; Greek Australian,
93–109 *passim*
self presentation and caste identity,
in Mukkuvar community, 3–12
passim
sexes, indigenous relations between,
58
sexism, and racism, 187–202
passim
sexual harassment, Australian
migrant women, 147
sexual liberation, and black women,
54–5
sexual politics, 199–200
sexuality, female, black women,
representation of, 197–9; control
of, in Bangladesh, 15–32 *passim*
Siva worship, 7
Smolicz, J., 116
social phenomena, objective and
subjective accounts, 95–7, 108
sociological studies, feminist
research, Marxist analysis,
160–4; Greek Australians,
97–105
Sope, Barak, 68
Soroakan women, 42
Soroako nickel project, 42, 45
South India, gender in cultural
power relations, 1–13; Mukkuvar
community, 2–13
South Sulawesi, 34, 35, 39, 42
State of Shock, 199
sterilisation, forced, in United States,
54